Dell deChant's book is fascinating, provocative, and far-reaching, and it is about much more than Christmas. With impressive theoretical grounding, deChant argues that our consumerist, "postmodern" culture is not a secular challenge to Christianity; it is a rival religion. And unlike many critics, he is interested in describing it, not attacking it.

Bruce David Forbes
Professor of Religious Studies
Morningside College, Sioux City, Iowa

Sacred Santa is a provocative and fascinating account of the role of Santa Claus in postmodern America. Dr. deChant provides us not with the usual and expected interpretation of a secular present and future versus sacred past but rather an affirmation of the sacred in what is perhaps the most self-serving and secular of venues: commerce. A thoroughly enjoyable book to read with a novel and illuminating approach to the sacred and to religion too often presented in a stereotypical and tedious style. This is one of the few books that will appeal to all segments of society because it both educates and entertains, with no compromises to either.

James A. Santucci, Professor
Department of Comparative Religion
California State University, Fullerton

The
Sacred Santa

Religious Dimensions
of Consumer Culture

Dell deChant

WIPF & STOCK · Eugene, Oregon

For Marilynn

Wipf and Stock Publishers
199 W 8th Ave, Suite 3
Eugene, OR 97401

The Sacred Santa
Religious Dimensions of Consumer Culture
By deChant, Dell
Copyright©2002 by deChant, Dell
ISBN 13: 978-1-55635-839-5
Publication date 2/1/2008
Previously published by Pilgrim Press, 2002

I went down to the Piraeus yesterday with Glaucon, the son of Ariston.
I intended to say a prayer to the goddess,
and I also wanted to see how they would manage the festival,
since this was its first celebration.

—Plato, *The Republic*

Contents

Part IV
RELIGIOUS DIMENSIONS OF CHRISTMAS
IN POSTMODERN CULTURE

Foreword

What does religion have to do with economics, the sacred with the secular, or postmodernity with premodernity? Unlike most who would see only "difference," Dell deChant also sees important similarities. What do modern scholars like Paul Tillich, Jacques Ellul, Eric Voegelin, and Mircea Eliade have to do with postmodernists like Frederic Jameson and Jean Baudrillard? Conversant with postmodern intellectual trends, deChant is no slave to current intellectual fashions but rather places historical eras and intellectual styles (premodern, modern, and postmodern) into critical dialogue with each other in order to illuminate the religiosity of contemporary postmodern secular culture.

Contrary to what some may expect, this book is not about putting Christ back into Christmas. Rather, it demonstrates that the scholarly and comparative study of religion offers unique perspectives from which to understand ourselves and our times. For deChant shows us that religious studies is about more than the study of religions; it is about the study of different ways of life and how, since the beginning of the human race, a sense of the sacred has shaped every culture, including postmodern secular culture.

While a struggle may be going on between Santa and Jesus for the meaning of Christmas, deChant rejects the thesis that this is best read as a struggle between the secular and the religious, between economics and religion. On the contrary, he tells us, what we see here is really a struggle between two different forms of religiosity. If Christianity sometimes seems to be losing this battle, it is not so much losing out to a secular society as it is to a society that has embraced another form of religiosity.

Deeply indebted to the thinking of Paul Tillich and of Jacques Ellul in the way he asks questions, but not necessarily in the way he answers them, deChant probes the religious dimension of contemporary secular and postmodern culture. He attempts to understand the religiosity of the economy much the way I attempted to understand the religiosity of technology in *The Ethical Challenge of Auschwitz and Hiroshima* (SUNY, 1993). While his interpretation puts us at odds on some key points concerning the religiosity of our culture, I am pleased that Dell credited that work as having an important influence on his project, and I find in his work an intellectual challenge worthy of the highest respect. Dell deChant asks us to see ourselves and our society with new eyes. Like Kierkegaard, he is a master of indirection. Without ever lecturing us, he challenges us to look at ourselves and decide for ourselves if the way we are actually living is what we really had in mind. He helps us understand ourselves and our postmodern culture.

A dominant theme of modern thought was that religion would disappear, to be replaced by the secular society of a scientific age. It is commonplace now to observe that a global religious resurgence since the 1970s has proved that claim false. What is still often missed is that, quite apart from the resurgence of religions, our everyday world of commerce and consumerism is saturated with religious myth and ritual. We fail to see this, says deChant, because we tend to identify religion with the transcendental religions like Judaism, Christianity, and Islam, where God is understood as different and distant from the natural world. But the religiosity of postmodern society is closer to the cosmological religiosity of premodern primal and early urban societies where the sacred manifests itself through diversity rather than uniformity, with rituals related to the many gods and spirits that influence every aspect of daily life. In this ancient type of society, religion is not a separate realm within society but an aspect of every cultural activity. To participate in the culture is to be religious.

In such ancient societies, human beings saw nature as the overwhelming and all-encompassing environment of powers and forces that governed their destiny. Experiencing themselves as totally dependent on these powers, human beings, overwhelmed by a sacral awe, sought to be in harmony with these forces through the myths and rituals of polytheism in all their contradictory diversity. Today the postmodern world mirrors that premodern world, deChant argues, except that now the environment that surrounds us and governs our destiny is the postmodern, multinational, global economy. The economy has transcended and encompassed nature in its marketing strategies, desacralizing nature and turning its abundance into raw materials for commodification while reorienting and secularizing its rituals in order to render consumerism a sacred activity serving the new powers that now govern our destiny.

Our problem is that we are blinded to the religious/ritual dimension of our economic life by our identification of religion with transcendental religions, seemingly unaware that cosmological, this-worldly religiosity has been far more typical and pervasive in the history of the human race. And so, in important ways, we fail to fully appreciate our own actions and the religious rhythms of our own culture, defined by a postmodern cycle of sacred festivals.

From the sacred stories conveyed by film, television dramas, and mass media advertising, on through the ritual activities of watching sports and visiting shopping malls as sacred places of intense religious activity, deChant takes us on a journey through postmodern religiosity. It is a journey through the eclectic amalgamation of postmodern myths conveyed by the mass media and the equally eclectic rituals of our postmodern holidays, from New Year's Day through Super Bowl Sunday, Presidents' Day, St. Patrick's Day, Easter, the Fourth of July, and on to the "High Holy Days" of Halloween-Thanksgiving-Christmas, peppered with many secondary festivals along the way.

Through his analysis of the stories and rituals that shape postmodern culture, Dell deChant shows us our sacred way of life — how the economic life of our postmodern world is permeated by the sacred and driven by mythic and ritual patterns as old as civilization itself. These patterns are intent on bringing us into harmony with the powers that govern our destiny, now perceived as the powers of the economy. After reading this book, you will never look at the world around you in the same way again.

DARRELL J. FASCHING
University of South Florida, Tampa

Preface

The Sacred Santa takes seriously the widespread perception that contemporary culture witnesses a profound struggle between two antithetical belief systems — a collision of two worlds. Unlike other studies that interpret this struggle in terms of dichotomies of religious and secular, this book reads the struggle as a conflict between two distinct religious systems.

The first of these systems, Christianity, has long been analyzed in the context of the "secularization thesis." In brief, this thesis argues that with the rise of modernization Christianity became increasingly marginalized in the West as secular institutions began to replace it as the source of cultural meanings and values. The question at the heart of this book is whether this traditional reading may not perhaps be a little too simplistic and a little too quick to discount the religious dimension of secular culture — especially in the contemporary *post*modern world. In response to this question, in *The Sacred Santa* I offer an alternative to the traditional interpretation, arguing that rather than being secular and nonreligious, America's late capitalist, postmodern culture is actually intensely religious, and best classified as a contemporary version of ancient cosmological religiosity.

In developing this argument, special attention is given to the religious function of contemporary holidays. And while American holidays have certainly become secular events, I contend that precisely their "secular" (materialist/commercial/consumerist) dimension makes them most obviously religious events in the context of postmodern cosmological culture. Christmas is certainly the most obvious example of a contemporary cosmological religious celebration, so it receives a detailed treatment in the book; other holidays also reveal the same sort of cosmological sense of the sacred.

The theoretic basis for the type of analysis I am doing in *The Sacred Santa* was first developed in two papers that I presented in 1996. The first, at the National Conference on Ethics and Popular Culture, focused on the function of Santa Claus as a cultural deity in a late capitalist, consumer-based society. In that paper, I drew connections between Santa and the cosmological gods of antiquity. The second, presented at the annual meeting of the American Academy of Religion, broadened my inquiry to include an analysis of the religious dimension of contemporary holidays (and Christmas in particular). Building on the analysis of Santa as a neocosmological god, I outlined the affinities between Christmas in contemporary consumer culture and the religious festivals of ancient cosmological cultures.

With continued research into the cosmological character of Santa Claus and the postmodern Christmas celebration, the same neocosmological religious elements that are so abundantly evident at Christmas became obvious during other holidays as well. This sort of religious activity is not confined to holidays, but actually is an elemental feature of our culture. The holidays simply intensify the religious experience. As the ancients saw nature as the ultimate sacred power and worshiped it in all of its various expressions, so we today see the economy as the sacred power of our culture and worship it in an even wider array of manifestations. As the ancients participated in rituals at temples and shrines, we participate in similar rituals at malls and department stores. Thus, rather than being functionally secular, our entire culture system begins to look profoundly sacred. Hence, my question about the secularization thesis and my subsequent answer in *The Sacred Santa: Religious Dimensions of Consumer Culture.*

Although this book is scholarly in its theoretical basis and premises, I have tried to write in a style and language that make it accessible to general readers. Persons interested in Christmas, holidays as a whole, and consumer culture should find much of interest here. Its professional audience will include Christian religious professionals, media professionals, and scholars working in disciplines and fields such as religious studies, American studies, humanities, popular culture, theology, and possibly anthropology and sociology. The book can function as a supplemental text in introductory courses in these fields or as a primary text in advanced courses.

A considerable number of people have inspired, encouraged, and assisted me in this project. Without their presence in my personal and professional life, *The Sacred Santa* would never have been completed. First and foremost is Professor Darrell J. Fasching, a person who has played many roles in my life — teacher, mentor, colleague, and friend. His support and assistance over the past twenty years have been invaluable. As regards this book, I am especially thankful to Dr. Fasching on three counts: first for introducing me to the thought of Jacques Ellul and Eric Voegelin, second for reading and critiquing the manuscript of this book, and third for agreeing to write the Foreword. In addition to Professor Fasching, I am appreciative of all the encouragement and assistance of each of the other faculty members in the Department of Religious Studies at the University of South Florida. Over the past several years, each has taken the time to discuss aspects of the book with me, raising issues I had not thought of, suggesting modifications in my interpretations, and helping me see the relationship between my work and their respective fields of inquiry. Of special note is Professor James F. Strange, who it seems I spoke with almost every day about the project.

Three talented graduate teaching assistants in the department were of tremendous assistance in the final stages of the project: Margo Smith, Michelle Demeter, and Jeffrey Thibert. Margo and Michelle not only proofread various drafts of the manuscript but also relieved me from a number of classroom and administrative tasks, which allowed me time to focus on the book. Jeff assisted in the review and analysis of economic data.

I also must thank all the students who have studied with me over the past sixteen years. Their interest in the study of religion has always inspired me, and their willingness to explore the religious dimension of consumer culture has quickened my own interest in this area.

Special thanks are extended to The Pilgrim Press and, especially, Editorial Director George R. Graham. I appreciate Mr. Graham's enthusiasm for the project and the willingness of Pilgrim Press to publish the book. In addition, I must express my gratitude to Mr. Graham for his helpful comments and suggestions on ways to improve the final draft.

For professional assistance in the assembly and analysis of economic data, I am indebted to Frank Y. Robson Jr., M.B.A. I would not have been able to grasp the relationship between holidays and consumer spending were it not for his exhaustive research, detailed computations, and coherent summaries of fluctuations in retail commerce. In this regard, I also wish to acknowledge Michael P. Niemira of the Bank of Tokyo-Mitsubishi (New York) for his willingness to allow me access to the bank's multiyear index of weekly chain store sales. For professional assistance in my analysis of advertising, I thank Eric Gerard, president, BigGross.com.

I would be remiss if I did not express my thanks to the Popular Culture Group of the American Academy of Religion and especially Professor Bruce David Forbes of Morningside College and Professor Jeffrey H. Mahan of the Iliff School of Theology. I am personally grateful for their acceptance of my paper on Santa Claus for the 1996 AAR program and their expressed interest in my work over the years. Beyond this, however,

I know I speak for many others in thanking them for their long-standing commitment to the study of religion and popular culture and for the considerable time and energy they devoted to establishing the Religion and Popular Culture Group within the AAR. I also wish to thank Professor Gary M. Laderman of Emory University for accepting for the 2001 AAR program my paper on the holidays and Professor Louis A. Ruprecht of Mercer University for his excellent response.

From the host of others who had an indirect relationship to my work on this project, I want to thank one unique individual who has been a source of personal inspiration and encouragement for many years: the Reverend Leddy Hammock of the Unity Church of Clearwater. Her friendship is one of the greatest blessings of my life.

Finally, and certainly most importantly, I wish to thank my wife, Marilynn, who was enthusiastically supportive from the outset. From listening to me talk about the thesis in its incipiency to helping with the final copy editing, Marilynn played a vital role in the project every step of the way. For this, I am most grateful. More than this, however, I thank her for allowing me to interrupt our togetherness to work on this book. There is no recompense that I can offer for this interruption. I can only express my deepest gratitude and witness it by dedicating the book to her.

— INTRODUCTION —

Sacred Worlds in Collision

Like many trite expressions, the observation of anguished Christians that Christmas has lost its religious meaning makes an important point, a point well known to most Americans — Christmas is not about religion but rather something else. Options for what this "something else" might be are numerous: shopping, tree buying and decorating, gift giving and receiving, bonus checks, "the children," office parties, going home for the holidays, and so on. While many millions do attend church during the Christmas season, it is usually not the most important event on holiday calendars.

The pious cant to "keep Christ in Christmas" is understandably as much a part of the season as carols on the radio, greeting cards in the mail, and fruitcakes in the stores. Also heard during the holiday season is the slogan, "Jesus is the reason for the season." Protest and critique also appear as a regular part of the American Christmas — an extended holiday period that enthralls and enchants virtually the entire culture. Regardless of what one makes of Jesus during the season and whether or when he comes into play, one would receive little argument that for vast numbers of the population Christmas in contemporary culture is a secular holiday, not a Christian holy day — that Santa, not Jesus, is the savior of this season. Santa and his celebration certainly save the bottom line on the annual reports for a great many merchants in this country. He is, in the words of Leigh Eric Schmidt, the "patron saint" of the modern Christmas bazaar.[1] Santa may be something more as well, and his relationship to Jesus might help us begin to understand just who he is and what he means to the holiday and culture as a whole.

As revealed by the dismal holiday sales of a nativity scene featuring Santa kneeling in prayer before the manger-crib of Christ,[2] Santa and Jesus are apparently not easily conjoined in the popular imagination. In fact, if the two are not engaged in mortal combat, as the pious would sug-

---

1. Leigh Eric Schmidt, *Consumer Rites: The Buying and Selling of American Holidays* (Princeton, N.J.: Princeton University Press, 1995), 130.

2. See Russell W. Belk, "A Child's Christmas in America: Santa Claus as Deity, Consumption as Religion," *Journal of American Culture* 10 (1987): 94.

1

gest, they are certainly involved in a rather vigorous competition — and Santa seems to be winning. The broader cultural context of this struggle and explanations for Santa's success are supplied by a now rather traditional interpretation of contemporary culture known as the "secularization thesis."[3] In brief, the thesis holds that concurrent with the emergence of secular institutions and worldviews associated with modernization, in the seventeenth and eighteenth centuries, a decline occurred in the cultural significance of religious beliefs and practices. The cultural contraction of religion and the rise of secular institutions have continued ever since and are witnessed in what Steve Bruce describes as three major changes: "the decline of popular involvement with the churches; the decline in scope and influence of religious institutions; and the decline in the popularity and impact of religious beliefs" (26).

In terms of this thesis, the competition between Santa and Christ is, thus, representative of the larger cultural struggle between secular and religious values — with Santa exemplifying secular values and Christ religious ones. To the degree that Santa is advancing as Christ is receding in terms of cultural significance, Santa's success conforms to the secularization thesis, offering yet another example of the replacement of traditional religious beliefs and practices with those more appropriate to a secular culture.

To read the seasonal struggle between Santa and Christ in the context of the secular-religious conflict may, however, represent a misinterpretation of Santa, the season, and the nature of contemporary culture. In fact, the erosion of the Christian significance of the season may be best understood not as a consequence of rising secularization and declining religiosity but as just the opposite. Rather than being a casualty of the struggle between secular and religious values for dominance in the commercial marketplace, the loss of Christian religious content in Christmas may actually be the consequence of Christianity's failure to successfully compete in another sort of marketplace — the marketplace of religion itself.

The Sacred Santa is based on the contention that Christmas has not lost its religious significance, only its *Christian* religious significance. Further, I argue that the initial presupposition that Christmas has become a secular event may overlook the ways and occasions in which events typically classified as secular are more accurately characterized as religious. Rather than a desacralized holy day or a purely secular one, in this book I propose

---

3. For a good overview of the secularization thesis, see Steve Bruce, "The Erosion of the Supernatural" (chapter 3), *Religion in the Modern World: From Cathedrals to Cults* (Oxford: Oxford University Press, 1996), 25–68. Bruce presents the main components of the thesis as well as major criticisms in an unapologetic "robust defense" (6) of the thesis.

an understanding of Christmas that sees it as not only decidedly religious but perhaps the best example of religiosity in our culture.

While one certainly can maintain that Christmas has indeed become a secular event, insofar as "secular" is intended to mean nonreligious in the academic and culturally normative sense of the word *religion,* this book proposes that the holiday's "secular" dimension (the materialist/ commercial/consumerist dimension) precisely makes it most obviously a religious event in the context of postmodern culture.

I might also add that Christmas is certainly a "Christian" event, but, again, not in the classical and modern sense of Christianity. Rather, by offering Christianity an opportunity both to define itself in the context of postmodern culture and to distinguish itself from that culture, Christmas allows Christianity to reinvent itself in terms of the logic of that culture and to do so through the use of its second greatest myth. Because this myth (the birth of Jesus) is now marginalized and this marginalization is generally legitimated in culture, when Christianity invokes the narrative, which is now one of social contrast and criticism (e.g., "keep Christ in Christmas"), it allows Christianity to affirm its actual identity as a marginalized social institution.

In short, Christmas is a religious event, but it is not recognized as such because the prevailing understanding of religion limits it to established traditions or activities, while the religious dimension of Christmas is revealed in its embodiment of a new (decidedly postmodern) sense of the sacred. The understanding developed in *The Sacred Santa* presents the American Christmas celebration as a profoundly religious experience sustained through normative rituals and legitimated by mythic narratives appropriate to this culture. The rituals allow participants inclusion in a collective performance of massive sacral significance while the myths illuminate the relationship between participants and the sacred realm.

The Christian loss, then, in what Stephen Nissenbaum has referred to as "the battle for Christmas,"[4] may not have been to commercialism, consumerism, late capitalism, or some other expression of postmodern secularization. Instead, Christianity has lost to another type of religion — one more suited to twenty-first-century America and one especially fitted for success in its emerging postmodern culture.

When seen in this way, the nativity scene with the praying Santa failed as a commodity not so much because it disturbed the sensibilities of Christian religionists (on the one hand) and Santa secularists (on the other), but

---

4. Stephen Nissenbaum, *The Battle for Christmas* (New York: Alfred A. Knopf, 1996).

rather because the product brought into alarming juxtaposition two anti-thetical religious systems. The praying Santa crèche was an unsuccessful commodity not because we do not want Santa praying but because in the popular imagination Santa does not pray at the shrine of Jesus. As a commodity it was a cultural surd that failed to sell for the same reason a nativity scene with a menorah would fail to sell. The two figures are simply from two different religious worlds, and by naively conjoining two of the most profound symbols of each system, the marketers brought the systems into conflict. The difference, however, between my fictive conjoining of the menorah and the nativity and the actual conjoining of Santa and Jesus is that in the latter conjunction, the systems in collision were represented by rival gods — one in cultural ascent, the other in cultural decline.

The Sacred Santa is about these rival gods, but only in part, because the conflict of these gods is merely the most salient witness to the religious struggle that may best explain the radical changes occurring in society and consciousness as the world lurches toward a thoroughly postmodern culture. This culture, which is typically interpreted as secular, in this book is reinterpreted as religious; but rather than being religious in the familiar *transcendental* sense, the culture is religious in a *cosmological* sense. In brief, "cosmological" refers to religions and cultural systems that locate the ground of being or ultimate concern in the natural world. "Transcen-dental" refers to religions and cultural systems that locate the ground of being in a supernatural dimension — literally, a realm beyond and radically different from nature.[5] As a representative religious event of this culture, Christmas necessarily reveals characteristics of a cosmological engagement with the sacred.

Christmas, however, is only the most obvious example of this cosmolog-ical engagement. As will be argued, other holiday periods and events also reveal the cosmological sense of the sacred. A critical assertion in this argu-ment is that the type of cosmological religiosity revealed in contemporary culture is historically unique and based on a fundamental shift in social structures and social values. This shift, which is most clearly articulated in postmodern interpretations of culture, serves to delegitimate the founda-tional faith claims of transcendental religions while simultaneously offering new and contrasting claims about the ultimate meanings and values of life.

Although these new claims are customarily understood as secular, and

---

5. The use of the terms *cosmological* and *transcendental* to distinguish between these types of cultures was introduced by Eric Voegelin in *The New Science of Politics* (Chicago: University of Chicago Press, 1952) and *Israel and Revelation* (Baton Rouge: Louisiana State University Press, 1956). These terms will be explicated more fully in chapter 1.

specifically defined in economic terms that accentuate their contrast with those asserted by religions, my contention is that they are not secular at all but just as fully religious as those they challenge and may today have eclipsed. If religion is the dimension of society and consciousness where ultimate concerns are encountered, as Paul Tillich told us in the 1920s, then consumption (certainly late capitalism's ultimate concern) must have a religious dimension in today's world. In this regard, and as is more fully discussed in chapter 1, the general approach of *The Sacred Santa* is in harmony with the sort of project Tillich introduced and first developed under the heading of "Theology of Culture," and as specifically explicated as a form of social ethics in the work of Darrell Fasching.[6] As Tillich was interested in "the religious dynamic at work in the diverse autonomous spheres of human endeavor that typify modern culture,"[7] this book is interested in the same dynamic as expressed in *post*modern culture. To encounter and analyze this dynamic in the contemporary world may help us better grasp how profoundly we have changed and how difficult it is for us to be other than we are.

To make my case, I have divided my argument into four sections, the four parts of the book. Part 1 introduces critical terms and concepts used in the text and offers a brief summary of the methodological approach. Although this book is not designed to be a theoretic study, the theorists and works from which the methodology is derived will be touched on briefly. Chapter 1 begins with a working description of religion and the role of myth and ritual in religious experience. Then the chapter explores the contrast between cosmological and transcendental religious systems followed by a brief survey of the historical trajectory of the secularization process from its biblical roots to the postmodern period. Chapter 2 advances an interpretation of contemporary postmodern culture as essentially religious, and specifically cosmological, given its veneration of consumption as a sacred activity. Chapter 3 offers an analysis of contemporary cosmological culture in the context of ancient cosmological religious systems, especially the primal and archaic.

Part 2 focuses on the critical religious features of postmodern cosmological culture. Chapter 4 specifies and analyzes the formal components

---

6. Paul Tillich, "Über die Idee einer Theologie der Kultur," in *Kanstudien* (Berlin: Pan Verlag, Rolf Heise, 1920). Found in translation in *What Is Religion,* trans. James Luther Adams (New York: Harper and Row, Harper Torchbooks, 1969). Darrell Fasching, *Apocalypse or Utopia?: The Ethical Challenge of Auschwitz and Hiroshima* (Albany: State University of New York, 1993), esp. 134–60.

7. Fasching, 139. My understanding of theology of culture as a form of social ethics is derived from Fasching's work, although my approach differs significantly from his.

of myth as they appear and function in postmodern culture, and chapter 5 focuses on postmodern rituals and religious specialists. Using Juliet B. Schor's study of contemporary consumerism as a base, chapter 6 offers an analysis of the religious dimension of personal consumption.

Building on the more general studies of the previous chapters, part 3 presents a detailed exposition of the religious dynamic of postmodern religious celebrations. Chapter 7 isolates and discusses the characteristic elements of postmodern holy days, using archaic cosmological New Year's celebrations as a model. Beginning with the various elements of holy days established in chapter 7, chapter 8 considers the role of myths and rituals in holy-day activities and deploys economic data as a measure of ritual activity to help define holy days apart from other holidays. Chapter 9 concludes part 3 with an analysis of the postmodern liturgical year (through Halloween), focusing on the function of holy days and other observances in the annual religious cycle.

Part 4 is devoted entirely to an exposition and analysis of the religious dimension of Christmas. Chapter 10 picks up with the end of the fall season and the beginning of the Christmas cycle. In addition to an analysis of Thanksgiving and the first Christmas rituals, this chapter uses the same criteria introduced in chapter 8 to determine the relative religious significance of the Christmas festival. In chapter 11, I examine a number of nonreligious seasonal narratives and traditions that support and enhance the religious celebration. Chapter 12 concludes the book and the argument with a study of the genealogy of Santa Claus and an examination of his status today as a postmodern god.

●

If the interpretation advanced in this book is correct, two antithetical belief systems are in collision not as dichotomies of religious and secular but rather as two distinct religious worlds. Each offers vivid visions of the sacred, but visions that differ radically with regard to what the sacred is and what it means to human life and social endeavor.

The substance of this argument, then, is that the culture we increasingly understand as *post*modern, while certainly antithetical to the modern, may not be such a novel cultural system after all. Our culture may actually be quite *pre*modern and have more in common with the grand imperial cultures of late antiquity than any seen in the West since the advent of Christianity. To overlook this possibility may overstate the extent to which Christianity still functions as a viable religion and understate the sacredness of our seemingly secular world.

Part I

THE SACRED GROUND OF POSTMODERN CULTURE

— O N E —

Religion from the Sacred Cosmos to the Secular World

Like other worlds and epochs before it, the postmodern world did not spring fully developed into life. Its roots are most directly traced to the modern period and its emergence predicated on cultural processes set in motion at that time. These processes, together with reactions to them, have had explicit and implicit religious consequences, and these consequences have served to form the sacred ground of postmodern culture. The precise character of this sacred ground and the religious ecology it fosters are the interests of this chapter. As a preface to this investigation, primary terms must be defined and the relationship between these terms explored.

Religion: myth and ritual

The first and perhaps most obvious term to define in the context of this inquiry is the concept of *religion* itself. This concept is notoriously ambiguous but theoretically unavoidable. The understanding offered here is essentially functional, but only insofar as a functional approach acknowledges the legitimacy of a sacred realm as an object of human intending. The other theoretic issues dealt with in this chapter, and the general argument of the book as a whole, are necessarily related to this working description:

> Religion is about power. It mediates our relationship with the source(s) of ultimate (sacred) power by suggesting, teaching, or commanding (1) a *belief* that the ultimate truth and meaning of human life is derived from and related to an order and purpose based on or decreed by the ultimate (sacred) power (e.g., gods, God, nature, cosmic principles, social order). (2) This belief is necessarily shared by a group or *community*. (3) This belief is *maintained* because of

9

(a) the community's participation in certain special and uniquely patterned actions, either personal or communal, typically called *rituals*, and (b) special (numinous) narratives, typically called *myths*, which deal with unique persons or events related to sacred concerns and elements. (4) This belief in the foundational truth and meaning of human life is understood by participants in the religion to allow them (as individuals and as a community) a certain degree of *power over material conditions* (in so far as they live and act in harmony with the ultimate power) and to supply them with *answers to ultimate questions* regarding nature and the human condition (such as death, the afterlife, evil, one's place in society, why one succeeds or fails).

Of special note here is the character and function of myths and rituals. Myths are narratives about the sacred and humanity's relationship to the sacred. Typically these narratives are set in a primordial time of origins and depict the actions and teachings of venerated ancestors, heroes, saviors, and gods. These actions and teachings disclose both the foundational reality of life and articulate the relationship of the believer to this reality. For the believer, myths communicate truths of such profundity that, even in the face of falsifying material or historical evidence, the believer accepts the reality of the myth. To the degree that a myth loses its radical truthfulness, it loses its primary religious function.

As will be discussed later, myths can be divided into three classes: "meta," secondary, and tertiary.[1] The meta-myth is the master story of a culture, which articulates "the true motivating and psychological foundations of [a] civilization . . . expressions of the very being of the collective and universal civilization in which we are living."[2] Secondary and tertiary myths are narratives that offer more accessible versions of the meta-myth, serving to personalize, vivify, and make it immediately relevant to individuals. In their secondary and especially their tertiary forms, myths guide and motivate religious activities. In their most formal sense, such activities are called rituals.

---

1. The specification of three classes of myth is derived, with some modifications, from Jacques Ellul. My meta-myth corresponds to what Ellul refers to as the "basic" or "essential" myth of a culture. My designation of secondary and tertiary myths is derived from Ellul, although, in my deployment, the two are more precisely distinguished from each other. See Jacques Ellul, *The New Demons* (New York: Seabury Press, 1975), 88–121, esp. 100–110.
2. Ibid., 109.

The general properties of rituals, as summarized by Sally F. Moore and Barbara G. Myerhoff, form the basis for understanding the term *rituals* as it is used here. These properties are:

1. *Repetition*

2. *Acting* (as in a play)

3. *"Special" behavior or stylization* (in actions or through the use of symbols)

4. *Order* (they are organized events at "prescribed times and places," "having a beginning and an end")

5. *Evocative presentational style; staging* (they "produce at least an attentive state of mind, and often an even greater commitment of some kind ... through manipulation of symbols and sensory stimuli")

6. *The "collective dimension"* (they have "social meaning" and carry "a social message")[3]

I would nuance this understanding by noting that although rituals are often collective, they may certainly be performed by individuals privately. Most importantly, to these general properties, I would add that those rituals that are specifically *religious* have a sacred dimension — a sacred meaning and message as well as a social meaning and message. In fact, in many religions, especially those focused on in this book, the sacred meaning/message is self-same with the social meaning/message. For the believer, rituals are the formal processes through which one participates in or otherwise affirms a proper relationship to the sacred. In this regard, the "texts" that religious rituals follow are the myths of the religion, since these narratives are the ones that articulate the sacred realm and humanity's relationship to that realm.

In a religious sense, then, rituals and myths are intertwined in such a way that rituals reenact myths and myths illuminate rituals. Through rituals, the believer experiences the sacred realm described in myths and is brought into communion with the foundational reality of life. In a practical sense, the interrelation of myth and ritual is revealed in the relationship between mythic narratives such as the Exodus story and the ritual of Passover; the narrative of the Last Supper and the ritual of communion;

---

3. For more detail, see Sally F. Moore and Barbara G. Myerhoff, "Introduction: Secular Ritual," in *Secular Ritual*, ed. Moore and Myerhoff (Amsterdam, The Netherlands: Van Gorcum, Assen, 1977), 7–8. Terms in italics and quoted material in parentheses are Moore and Myerhoff's.

or the narrative of the Buddha's enlightenment and the ritual of medita-
tion. A dynamic nexus thus occurs when the sacred reality disclosed in
myths is fully experienced through the performance of rituals. In a discussion of New Year's festivals of the ancient world, Mircea Eliade uses the
term "mythico-ritual" to characterize this synergy.[4] As will be seen later
in this book, many of our contemporary holidays reveal this same sort of
mythico-ritual dynamism.

Although healthy religions routinely reveal the positive dimension of the
synergy of myths and rituals, this synergy can also be reflected negatively
since the loss of plausibility for one may undermine the meaningfulness of
the other. In other words, when believers begin to doubt either the radical
truth of the myths or the re-creative power of the rituals, the religious
significance of both may decline. Doubting the truth of the myths leads
to a weakening of the significance of rituals just as doubt of the power of
rituals causes a corresponding erosion in the plausibility of mythic verities.
As such doubts become more widespread among participants, religious
communities decline.

•

This exploration and analysis of myth and ritual is undertaken in the context of what Paul Tillich introduced and first developed under the heading
of "Theology of Culture" and as further detailed in Darrell Fasching's contemporary interpretation of Tillich's method as a form of social ethics.[5]
There are two crucial elements in this approach. First, as Tillich recognized, "every culture has an inherent religious dimension, even as every
religion is shaped by the culture in which it emerges [and] culture is
driven by its religious 'substance,' which is the human need for meaning expressed and embodied in its...'ultimate concerns' "; and second,
theology of culture is specified as "a critique of the religious dynamic at
work in the diverse autonomous spheres of human endeavor that typify modern culture."[6] I argue that this religious dynamic is found in the
myths and rituals of a culture and most explicitly in their synergy — the
mythico-ritual dynamic. Following Tillich's proposal, then, as a theology
of culture, my subsequent inquiry into contemporary myths and rituals

---

4. For example, see Eliade's usage of the term in *Cosmos and History: The Myth of the Eternal Return*, trans. Willard R. Trask (New York: Harper and Row, Harper Torchbooks, 1959), 68–70.

5. See Darrell Fasching, *Apocalypse or Utopia: The Ethical Challenge of Auschwitz and Hiroshima* (Albany: State University Press of New York, 1993), chapter 4, esp. 134–41.

6. Tillich as explicated by Fasching in ibid., 137, 139.

can be understood as a "theological questioning of all cultural values,"[7] because the myths and rituals of this culture form the religious "substance" of these values — affirming their basis in truth and allowing experiential interaction with the reality of this truth.

As Tillich understood theology of culture to be a "critique of the religious dynamic at work in... modern culture," in my application, the critique is of the religious dynamic at work in a *post*modern culture, which is seemingly secular. Two other terms require contextual explication at this point: secularization and *post*modern. Secularization, as it relates to this study, is the focus of the remainder of this chapter. Postmodernity is taken up in the following chapter.

Secularization and modernity

To better understand postmodernity, some engagement with modernity is necessary, and this engagement leads inevitably to an encounter with the great cultural engine of modernity — secularization. The most obvious causes and earliest manifestations of secularization can be found in the Reformation, and its first flowering in the Enlightenment, but its true womb was the biblical worldview and specifically the worldview of ancient Israel.[8] Thus, in briefly considering its process and its function as the engine of modernity, we must look at secularization in three historical contexts: (1) its origin in the biblical worldview, (2) its eruption in Europe between four and five centuries ago, and (3) its rise to cultural dominance during the Enlightenment.

Even before examining the process of secularization, we must first equip ourselves with a working definition of this term. The most economical definition available comes from the work of Peter Berger, who explains it as "the process by which sectors of society and culture are removed from the domination of religious institutions and symbols."[9] Importantly, he goes on to say that secularization manifests itself in both the material and intellectual realms. The material impact is well known, being revealed in prohibitions on religious activity in government and public education (sep-

---

7. Paul Tillich, "Über die Idee einer Theologie der Kultur," in *Kanstudien* (Berlin: Pan Verlang, Rolf Heise, 1920). Found in translation in *What Is Religion,* trans. James Luther Adams (New York: Harper and Row, Harper Torchbooks, 1969), 165.

8. The inclusion of the biblical worldview in the interpretation of secularization is found in several sources, including Max Weber, Julius Wellhausen, Richard Rubenstein, and especially Peter Berger. For the fullest and most accessible sketch of this interpretation, see Berger, *The Sacred Canopy* (Garden City, N.Y.: Anchor Books, 1969), chapter 5.

9. Ibid., 107.

aration of church and state), and more radically in the expropriation of religious property and prohibitions of religious practices. The intellectual impact is even more significant, for in this way secularization influences culture as a whole, affecting the arts, philosophy, literature, economics, and human self-understanding. Perhaps the most significant consequences of secularization's modification of culture are witnessed in the rise of science as an autonomous power in the modern world and the economic application of science in the technological revolution.

Secularization, then, is a process, not an institution; and precisely the social and cultural process that relegates traditional religious affirmations and values to secondary status. As a process, secularization is most crucial to both the emergence of the modern worldview during the Reformation as well as its expansion and maintenance from that time up to our own.

What secularization does is loosen the grip of religion on society in general and individual consciousness specifically. In the case of the Reformation, it first loosened the grip of medieval Catholicism and later of religion itself on the societies and minds of Western Europe. Before isolating the forces that triggered the decisive eruption of secularization in the sixteenth and seventeenth centuries, a word must be said about its deep taproot, and to do so we must return to a far earlier time when the impulse to desacralize the world was born.

Desacralization and the biblical worldview

Central to the process of secularization is what Max Weber called "Entzauberung der Welt," the disenchantment of the world. This disenchantment, or desacralization, has long been thought to have its roots in the biblical worldview.

Following Eric Voegelin, Berger discusses the disenchantment process witnessed in the Old Testament and the religious tradition of ancient Israel by noting the difference between the biblical worldview, which was transcendental in character, and the worldview of other cultures existing in the ancient Near East, which was cosmological in character. The cosmological worldview of the indigenous cultures of the Near East was challenged by the religion of ancient Israel, and their "world" was disenchanted — at least in terms of Israelite theology. The key to understanding the disenchantment process, then, is to be found in the profound difference between the transcendental and cosmological approaches to life and meaning. As noted in the introduction, "cosmological" religions locate the ground of being or ultimate concern in the world of nature. In contrast, "transcendental" religions locate the ground of being in a supernatural dimension — literally, a realm beyond and radically different from nature.[10] The relationship of these two religious systems can now be considered in somewhat greater detail.

The eclipse of cosmological religion by transcendental systems began during the Axial Age (800–200 B.C.E.), but not until the Christianization of Rome in the fourth century C.E. did the transcendental worldview become a large-scale cultural force in the West. These religions, of which Judaism was an important early expression, recognize the highest meaning of life, the divine font of existence, the cause and principle of creation (in short, the foundation of ultimate concern) as un-natural; beyond, above, and utterly different from the world of nature. In addition, these religions affirm that humanity has some sort of relationship with this supernatural power, which in the monotheistic systems is called God, and this relationship in various ways legitimates humanity's dominion over nature. This relationship also adds what Voegelin calls the anthropological component to transcendental systems.

As these new transcendental religions developed, the old gods themselves were destroyed and the sacredness of natural elements (even nature itself) was increasingly denied. Weber calls this process " disenchantment."

Importantly, the Western forms of transcendental religiosity (Judaism, Christianity, and Islam) have tended to be extremely hostile toward cosmological religions. Relativizing the natural order to the transcendent order, as in the opening chapter of Genesis or the Gospel of John, Western monotheism attacked the sacred reality of cosmological religion and rejected the legitimacy of its myths and rituals. From strident missionary activity to forced conversions and legal prohibitions against cosmological religious practices, the history of the rise of transcendental monotheism has included an aggressive and at times violent antagonism toward cosmological religions. The mythic background of this antagonism can be found in the Old Testament and its various narratives pitting the God of Israel against various nature deities, condemning "idol" worship, and celebrating the victorious struggles of Israelite heroes against their cosmological adversaries. With the rise of Christianity and later Islam, the monotheistic assault on cosmological religion continued; with their enormous success, the assault became more widespread. Following Judaism, Christianity and Islam came on the historical scene bristling with critique and condemna-

---

10. See Eric Voegelin in *The New Science of Politics* (Chicago: University of Chicago Press, 1952) and *Israel and Revelation* (Baton Rouge: Louisiana State University Press, 1956).

tion of the old cosmological systems, their gods and sacred orders, their shamans and priests, their myths and rituals. History has revealed them to have been enormously successful.

Until the rise of these new religions, human religiosity (in fact, all of human culture) was cosmological. In such systems the divine was immanent in the world and the sacred was encountered in the context of nature: the flight of the sun and journey of the stars, the ebb and flow of seasons, the rise and fall of rivers, the cycles of the moon. No intrinsic separation existed between humans and the natural world that sustained life; so too the social order and the order of the cosmos itself were indistinguishable. Life was a continuous harmony. Religion and the other institutions of culture were not separate, and all of what we would call culture was integrated into the grand order of the cosmos.

Such religions served to mediate the relationship between human beings and the awesome and enchanted cosmos. They articulated the sacredness of places, objects, power spots, holy mountains, sacred groves, totems, male sky gods, and female gods of the earth. Their festivals were celebrations of the earth and its bounty; their myths were stories of ancestors and heroes who exemplified the norms of humanity's relationship with the divine; their rituals celebrated this relationship in the context of nature's ceaseless cycles. The changing of seasons was of religious concern for everyone and needed the religious attention of the entire culture, the ending of droughts a cause for collective sacrifice, a prosperous harvest an occasion for massive culturewide celebration.

Unlike the religions of today, which are discrete institutions, these religions were collective enterprises based on deeply rooted cultural beliefs about the order and process of the cosmos and humanity's right relationship with it. With the order and process of the cosmos as the ground of sacred meaning, religion served as the source and force of legitimation and guidance for culture and human activity relative to the sacred ground. Rather than standing apart from the everyday life of their cultures, cosmological religions were embedded in their midst, sacralizing their political and economic processes and cosmicizing their social structures. Myths were universal and rituals were collective. Through them, religion affirmed and acted out the truth of the cosmic order that was already revealed in everyday life: the way things are is the way they ought to be. These religions were structured for an enchanted world we do not know today and can hardly even imagine. This specific world began to be disenchanted with the rise of transcendental religions.

Cosmological religion goes by many names today: naturalism, animism, primal, and archaic. Its most sophisticated expression is probably best known as polytheism; and in this form cosmological religiosity made its last great stand against transcendental religiosity in the institutional polytheism of the Graeco-Roman world, a world that eventually was overcome by what would become the largest religion in the world—Christianity.

In summary, the transcendental worldview, rooted in biblical notions of transcendental monotheism, supernatural creation myths, and human dominion over nature, disenchanted the natural world and eviscerated cosmological religion. By removing its gods and the ambient sacredness of the world and placing a single God above and beyond the world, transcendental monotheism replaced a reverence for the cycles of nature with a reverence for the events of history, and instead of the magical and mysterious potentiality of nature, the rationality of God and elevated rationality in human beings were positioned in an exalted plane. While this early expression of desacralization cannot be called the beginning of secularization as we know it today, we can nonetheless learn something about the ground from which the process seemed so suddenly to explode at the close of the Middle Ages.

The eruption of secularization

The secularization process proper is correctly traced to the Reformation period of the sixteenth and seventeenth centuries. Although the ground was prepared by ancient transcendental religious notions, secularization in the modern period took new and more radiant forms.

To understand the modern secularization process, we might best proceed much as we did in our approach to the disenchantment process initiated by the biblical worldview, by comparing the new worldview with the resident one that it challenged and rather swiftly delegitimized. In the case of modern secularization, the worldview that it challenged and soon replaced was that of medieval Catholicism—a religion with certain salient features reminiscent of the cosmological religions of antiquity.

In looking at late medieval Catholicism, we are at once struck by its affinities with cosmological religions. Although the triumph of the Catholic form of Christianity over the polytheism of the Roman Empire can be seen as the victory of the transcendental religious vision over the cosmological, the triumph was paradoxical, for with the rise of Catholicism a process of recosmicization began. The process would not reach fruition because the Protestant Reformation decisively interrupted it.

Again following Berger's analysis, we have a good picture of how the

Catholic recosmicization process unfolded. As regards transcendentalization, Catholicism takes a significant retrograde step when positing Jesus
as the incarnation of God. Suddenly, God was not so transcendent after
all, for Jesus, who is fully God and fully human, was (at least for a time)
a living resident of the planet. Expanding on this retrograde notion, Catholicism reenchanted the world as it "brought in its wake a multiplicity of
other modifications . . . the whole host of angels and saints . . . culminating
in the glorification of Mary as mediatory and co-redeemer."[11] Other cosmological motifs include the rigid hierarchical structuring of society, the
decline of autonomous political authority and the ascent of religious dominance, the development and expansion of the sacramental ordering of the
life experience, the veneration of sacred images and relics, the notion of
transubstantiation, the recognition of theophanic and hierophanic physical locales that became pilgrimage sites, and the general subsumption of
culture as a whole in the categories and rituals of religion. Perhaps only in
the transcendentalization of history did Catholicism maintain a fairly consistent transcendental position; this notion, the idea of a divinely guided
historical progression, would, under the impact of secular reinterpretation,
become decisive to the emergence of modernization.

Luther, Calvin, and other reformers were reacting to this medieval Catholicism, and in effect, the Reformation replicated in Western Europe the
disenchantment process of antiquity. As had been the case in that earlier
time, a thoroughly mediated and unified religious worldview was challenged on the basis of a radically transcendental understanding of divinity.
Berger captures the full seriousness and extent of the situation:

> The Protestant believer no longer lives in a world ongoingly pene-
> trated by sacred beings and forces. Reality is polarized between a
> radically transcendent divinity and a radically fallen humanity. . . .
> Between them lies an altogether "natural" universe. . . . The radical
> transcendence of God confronts a universe of radical immanence, of
> "closedness" to the sacred. . . . Protestantism abolished most . . . medi-
> ations. It broke the continuity, cut the umbilical cord between heaven
> and earth, and thereby threw man back upon himself in a historically
> unprecedented manner.[12]

What Protestantism also did, especially in Luther's modification of Au-
gustine's concept of the two cities, was grant religious sanction to the

---

11. Berger, *The Sacred Canopy,* 121.
12. Ibid., 111–12.

secular world. No longer was the secular city relegated to secondary status beside the city of God; now the secular city was a place in which God could be served. Calvin would take this religious validation of secular activity even further by equating the concept of divine election with material prosperity and economic success.

By validating the secular world, Protestantism also devalued the world of religious meaning. In one sense this tactic was theologically cunning, for by challenging the Catholic assumption that life's ultimate meaning could be found only through the church, the Protestant impulse to legitimate the secular world served to delegitimate the Catholic religion. In a more profound sense, this tactic was a colossal blunder because the recognition of the viability of a secular society was a de facto recognition of the autonomy of secular society apart from any religious affirmation, Catholic or Protestant. To combat Catholic claims of religious ultimacy, Protestantism aligned itself with forces outside the religious sphere. In the case of Luther, the alliance was with the forces of nationalism in Germany; in the case of Calvin, with the forces of emerging capitalism in Geneva. In both cases, the alliance was efficacious to the cause of the new religion. But the alliance between Protestantism and the emerging forces of secularization would turn out to be a Faustian bargain, for ultimately, secularization would delegitimate all religious claims to ultimacy and subsequently religion itself.

The Protestant attack on Catholicism can be seen as the spark that triggered the modern secularization process, and while that attack has certain similarities with the biblical challenge to cosmological worldviews, there is an important distinction. What makes the Reformation different from the ancient situation is that in the Reformation religion itself affirmed the legitimacy of a nonreligious (secular) world. Initially, this legitimacy was tacit and perhaps only expedient; over time, this legitimacy increased until, by the Enlightenment, the secular world had the power to assert not only its full autonomy from religion, but also a greater legitimacy than religion. Unlike the ancient struggle, the encounter here was not between two rival religions, but rather between religion and an irreligious ideology — at least that is how the struggle has been interpreted traditionally.

Citing the Reformation as the spark of the secularization process is only the beginning of the story. The process itself extends well beyond the Reformation and, in fact, up to the present day. Between then and now the process has continued unchecked, although certain significant events accelerated its early development.

The first event of note actually occurred before the Reformation, in

1454. In that year Johann Gensfleisch of Gutenberg perfected movable type and the printing press was born. Arguably, Luther's Ninety-five Theses of 1517 would never have touched off the Reformation had it not been for the printing press. Equally arguable is the decisiveness of the press to the secularization process. The press did nothing less than transform society. Suddenly, access to knowledge was tremendously expanded. Before this invention, written documents had limited distribution, and as a corollary, few people could read and few had the opportunity to study and learn. Before the press, only a handful knew the events of the past — what Rome was, what history was all about. Before Gensfleisch's breakthrough, few knew geography — the location of nations and peoples, rivers and oceans. Before the press, few knew mathematics of even the simplest sort. Whatever the common person knew was probably received from the Church and the Church as an institution strongly resisted change. Once the press came into existence, however, change was inevitable and the Church could go along or be left behind. That it was left behind is part of the secularization process.

The next decisive event was the Thirty Years' War and the Peace of Westphalia of 1648. As a result of this war, which was fought largely on the basis of religious differences, the importance of religion was drastically reduced and its practice became a private rather than a public one. For over a thousand years the central feature of cultural life and individual existence had been the Church. Beginning with the Reformation, and fueled by the terrible religious wars it spawned, Christianity began to lose its hold on the minds and hearts of Western Europeans. Just as after the Peace of Westphalia, religion was not something worth killing or being killed for, so too did it cease to be a driving force in cultural life. This change is another part of the secularization process.

In the wake of the Thirty Years' War and with the erosion of religion as a motive force in cultural life, new institutions of a decidedly secular character arose. Some of the major new institutions that vied for the interest and devotion of the masses were education, politics, nationalism, and economics. In the case of each of these institutions, persons were given opportunities for self-identification apart from religion. In each case, persons who once would have identified themselves in religious terms and looked to the Church to explain their role in society now could look elsewhere for self-legitimation. As a consequence, religion was devalued in society and its sphere of cultural influence drastically contracted. While I might be a Christian, I was first what I was educated to be, perhaps a lawyer, or a scientist, an engineer, a teacher. If I was a politician or involved in political issues, I might still be a Christian, but I was first a Democrat, a Monarchist, or later a Socialist or a Marxist. If I was a nationalist, I might still be a Christian but I was first a Frenchman, a Pole, an Englishman, a German, a Serb. If I was involved in economics, I might still be a Christian but I was first a capitalist, a merchant, a tenant, an investor, a landlord, an employee. The great change, and the turn toward secularization revealed by these new institutions for self-definition, is that until this time, the vast majority of Europeans did not identify themselves apart from religion and religious categories of existence. Additionally, most people were uneducated agriculturalists with few material possessions and no property, usually ruled on one hand by a powerful lord and on the other by an even more powerful Church.

The Enlightenment and the first flowering of secularization

Beyond the crucible of the Reformation, the next great era of consequence to the secularization process was the Enlightenment. Secularization became fully established at this time, as the secular vision forcefully asserted its dominance over society and religion. Whether the Enlightenment is over or not is debatable, but even if it is simply a historical era (i.e., seventeenth and eighteenth centuries), the Enlightenment's chief themes and forces continue to powerfully influence the contemporary world.

The origin of the word tells us much about the ideology of the Enlightenment: "The Enlightenment" (*die Aufklärung*) was first used by eighteenth-century thinkers to characterize their times over and against the medieval period, which in contrast came to be known as the "Dark Ages." In its most forceful denotation, the term expressed an antireligious stance, since the "darkness" of medievalism against which the "light" of eighteenth-century culture was contrasted was a darkness of superstition and ignorance attributed to religious domination of society. In its social and cultural vision, the Enlightenment stressed secular ideals, and just as the social, political, and academic leaders of ancient Rome left their polytheistic religions for the new religion of Christianity during the Christian revolution of the second through fourth centuries, so the leaders of eighteenth-century Europe left the Christian religion for the various movements in the orbit of secularization.

In the Enlightenment, science bloomed, the horizons of intellectual inquiry expanded, and everything was questioned and doubted until proven true according to the emerging materialist ethic of the time. New inventions and technologies proliferated, and they continued to change the

world just as the printing press had done at the beginning of the secularization process. Concurrent with the Enlightenment were three revolutions:
the American Revolution, the French Revolution, and the Industrial Revolution — each representing important motifs of modernization. In the
American Revolution, we see the institutionalization and legalization of
the separation of the religious and secular realms, the beginning of state-
supported pluralism, and, in the name of religious freedom, the free and
open competition between religions for the allegiance of believers. In the
French Revolution, we find features common to many other modern political revolutions: the proclivity to violence (and often antireligious violence),
the aggressive assertion of a secular worldview, and the rise of an au-
thoritarian leader (i.e., Napoleon). Finally, in the case of the Industrial
Revolution, itself inspired and accelerated by the scientific revolution and
the capitalist revolution, we witness the expansion and complexification
of manufacturing, the intensification of the urbanization process, the up-
rooting of peoples, the destruction of traditional forms of human solidarity
and unity (i.e., family, church, local communities), and the stratification
of society along economic lines.

These great revolutions of the Enlightenment were not restricted to
the material realm alone. In addition to the three already noted, a fourth
revolution, an intellectual revolution, had perhaps the greatest long-term
negative impact on religion. This book is not the place to go into extensive
detail about the many thinkers who critiqued religion and its claims. Still,
a few must be mentioned, for they exemplify the process through which
the intellectual community effectively removed the plausibility structures
for religion. Each of these thinkers, and the intellectual milieu as a whole,
dealt religion a devastating blow by attacking the certainty and finality of
religious assertions. In an age of aggressive inquiry, such assertions were
rendered empty for all but the "unenlightened."

To set the strategy, although not necessarily the main religious theme
for the intellectual revolution of the Enlightenment, we can look at the
work of René Descartes, who introduced systematic doubt as a working
philosophic methodology. Of course, Descartes is best remembered for
the "Cogito," but his real importance to the Enlightenment and the entire
intellectual ambiance of modernity is his preface to *"Cogito ergo sum"*
(I think, therefore I am) — namely, the *"Dubito"*: *"Dubito ergo cogito"*
(I doubt, therefore I think). For Descartes, all things could be doubted,
except, initially, the fact that he doubted. How important and central to
the course of intellectual history is the fact that Descartes predicated his
existence and all his philosophy not on the fact that he thought, but rather

on the fact that he doubted; if he had not doubted, he would never have concluded that he thought. Doubt, then, was the key to the Cartesian system and a critical element in the foundation of modern intellectual history. Descartes did go on to construct arguments for God not unlike those of the great Church leaders before him, Anselm and Aquinas, but the arguments did not set the tone for modern thought. What set the tone was the doubt, and the thinkers of the Enlightenment picked up where Descartes left off and moved on to find the limits of human knowing and meaning.

The Western intellectual tradition has been following Descartes's strategy in one way or another ever since. In the wake of Descartes came Hume, Kant, Hegel, Kierkegaard, Nietzsche, and Marx. Each of these figures found pre-Enlightenment religion somehow unfulfilled and inauthentic. Each tampered with traditional Christian assumptions, and Hume, Kierkegaard, Nietzsche, and Marx blasted institutional Christianity from pillar to post. Each of these thinkers is critical to what becomes the secular-modernist understanding of religion, and each informs us that something is decisively wrong with religion in theory or practice or both. Most emblematic perhaps of the secular-modernist stance toward religion is this passage from Nietzsche:

> The madman jumped into their midst and pierced them with his eyes. "Whither is God?" he cried; "I will tell you. *We have killed him —* you and I. All of us are his murderers. . . . God is dead. God remains dead. And we have killed him.[13]

What started with Descartes as a doubt of all things and moves to his philosophic proof for the existence of God leads to Nietzsche's philosophic rejection of religion and his affirmation that God is dead. What Nietzsche affirmed remained for the most part a central tenet of the secularization process and a central premise in inquiries into religion undertaken in the wake of the intellectual revolution of modernity.

Whether or not this premise is still valid in the postmodern period is one of the questions of this study. This question has been asked before with no dearth of answers, pro and con, ranging from the fiercely academic to the rabidly devotional. What seems common to so many of these responses is a perspective that takes all too seriously the God that Nietzsche's madman

---

13. Friedrich Nietzsche, *The Gay Science,* trans. Walter Kaufmann (New York: Vintage Books, 1974), 181.

claimed had died, but perhaps not seriously enough the possibility that younger, more vigorous gods have taken his place. The madman could well have been correct in claiming that we have killed God, but we may err in ignoring the vastness of the sacred sphere and missing the presence of other gods, some of which may be quite near.

— T W O —

From Modern Secularization to Postmodern Sacralization

My intent in this chapter is not to resolve the complex nest of issues commingled in and around the term *postmodern*. The term is in extreme flux today, in part due to its magnificent popularity in both popular and academic culture. One of those ferociously alluring labels, *postmodern* can at once classify an incredibly vast array of cultural phenomena while simultaneously (and necessarily) defying any and all efforts to stabilize its meaning with anything close to precision. It is a term of conjure and conjecture, and ultimately, I suspect, uncertainty for many. This uncertainty may not be diminished here, although my hope is to approach postmodernism from a new direction that brings into focus an overlooked element in the ever expanding discussion of its meaning. For this purpose, a helpful place to begin is with Fredric Jameson's explication of postmodernism. Jameson is introduced here with some hesitancy because his work has become virtually iconic in some communities of inquiry, and in such instances, even brief references can lead to misinterpretations of an author's intent. Although it should be evident that my use of Jameson's approach here is hardly dogmatic, I do find his historically based socioeconomic reflections on the advent of the postmodern period insightful and coherent — and especially relevant to this study.

The development of life and consciousness inside the culture of consumption

Jameson's theory of postmodern culture follows Ernest Mandel's thesis in his *Late Capitalism,* and in a good Marxist reading, Jameson argues that cultural changes follow changes in modes of production and technology. Thus, Mandel's *market capitalism* corresponds to the cultural period Jameson refers to as *realism;* Mandel's monopoly capitalism corresponds to Jameson's *modernism;* and Mandel's third stage (variously termed *postin-*

dustrial capitalism, multinational capitalism, late capitalism, or *consumer capitalism*) corresponds to Jameson's *postmodernism.*[1]

This sequence of events in capitalism's evolution takes us from 1848 (Mandel's date for the beginning of market capitalism) to the present, with the 1940s cited as the beginning of the postmodern period. This evolution also measures the trajectory from the production-based economic system of the Industrial Revolution to today's consumption-based economic system. During this period of approximately a century, technological advances and manufacturing capacity transformed the economic equation from one in which the social focus of capitalism was on production of commodities to one in which the social focus was on the consumption of commodities.

Of primary interest here are Jameson's comments on changes in popular attitudes toward consumption in postmodern culture brought about by late capitalism's incredible capacity to produce and reproduce both material objects and images. For Jameson, late capitalism or "consumer capitalism...the purest form of capitalism yet to have emerged, [witnesses] a prodigious expansion of capital into hitherto uncommodified areas," such as the "unconscious" through "the rise of the media and the advertising industry" (36).[2]

In the postmodern world, "commodity production [is based on the] frantic economic urgency of producing fresh waves of ever more novel-seeming goods (from clothing to airplanes), at ever greater rates of turnover," in which there is "an immense dilation of...the sphere of commodities...a commodity rush, our 'representations' of things tending to arouse an enthusiasm and a mood swing not necessarily inspired by the things themselves" (5, x). The "culture of consumption" is presented as a dynamic force, which when "unleashed" consumes persons "to the point of being unable to imagine anything else" (207). Moreover, "we are *inside* the culture of the market and...the inner dynamic of the culture of consumption is an infernal machine from which one does not escape by the taking of thought (or moralizing positions)." It offers "an infinite propagation and replication of 'desire' that feeds on itself and has no outside and no fulfillment" (206). He notes that "the force, then, of the concept of the market lies in its 'totalizing' structure...: that is, in its capacity to afford a model of a social totality" (272).

---

1. Fredric Jameson, *Postmodernism, or The Cultural Logic of Late Capitalism* (Durham, N.C.: Duke University Press, 1991), 35–36.

2. See also his earlier work, "Postmodernism and Consumer Society," in Hal Foster, ed., *The Anti-Aesthetic* (Port Townsend, Wash.: Bay Press, 1983), 111–25.

Jameson's reading of consumption as the dominant characteristic of postmodern culture is affirmed and advanced by Jean Baudrillard. As noted by his critical exegete, Douglas Kellner, Baudrillard interprets postmodern culture as a culture of consumption in which "participation... requires systematic purchase and organization of domestic objects, fashion and so on into a system of organized codes and models."[3] In Baudrillard's own words:

> We have reached the point where "consumption" has grasped the whole of life, where all activities are connected in the same combinatorial mode.... In the phenomenology of consumption, this general climatization of life, goods, objects, services, behaviors and social relations represents the perfected, "consummated" stage of evolution which, through articulated networks of objects, ascends from pure and simple abundance to complete conditioning of action and time and finally to the systematic organization of ambience, which is characteristic of the drugstores, the shopping malls, or the modern airports in our futuristic cities.[4]

Kellner further interprets Baudrillard: "The consumer... cannot avoid the obligation to consume, because it is consumption that is the primary mode of social integration and the primary ethic and activity within the consumer society." For him, consumerism requires "active labor, incessant curiosity and search for novelty, and conformity to the latest fads, products and demands to consume"; and through the acquisition of commodities "our entire society *communicates* and speaks of and to itself" (16). Finally, and most significantly, Baudrillard characterizes the consumer's mental attitude toward consumption as *"magical thought"*: "a miraculous mentality which rules everyday life, a primitive mentality in the sense that is defined as a belief in the omnipotence of thoughts: in this case, belief in the omnipotence of signs" (14).[5]

I believe that Jameson and Baudrillard (and others who follow this general reading) are correct in their interpretation of postmodern culture as fundamentally a culture of consumption that is defined materially and psychically in and through the consumption of objects and images. Moreover,

---

3. Douglas Kellner, *Jean Baudrillard: From Marxism to Postmodernism and Beyond* (Stanford, Calif.: Stanford University Press, 1989), 13.
4. As cited in ibid., selection from Jean Baudrillard, *Selected Writings*, ed. Mark Poster (Cambridge and Palo Alto: Polity Press and Stanford University Press, 1988), 33.
5. From Baudrillard, *La société de consommation* (Paris: Gallimard, 1970), 27 (Kellner's translation of passage).

this interpretation should be expanded and further clarified to include the observation that mere consumption does not adequately describe our relationship with objects and images. The association is more complex.

Rather than simply consuming objects and images, postmodern culture can be understood as explicating meaning and value through a three-stage process, which begins with (1) acquisition of products, is clarified in (2) consumption of products, and finally is fulfilled in (3) disposal of products. In critical texts dealing with consumer culture, the first and third stages are typically subsumed by the second,[6] but the first and third make both logical and psychical claims to equal importance. The first stage is of absolute importance, for without it actual consumption cannot occur. One must first acquire the item before the item can be consumed. In this regard, studies of compulsive/addictive behavior indicate that the compulsive/addictive subject is often driven as much (or more) by the thrill of acquisition of the desired item as by its actual possession/consumption.[7] The final stage is equally important because it allows the process to begin again, and preferably, with a higher-quality object or image within a particular class of items. Although researched studies of compulsive behavior have not revealed particular interest in this feature of the process, the gratification of disposing of the consumed item may well equal the gratification of acquiring it initially, since only when the item is disposed of can the process begin again.

A note on consumption and the acquisition-consumption-disposal process

The reason for the general tendency to subsume the other two parts of the process, especially acquisition, under the heading of consumption seems to be a consequence of the way the term "consumption" is used in economic literature. As explained by Juliet B. Schor, for economists, "consumption" refers to "all monetary expenditure."[8] In my own diagnosis, however, this concept of "consumption" would refer to the acquisition phase of the

6. See Jameson, *Postmodernism,* and Baudrillard in Kellner, *Jean Baudrillard.* See also Daniel Miller, "A Theory of Christmas," in *Unwrapping Christmas,* ed. Daniel Miller (Oxford: Clarendon Press, 1993), 18–19; and Juliet B. Schor, *The Overspent American: Upscaling, Downshifting, and the New Consumer* (New York: Basic Books, 1998).

7. See Anne Wilson Schaef, *When Society Becomes an Addict* (San Francisco: Harper and Row, 1987), 74–78; Janet E. Damon, *Shopaholics: Serious Help for Addicted Spenders* (Los Angeles: Price Stern Sloan, 1988), 12; and Donna Boundy, *When Money Is the Drug: The Compulsion for Credit, Cash, and Chronic Debt* (New York: Harper Collins, 1993), 128.

8. Schor, *The Overspent American,* 217.

acquisition-consumption-disposal process. Having said this, and not to quibble too much over semantics, here and elsewhere in the book I will generally follow the standard usage of "consumption," as a covering term for the threefold process described above, and more specifically for the initial acquisition phase of the process. In order to clarify certain points or to draw specific attention to the acquisition phase, however, I explicitly link consumption with acquisition or the threefold process. I also use "acquisition" rather than "consumption" when acquisition is the more suitable term.

The cosmological character of contemporary culture

Aside from subsuming acquisition under consumption, what is missing in most examinations of the process of consumption in postmodern culture is the recognition that the process may be decidedly religious in character, or that it has anything to do with religion at all for that matter. The works of Eric Voegelin and especially Jacques Ellul are helpful here. While offering a departure from the rather traditional interpretation of religion found (at best briefly) in Jameson and Baudrillard, what Voegelin and Ellul supply are the missing features of the analytic model necessary to designate the religious character of postmodern culture and the base from which to develop the analysis of consumption as a religious activity. Although I do not entirely agree with Voegelin and Ellul, and at certain critical points I believe their analysis is flawed, their designation of the religious dimension of contemporary culture is fundamentally correct.

Unlike Jameson and Baudrillard, Voegelin and Ellul do not minimize or marginalize the religious character of what typically is presented as secular culture. Rather than relegating religion to its classical forms and discussing it in the context of its eclipse or its problematic status in postmodern culture, Voegelin and Ellul allow interpreters to recognize what Tillich calls the "religious dynamic" in seemingly secular processes. Both Voegelin and Ellul advance the notion that the religious substance of contemporary culture may well be quite different from what ordinarily passes for religion. Furthermore, institutions typically recognized as religious may be neither the dominant material embodiments of contemporary religiosity nor the belief systems that accurately serve to mediate human relations with the sacred.

For Voegelin and Ellul, those material institutions and theoretic assemblages normally classified as religion (namely, classical and modern embodiments and sectarian variations of traditional transcendental reli-

gions [Judaism, Christianity, Islam, Buddhism, and post-Vedic Hinduism])
face serious challenges from alternative forms of religiosity that are at once
uniquely contemporary in form and function while also being incredibly
ancient in foundational structure. Voegelin and Ellul argue that although
these alternative faiths are not completely unrelated to the religions with
which culture is most familiar, their primary beliefs are markedly different.
Where traditional/normative religions are transcendental (in their locus of
the divine) and anthropological (in their locus of human meaning and
value), the alternative religions recognized by Voegelin and Ellul are cosmological (in their locus of the divine) and sociological (in their locus of
human meaning and value).

The contours of the cosmological worldview (discussed in the first chapter) is where Ellul begins his analysis of religion in contemporary culture.
Illuminating the character of the sacred in cosmological societies, he writes:
"In a world which is difficult, hostile, formidable, man . . . attributes sacred
values to that which threatens him and to that which protects him, or more
exactly to that which restores him and puts him in tune with the universe."[9] In ancient cosmological societies, which depended on the cycles
of nature and fertility of the natural environment, nature and the natural environment were the ground of the sacred — the ground of ultimate
concern, awe and fascination, dread, and enchantment.

Today, however, Ellul argues that technology has replaced nature as the
sacred ground and locus of ultimate concern. As he notes: "The novelty
of our era is that man's deepest experience is no longer with nature. . . .
Hence [nature] is no longer the inciter and place of the sacred" (100).
Instead, "the modern western technical and scientific world is a sacral
world" and "technology is the god who saves" (70, 73). In essence, in
today's world, technology has come to occupy a place analogous to that
of nature in antiquity: the source of ultimate power and ultimate dread,
what Otto would call the *mysterium tremendum et fascinans*. As a result,
like nature of old, technology elicits a religious response. Importantly, although Ellul analogizes the sacred power of this era (technology) with the
sacred power of traditional cosmological religions (nature), he does not
equate it with the sacred power of the traditional transcendental religions
of the West (God), at least not in a conventional manner. While Ellul is
correct in his general approach, I believe he errs in specifying technology

---

9. Jacques Ellul, *The New Demons*, trans. C. Edward Hopkin (New York: Seabury Press,
1975), 50.

as the sacred ground. For reasons that are discussed later, the economy rather than technology may best embody the sense of the sacred in our culture.

As with the cosmological attitude of yore, modern cosmological religious expressions seek to relate persons and all of culture to the source of sacred power. Just as the ancient cosmological religions utilized myth and ritual to establish and legitimate this relationship, so too does the modern cosmological religion; but since the source of sacred power has changed, so too have the myths and rituals. In Ellul's reading, where once the myths told of a sacred time of ancestors, heroes, and gods of nature and fertility, today they tell us of the sacred origins and mysterious processes of our technological world and our right relationship with technology (113). Here again, Ellul's commitment to technology as the ground of the sacred may lead him to a mistaken analysis of contemporary myths.

In primal societies, the medium of myth was the storyteller, perhaps the shaman, the one who revealed the meaning and order of life in a world that nature dominated. In later archaic culture, after the dawn of literacy, myths were written down, as in the epics of Hesiod and Homer. Much later came the written form of the Vedas, which existed in an oral form long after the development of writing in India.

Following his specification of technology as the sacred, Ellul designates the "two fundamental myths of modern man" as "history and science" (98) and the sacred texts of the "secular religions" as *Das Kapital, Mein Kampf,* and *The Little Red Book.* Importantly, he also recognizes advertising as "the liturgy and the psalmody of the consumer religion" (146), but he does not quite tell us how the liturgy relates to the myths or the sacred texts. Ellul may be somewhat off the mark in designating history and science as the dominant myths of today and quite a bit off the mark in his designation of the sacred texts. He comes closer to the mark in citing advertising as the liturgy of the consumer religion, but his failure to clearly show how the liturgy relates to the myths points up a fundamental problem in his analysis. Consumption as a religious expression is not legitimated (mythically) by history and science, and while its liturgy may well be advertising, this liturgy seems significantly disconnected from Ellul's sacred technology — notwithstanding Ellul's own observation that showing "how [advertising] is planted in the sacred and in the religious structure" would not be difficult (146). Rather than history and science being the dominant myths of today, we might look to mythic narratives that articulate the meaning and order of life in a world dominated by the economy — perhaps focusing on myths of economic success and material acquisition. The delivery system for these myths is the mass media, and television is the primary vehicle.

For Ellul, religious ritual takes the form of political activity, since politics has become the functional religion of a culture in which technology is sacralized. In fact, in chapter 6 of *The New Demons*, Ellul offers a rather elegant argument supporting his claim that politics is the religion of the contemporary world. As noted above, the sacred scriptures of today are political texts; looking more closely, Ellul finds messiahs (for example, the proletariat, in Marxism), theories of resurrection (of the race and the *Volk* in Nazism), millennialism (as with the Chinese cultural revolution), dogmas (Marxist theory), clergy, and heretics. Of course, worship and liturgy occur in the great political festivals, such as those at Munich and Nuremberg or "Chinese assemblies of Tien Am Mem." Curiously, and somewhat inaccurately I believe, Ellul finds these political religions to correspond perfectly with Christianity (189), and their modification from radical movements to "guarantors of the established order" (circa the mid-1970s) to be analogous to the modification of Christianity when it became politically successful (196–97). Although his primary focus is on totalitarian states, he observes: "there is a sacralizing of all political activity elsewhere, in the liberal democratic, bourgeois and capitalist countries" (197). He does not support or develop this observation, but following his thesis this extension could be accomplished easily enough. Especially keen is Ellul's analysis of the ritualistic function of politics in the technological society. As he writes:

> The political behavior of the modern citizen makes manifest the sacred of the state, and the fact that the participating citizen is endowed with an exciting grandeur. Politics has become the place of final truth, of absolute seriousness, of radical divisions among men, of the separation of good from evil.... In the end it is there [in the political domain] that people experience the deepest conviction that everything is at stake. (198)

Thus, as with the source of sacred power and the myths that illuminate it, the religious rituals that relate us to this power are decidedly different from those of traditional religion. But is Jacques Ellul correct? Only up to a point.

Like Baudrillard, whom he cites, Ellul observes: "Consumption...is no longer a materialistic fact. It has become the meaning of life" (144). He also recognizes a distinctive religious quality to consumption. Still, for Ellul, politics functions as the decisive form of religious expression in technological societies, and these political religions are presented as essentially variations on Christianity, a transcendental religion.[10]

Voegelin also sees modern political movements as religions.[11] In his analysis of contemporary culture and his reading of politics as religion, Voegelin, like Ellul, recognizes that the fundamental impulse of such cultures is harmonial and integrative, and like Ellul, he cites Soviet Marxism and Nazism in this regard. But what Voegelin does, and Ellul does not (at least not thoroughly or convincingly), is recognize the similarities between these and other contemporary social and political systems and the cosmological religions of antiquity.[12] In his words:

> The self-understanding of a society as the representative of cosmic order originates in the period of the cosmological empires in the technical sense, but it is not confined to this period. Not only does cosmological representation survive in the imperial symbols of the Western Middle Ages or in continuity into the China of the twentieth century; its principle is also recognizable where the truth to be represented is symbolized in an entirely different manner. In Marxian dialects, for instance, the truth of cosmic order is replaced by the truth of a historically immanent order.[13]

In ancient cosmological cultures, religion functioned to integrate society and internal social structures with the cosmos and the immediate natural

---

10. Ibid., chapter 6. Ellul notes that he is following Aron and Simondon in his discussion of politics as "secular religion," and this approach may ultimately account for his too-brief depiction of consumption as a religion (144–47) and the internal contradiction this depiction sets up with this argument that politics is the religion of the contemporary world.

11. See Voegelin, *New Science: Science, Politics, and Gnosticism* (Chicago: Henry Regnery Co., 1968), and his early work, *Die Politischen Religionen* (*The Political Religions*) (Vienna: Bermann-Fischer, 1938). Curiously, Voegelin interprets political religions as variations of ancient Gnosticism.

12. There are important similarities between Ellul and Voegelin, and I think that when used together, as here, they disclose much more than either of them when used independently. Darrell Fasching has done the best job yet of revealing the significant affinities between the work of Voegelin and Ellul and then successfully deploying both their theories, essentially in tandem, to illuminate contemporary ethical dilemmas. See especially, *Ethical Challenge,* chapter 4. In short, Fasching argues that Voegelin's distinction between cosmological and anthropological is the same as Ellul's distinction between sacred and holy, with the latter term in both being essentially analogous to what I have termed "transcendental" and the former term functioning essentially as Voegelin and I (here) have used the term. I think the analogy works well in terms of the sort of ethical analysis Fasching is doing, and could possibly work here to reconfigure Ellul's analysis of political religion. But it would take a *reconfiguration* of Ellul, which is hardly necessary when Voegelin's theory works perfectly well as a *clarification* of Ellul.

13. Voegelin, *New Science,* 59–60. Voegelin's explication of ancient cosmological civilization can be found in part 1 of *Israel and Revelation.* Although he much prefers to characterize the contemporary political and social movements as Gnostic, his depiction of them seems essentially cosmological (see n. 11).

environment. It also served to maintain collective unity in the society. In fact, and in distinction to contemporary transcendental religions, religion was not a discrete institution in these cultures. It simply *was*, and through myth and ritual it affirmed and acted out (in a heightened and intensified sense) the truth that the way things were, was the way they ought to be. For these cultures, *is* was *ought*.

Like Ellul, Voegelin clearly recognizes that contemporary culture evinces this same sort of worldview. Also like Ellul, he misdiagnoses the religious character of this culture by looking to politics as the religious institution that typifies this worldview. Again, like Ellul, he nicely analyzes the structures of politics and other cultural institutions as religious in character, but then, in spite of what would seem to be his own overwhelming evidence, he concludes that these institutions are Gnostic — dependent on a mystical sort of salvific knowledge about history and human destiny because of their ideological nature. This approach is no more satisfying or accurate than Ellul's efforts to analogize these institutions to Christianity. Although Voegelin labored long and hard to make this argument, ancient Gnosticism itself was, at best, minimally cosmological, while in Voegelin's own presentation, contemporary Gnosticism is clearly cosmological, with myths of history and progress serving to illuminate the sacred realm and political movements serving the religious function of integrating persons and whole societies with this realm. Voegelin's much-disputed "Gnostic thesis" is probably the greatest flaw in his far-reaching and highly regarded inquiry into the order and process of history. How much better it would have been had he forgone the problematic Gnostic thesis altogether and expanded his brief and passing analogies of contemporary culture with cosmological civilizations into a working argument.

In spite of their flaws, Ellul and Voegelin, when used together in a complementary fashion, supply what was missing in Jameson and Baudrillard — the basis for an analysis of the religious dimension of contemporary culture. The question remains, however: what is the proper way to interpret this dimension? This is a fundamental question, because if Voegelin and Ellul are correct about the cosmological character of our culture (and this book presumes that they are), then the religious expression of our culture is cosmological and so the rituals and myths of this culture should reveal characteristics of a cosmological engagement with the sacred. The Voegelin-Ellul theory seems to fall apart here, for although they both seem to strongly suggest that the essence of contemporary culture is cosmological (notwithstanding their clumsy attempts to Christianize or Gnosticize specific religious expressions), they fundamentally misdiagnose the religious dimension itself by looking to politics rather than to consumption, a more clearly cosmological phenomenon.

The idea of sacred consumption

The central problem with designating politics as the religious dimension of contemporary culture is found in the failure of politics to generate sustainable representative myths and associated rituals. If what we are dealing with in the postmodern era is a cosmological culture, politics does not offer a reasonable approximation of religion because the myths and rituals of political reality lack the sort of massive plausibility and culturally unifying dynamic demanded of the religious expressions of such cultures. While Ellul is accurate in recognizing the quasi-religious role of consumption, his designation of politics as the process through which moderns "manifest the sacred," experience "exciting grandeur," and find the basis of "final truth" simply overstates the religious function of politics. Today, politics is typically dismissed as a charade at the level of popular culture and its substance (the quest for and maintenance of social power) tends not to generate community-sustaining myths and rituals, but rather community-destroying narratives and socially disorienting activities, often of the most disconcerting type.

The search for the religious character of postmodern culture must therefore lead elsewhere, specifically back to Jameson and Baudrillard and their carefully articulated study of the social function of commodity consumption. Following Baudrillard (and entirely in the context of Jameson), Kellner observes:

> [T]he consumer . . . cannot avoid the obligation to consume, because it is consumption that is the primary mode of social integration and the primary ethic and activity within the consumer society. The consumer ethic and "fun morality" thus involve active labor, incessant curiosity and search for novelty, and conformity to the latest fads, products and demands to consume.[14]

In this regard (to the degree that he follows Jameson and Baudrillard), Ellul is absolutely correct when he writes that "consumption . . . is no longer a materialistic fact. It has become the meaning of life"; he errs, though, in not recognizing that consumption, as the "meaning of life," is (much more so than politics) revealed to be the basis of ultimate legitimation for individuals and society as a whole. Through consumption, which

---

14. Kellner, *Jean Baudrillard*, 16.

begins with ritual acquisition, one gains significance in the cosmic scheme of existence by engaging in a sacred activity and actually penetrating the sacred realm itself. The economy, rather than technology, serves thus as the sacred ground of our culture, and rather than politics functioning as the religious mediation of sacred reality, consumption, or more accurately, the experience of acquisition-consumption-disposal, holds that place.

Using our initial description of religion as a guide, we may describe consumption as that which relates us to the sacred (economy) through the shared myths and rituals of our community, which, in the case of cosmological religion, is our entire culture. Religion, in this case, is the phenomenon that harmonizes individual and collective activities and integrates them with the order and process of the sacred (economic) realm. In cosmological cultures this phenomenon is not isolated in discrete institutions, but is rather embedded in the collective beliefs of the entire culture. These beliefs give order, guidance, and legitimation to culture as a whole and its residents specifically. In this context, then, consumption as a religious activity articulates our right relationship with the sacred and reveals the cosmic meaning of existence, which is also the culturally normative way of life and living. The Sanskrit term and Hindu religious concept of *dharma* (sacred/social duty) perhaps best approximates this notion.

Thus, if the order and process (or order-process) of the economy can be read as the ground of the sacred, then religion in its cosmological form and function is the interrelated, comprehensive, and incredibly complex collection of cultural beliefs and practices that explain and motivate our right relationship with the economic order and its process. This right relationship is illuminated and vivified in culturally embedded myths. Such myths must be at once believed as elemental (unquestioned) truths of existence. This characteristic, by the way, is true of all myths, whether cosmological or transcendental, but is not true of Ellul's myths of history and science and Voegelin's similar myths of history and progress, which seem to function mythically only in some sort of abstract, academic manner. Rather than myths of history, science, or progress, the myths that relate us to the sacred realm of the economy are the much more vital, robust narratives of our postmodern culture.

The meta-myth of success and affluence

We can refer to the paradigmatic model of these narratives as our meta-myth: the overarching story that communicates the sacred ideal of our culture and the myth that contains and generates all other myths and to which all other myths in some way refer. In short, the great meta-myth of postmodern culture is the myth of success and affluence, gained through a proper relationship with the economy, and revealed in the ever-expanding material prosperity of society and through the ever-increasing acquisition and consumption of products by individuals. As is discussed further in chapter 4, from this meta-myth all our other (more accessible, relative, and domestic) myths derive.

Although the meta-myth is seldom articulated, the secondary and tertiary myths it spawns are communicated through narratives embedded in popular culture and told as much through images as words. Secondary myths are narratives about the masters of business and finance; the stars of movies, sports, and the music industry; persons who win lotteries, make fortunes off of e-trading, win game shows — and then "live large" as a consequence of their success. Secondary myths are the stories of Bill Gates, Michael Jordan, Madonna, Mark McGwire, Ricky Martin, Britney Spears, the person on TV we never heard of who receives the check for millions of dollars, or the one who catches some record-breaking home run ball and rushes home to post its availability on eBay. Each of these stories, in its own way, constantly tells and retells the meta-myth — the myth of material success and achievement, gained through mastery of the mysteries of the economy. Besides these stories there is the wide range of tertiary myths. These generally tend to focus on representative persons from the public at large and reveal how they too may participate in the sacred reality of prosperity and abundance through rituals of acquisition and consumption.

Like the myths of any era, the myths of our time are the stories that we know the best, that we listen to most closely, tell each other, and never tire of hearing. We want to be like these people, we want to experience the world as they experience it; see as they see, live as they live, do what they do, and, in some way, consume as we know they must consume. Stories of history, science, and progress are not in this category; they are academic explanations, theoretic maneuvers. Religious myths are much more vital than these. So too are religious rituals.

As noted earlier, rituals engage religious participants with the sacred realm disclosed by the myths. In their most distinctive cosmological form, these rituals are massive collective experiences that enthrall and enchant the whole of culture and serve to integrate persons and the most important activities of their everyday commonsense world with the sacred order. For us, the rituals that integrate us with our myths are those activities that allow us to symbolically experience mastery of the mysteries of the economy, activities that offer luminous witness to our own material success and achievement. As the recently popular TV commercial affirmed: "If I could be like Mike [Michael Jordan]," I would consume a particular commodity. So, to be like Mike, I acquire, consume, and dispose of the product. Then, I acquire another. In this way, I *am* like Mike, the hero of the myth. I hear the narrative of what the mythic heroes acquire, consume, dispose of (houses, cars, boats); I see the clothes they wear and/or advertise; I learn about the foods and beverages they consume. They are consumers too, and the grandest consumers of all. To be like them, to be close to the sacred world they have mastered, I too consume — as often as I can, in as many ways as I can, and preferably I consume products that are like those that they consume as well. In this way, citizens of postmodern culture are ritually integrated with the sacred order articulated in their myths and, as is typical of cosmological cultures, the highest form of this ritual integration occurs when the entire culture shares in events of consumption.

In the context of this analysis, Ellul and Voegelin appear to err not in their designation of certain elements in contemporary culture as cosmological, but rather in their specification of both the sacred realm and the religious dimension of this culture. In short, neither understands it quite "cosmologically" enough.

Technology is not the sacred ground because, to use Ellul's own terms, it lacks the requisite capacity to "threaten," "protect," "restore," and "put [us] in tune with the universe." Technology can do these things to some extent, just not with the same decisiveness, enormity, and grandeur as the economy. Technology is the servant of the economy, as is every other institution and enterprise in our culture. When the economy fails, it brings disorder, even chaos, to every other institution and enterprise of meaning and value — education, science, the media, government, and technology. On a national scale, technological failures are resolved economically. A nation that possesses adequate economic resources can quickly and relatively easily resolve technological challenges that war or natural calamity may cause. On the other hand, if a nation is not economically powerful, resolving technological challenges is considerably more difficult. Compare the way in which the United States quickly and effectively responded to the (technological) destruction of Hurricane Hugo and Serbia's inability to respond to the destruction wrought by NATO bombing, or Turkey to the August 1999 earthquake. Economic power can solve problems in all other enterprises that might be claimed to have a sacred significance, but those other enterprises do not exercise a similar power over the economy. They are the economy's servants and the economy does use them.

The same is true at the personal level. When my personal engagement with the economy is interrupted (when I lose my job or am laid off, or if I take a cut in pay because my company is "downsized" or acquired by another), disorder and chaos enter my personal life. This disorder is registered in my inability to participate in the rituals of acquisition and consumption that are religiously necessary to my identity as a citizen of the postmodern world. Only when I am again able to ritually enter into the sacred world, mythically disclosed by narratives of acquisition, can I again be a legitimate member of the culture.

The role of the economy in postmodern culture is every bit the same as the role of nature in primal and archaic cosmological cultures — if not more. Its order and process are beyond my grasp or anyone's for that matter, including the chair of the Federal Reserve. The ways of the economy are at times capricious, ruthless, sudden, uncompromising, and uncontrollable. Its interest in me is indifferent at best; it colors all of my activities, even if I am not immediately aware of it. It tells me who I am, what I am, and what I am able to do. It defines my dharma. James Carville was right when he said (regarding the need for Bill Clinton's 1992 presidential campaign to focus on what was most important to Americans), "It's the economy, Stupid."

By the same token, and I think as a consequence, politics is not the religion of our postmodern culture. Politics simply is not a cosmological religion for it is too distinct an institution, existing as a separate entity in society and not usually a part of everyday life for most persons; in fact, for many, politics is something to be avoided. Hardly an institution that promotes integrative experiences, politics at best is a divisive social enterprise. Likewise, technology is not sacred in a cosmological sense, for it is too transcendental. Technology is one of the grand abstractions (even an ideal) of our culture and best understood as a critical explanation for the type of societies that have emerged in the postmodern period. Yet technology serves more as a term of analysis and classification of the physical/material world as we know it than a sacred reality that one might experientially encounter in a religious sense.

Remember, in cosmological cultures, as distinguished from those in which transcendental systems dominate, religion is not a discrete institution and the sacred is close at hand. In these cultures, such as our own, religion is indistinguishable from culture itself, indistinguishable from the normative way of life and living, which it legitimates as an expression of the sacred order. Ellul's analysis of politics noted earlier may thus be modified to read:

Consumption by the postmodern citizen makes manifest the sacred of the economy, and the fact that the consuming citizen is endowed with an exciting grandeur. Consumption has become the place of final truth, of absolute seriousness.

Let us be honest and admit it: have we not at times (and perhaps more often than not, more often than we realize, and surely more often than we would like to admit) had a sense of this grandeur as we engaged in the ritual of consumption (acquisition-consumption-disposition) and gone about our activities with a seriousness that in earlier times was restricted to religious activity? Still, most of us do not think about this ritual much, which is exactly the point. It is just the way things are. What *is* is what *ought* to be. To say otherwise, or to think too hard about it, is not appropriate, not normal, not in harmony with the sacred order and process of the economy.

Given this integration, although consumption is ubiquitous — as the specifically *religious* expression of our postmodern, cosmological culture — it is nonetheless difficult to find. Moreover, once found, distinguishing consumption from the rest of culture is hard to do. Consumption simply *is*, and through myth and ritual it affirms and acts out (in a heightened and intensified sense) the truth of the cosmic (economic) order that is already revealed in everyday life. This truth is that the way things are is the way they ought to be; and the way things are in our culture when things truly *are*, is the way things are when we consume. Thus, we as individuals serve the economy, as does every other entity in the culture; furthermore, when we serve rightly, we prosper. Why? Because of the sacred order and process of the economy itself. Carville was right and more religious than he could imagine.

As we seek to isolate the religious essence of our culture, our attention should not be directed to discrete, specialized institutions that can be distinguished from other institutions because they are somehow *religious,* but instead to the everyday stories (myths) and activities (rituals) that we share as a whole and that we communicate and experience in heightened and intensified ways at specially designated (sacred) times. In these sacred times, we can find what may well be the actual religious phenomena of our culture, and in the finding discover just how religious we may really be and how hard it may be to be different than we are.

— THREE —

Cosmological Communities
of Antiquity and Today

Building on the working understanding of the religious dimension of post-modernity and the earlier description of religion, we may now observe that the sacred is experienced in the process of acquisition-consumption-disposition. The key to the process is ritual acquisition, and here the experience of the sacred is the greatest. The process is vivified through mythic narratives that communicate the ultimate truths of culture and the necessity of acquisition to human existence. The myths are then acted out in our everyday rituals of acquisition and in massive collective rituals that occur during especially sacred times of the year — our cultural holy days. These rituals integrate persons and the most important activities of their everyday lives with the sacred truths articulated by the myths.

This being so, religion in the postmodern world is the culturally em-bedded pattern of mythico-ritual activity through which we discover and experience the sacred power of the economy on an ongoing basis. Religion, thus, becomes not a collection of distinct beliefs, objects, and practices (texts, doctrines, rituals, special locales, material items, and aesthetic cre-ations), but rather a comprehensive way of being and living. In this way, the heretofore noun, *religion,* becomes a verb; not a discrete thing but an action, or, better, an ongoing way of acting — a dharma.

The order and process of the economy, which defines the sacred ground and locus of absolute power, is thus mediated in two ways: first through myths that vivify its power and our relationship with it, and second through rituals that allow us to fully experience the truth disclosed in the myths. The basis for the entire mythico-ritual dynamic can be called a *meta-myth,* a dominant and overarching sacred narrative. In postmodern culture, the meta-myth that informs and guides the mythico-ritual ex-perience is the myth of success and affluence, gained through a proper relationship with the economy, and revealed in the ever-expanding material prosperity of society and through the ever-increasing acquisition and con-

41

sumption of products by individuals. Though seldom articulated formally, the meta-myth is always with us, most often in the form of secondary and tertiary myths. All affirm acquisition and consumption as the foundational acts of existence.

A detailed study of the religious components that constellate around this meta-myth is presented in part 2 of the book. Before considering these elements, however, we must consider their expression in earlier cosmological communities and specify the general points of congruence between those communities and ours of today.

The cosmological communities of antiquity

Ancient cosmological religion took two general forms, which Robert N. Bellah has defined as primitive (for which we use the term *primal*) and archaic.[1] Both conform to our working description of the cosmological religions of antiquity insofar as nature functioned as the sacred ground, and religion served to integrate humans with the cosmos and their immediate community. In these systems, religion, per se, was indistinguishable from society as a whole; and although the primal and archaic differ in their social structures and material expressions, as Bellah explains, "the myth and ritual complex characteristic of primitive [primal] religion continues within the structure of archaic religion, but it is systematized and elaborated in new ways" (29).

Key distinguishing features between the two systems can be traced to material developments in human culture, with the deciding event being the first great agricultural revolution, beginning around 8000 B.C.E. Prior to this revolution, which allowed for the development of sedentary societies and vast increases in population, human communities were tribal, nomadic, and organized around the vital, all-consuming quest for sustenance. This quest served as the basis for the well-known "hunter-gatherer" socioreligious system, here classified as primal.

Primal culture

In primal communities the elemental threat and promise of nature were ever-present realities, and right relationship with the power of nature an ever-present concern. As with all ancient cosmological systems (including

---

1. Robert Bellah, *Beyond Belief* (Berkeley: University of California Press, 1970), 25–32. He also includes phases he terms "Historic," "Early Modern," and "Modern."

the archaic, to be discussed later in the chapter), the meta-myth of primal communities told the story of nature and the right relationship of humans with it. More explicitly, the meta-myth affirmed success and well-being in the context of the natural world, which was gained through a proper relationship with the forces of nature, and revealed in the maintenance of social (in this case, tribal) order and the fulfillment of social (tribal) duties by individuals.

Rather than discrete and individualized deities, primal communities articulated the sacredness of nature as what is generally termed *mana,* the mysterious power and potency present in all things — more present in some than others. Beings and elements possessing considerable mana might bring great harm or benefit to the tribe: the thundercloud or the bear, on the one hand, the gently flowing brook or the caribou herd on the other. Mythically, primal communities affirmed kinship with the sacred power of nature through narratives of hero-ancestors whose ideal relationships with the forces of nature and mana-rich entities prefigured those of their descendants. Ritually, primal communities sought to reenact the mythic experiences of their forebears. As Bellah explains:

> Just as the [primal] symbol system is myth par excellence, so [primal] religious action is ritual par excellence.... The distance between man and mythical being, which was at best slight, disappears altogether in the moment of ritual when everywhen becomes now. (28)

And crucially:

> the symbolism is so compact that there is almost no element of choice, will, or responsibility. The religious life is as given and as fixed as the routines of daily living. (28)

The being with perhaps the greatest mana of all was the shaman; this was the religious specialist of the primal tribe, chosen not on the basis of heredity or class but rather on the basis of sensitivity to the sacred realm of natural powers and the mysteries of mana. He or she was the storyteller; the narrator of primal myths; the one who told of ancestors, the origins and order of the world, and the place of human beings in it. The shaman was also the healer, the visionary, the instructor. She or he would be consulted and give guidance regarding what was right and wrong to do, for the shaman knew the ways of mana and the proper manner to approach it and its manifestations. The directions of the shaman guided the community in ritual behavior: what needed to be done for the good of the tribe; where to hunt and gather; how to call the spirit of the animals, invoke the power of mana, and initiate the young; and when to leave one locale for another.

Chief among the rituals were those dealing with transition. In the human community these rituals dealt with birth, puberty, old age, and death. But human transitions were not the only ones of concern to these communities. Equally important were transitions in the natural world: the mating, birth, and death of animals (especially those taken in the hunt); the revival of plants in the spring, their fruiting, and their death in winter. Overarching all other transitions were the grand transitions of the cosmos itself: the wandering of planets and constellations across the heavens, the waxing and waning of the moon, and perhaps most critically, the changing of seasons. In primal communities these transitions were matters of the gravest importance, for life had to be lived in accord with the sacred norms of the cosmos. To miss or misunderstand these processes was to risk the disaster of disorder. Times and events of transition thus required the greatest ritual attention so they might be experienced in ways consistent with the myths of the ancestors, respectful of the manifestations of mana, and in harmony with the order and processes of the cosmos.

As the primal gave way to the archaic, we do not see so much of a revolution as an increase in complexity, specialization, and individuation in the social forms and religious symbolism of humanity's relationship with the sacred. Nature remained the sacred ground of ultimate concern, for from nature humanity derives its sustenance, its very existence. At the material level, only the means of gaining nature's blessings changed — from foraging for edible vegetation to farming, from hunting animals to harvesting them and their byproducts. Religiously, as Bellah explains, the general worldview and meta-myth of archaic cultures remained essentially the same as those of primal cultures, with major modifications being the advent of "true cult with the complex of gods, priests, worship, sacrifice, and in some cases divine or priestly kingship" (29). In this system,

> mythical beings are more objectified, conceived as actively and sometimes willfully controlling the natural and human world, and as beings with whom men must deal in a definite and purposive way; in a word they have become gods. (29)

Still, the cosmological conception of human religious life continued as the norm. As Bellah observes:

> The individual and his society are seen as merged in a natural-divine cosmos. Traditional social structures and social practices are consid-

ered to be grounded in the divinely instituted cosmic order, and there is little tension between religious demand and social conformity. Indeed, social conformity is at every point reinforced with religious sanction. (31)

Archaic culture

Although clearly discernible expressions of archaic culture are not present until around 3000 B.C.E., the roots of archaic culture can be traced back to around 8000 B.C.E. when animals and plants began to be domesticated. With the rise of large-scale agriculture and subsequent urbanization, history's earliest civilizations began to emerge, initially as city-states and later as widely extended empires. The earliest forms of these civilizations were located in river valleys of eastern, south central, and western Asia, and along the Nile in north Africa. By the turn of the eras, this type of culture had come to dominance in large parts of China, India, eastern Asia, and around the Mediterranean Sea.

These new urban civilizations differed culturally from their primal precursors in numerous ways. Among the major innovations that occurred with the development of archaic culture were rigid hierarchical class stratification, literacy (at least among the social elite), patriarchy, and governmental bureaucracy. What was once called the rise of civilization can now be seen as essentially a tracking of the increasing material and institutional sophistication in these archaic cultures.

The catalyst for archaic cultures, of course, was the domestication of plants and animals, which led to population increases and sedentary communities. The key to their emergence, however, was the advent of writing — as early as 4,000–3,500 B.C.E. in Sumer. Soon after this discovery came a host of other cultural innovations: wheels, bricks, mathematics, city-states, large-scale commerce, law codes, money, tombs for departed royalty, geometry, astronomy, sophisticated solar calendars, mastery of metals (bronze, then iron), and so on. The trajectory of material development and major innovations is relatively consistent cross-culturally during the archaic epoch, with some cultural systems advancing materially and technologically more rapidly than others at different times during the period.

In the religious sphere, however, the cosmological sense of the sacred remained virtually unchanged from the primal period. Religious innovations that did occur seem essentially contingent on sociological modifications brought on by urbanization and its attendant class stratification and individuation: the establishment of priest classes as part of the social hierarchy and the emergence of gods as individualized personifications of the sacred forces of nature or divine patrons of human activities dependent on nature. These changes tended to systematize, bureaucratize, and institutionalize the relationship of humanity to the sacred, but the sacred per se continued to be the force(s) of nature and the meta-myth continued to be the story of nature and the right relationship of humans with it. Again, more explicitly, the meta-myth affirmed success and well-being in the context of the natural world, gained through a proper relationship with the forces of nature, and revealed in the maintenance of social order and the fulfillment of social (class or caste) duties by individuals.

Only with the transcendental revolution of the Axial Age (800–200 B.C.E.) did any substantial changes in religiosity occur, and even then, it took centuries for the new transcendental systems to influence archaic culture and even longer for them to eliminate large-scale expressions of cosmological religiosity.[2] In fact, in its most fundamental characteristics, archaic religion was little different at the turn of the eras from the time of its emergence. Archaic religion also varied little from one cultural system to another.[3]

In its general form, archaic religion's sacralization of nature and the cosmos was articulated as hierarchically stratified pantheons, in which various deities performed specialized functions, just as humans did in the archaic world's newly emerging urban centers. The gods were thus instrumentalities of nature, the ultimate power and sacred ground of being; so too were human beings, only on a smaller, less significant scale. The myths of archaic cosmological cultures were narratives about these gods, their origins, their relationship with the order-process of the cosmos and human society, and their importance to the everyday lives of human beings. Each of the myths were variations on the meta-myth, for each was

---

2. See chapter 1 for a sketch of the rise of transcendental religion. The earliest possible date for a major and distinct influence of transcendental religion on archaic culture is perhaps no earlier than the third century B.C.E. in east Asia, with Ashoka and Buddhism, and certainly no earlier than the late third or early fourth century C.E. in west Asia and the Mediterranean basin, with the rise of Christianity. An argument could be made for the sixth century B.C.E., with Zoroastrianism in the Persian empire, but I think we must really wait for the rise of Islam for central Asia to become transcendentalized.

3. The one possible exception here would be China, which seems to have maintained much more of its primal animism and ancestrism, in spite of the deification of the emperor and large-scale seasonal rituals in archaic times. Although many of the ancient myths have been preserved, their original character and relationship to ritual seem to have been compromised because of their transmission through Confucian and Daoist texts. In this regard, see Maxime Kaltenmark's articles on ancient Chinese myths and mythology in *Asian Mythologies,* comp. Yves Bonnefoy, trans. under direction of Wendy Doniger (Chicago: University of Chicago Press, 1993), 233–63.

contingent on the story of nature's sacred power and the right relationship of humans with it. To the degree that the myths concerned exploits of the gods themselves, they have affinities with our secondary myths of today, insofar as they deal with ideal representatives and personifications of the meta-myths. Moreover, to the degree that they relate to human beings, they have affinities with our tertiary myths, insofar as they articulate the right relationship of humans to the sacred order.

Rituals were essentially economic transactions between the gods and individuals or entire communities; again, no different from the immediate social activities of persons and social classes in these times. Transactions with the sacred beings were mediated and directed by religious specialists (priests). These rituals generally involved sacrifice of precious commodities (food and libations) to the gods at geographically discrete locales or mythically specified calendrical times when expressing appreciation or addressing petitions to the deities was appropriate. While specific rituals varied widely, based on the specific desires of individuals and communities, the ultimate purpose of rituals was always the reestablishment of the right relationship between individuals and whole communities with the sacred realm.

The grandest rituals occurred at the transition of seasons and years, when entire cultures would join in massive collective events celebrating the harmony of all creation and affirming a society's continuity with the sacred cosmos and its agents (the gods). In these rituals, the great myths were reenacted and the meta-myth revivified, thus affirming and assuring the regeneration of the cosmic cycle and bringing success and well-being for all.

Affinities and continuities in ancient cosmological cultures

With the rise of archaic religions, the primal notion of mana seems to have been replaced or translated into polytheistic pantheons, but only insofar as the sacred had become personified as anthropomorphic deities, rather than generalized throughout the natural world and concentrated in classes of beings and elements of considerable power. The gods were the forces of nature, individualized and personalized, to be sure, but still fundamentally expressions of nature's vast and awesome power. In short, the great mana of the heavens became the god Uranus or Varuna; the thunderstorm became individualized as Zeus, Marduk, or Indra; the mana of powerful animals became personified as the Sphinx (the lion god of Egypt and

Greece), Ganesh (the elephant-headed god of India), or the Minotaur (the bull-headed denizen of the Labyrinth in Greek culture).

Like their primal forebears, archaic peoples needed to know and maintain their proper relationship with the sacred cosmos. This relationship was articulated in myths and reaffirmed in ritual. Where primal societies had shamans to remember the myths and give guidance in ritual, archaic cultures had priests to guide ritual, and by the second millennium B.C.E., some societies also had written versions of their myths, thus leading to a compartmentalization of religious activity.[4] Unlike the shaman, the office of priest was highly specialized; people who filled the office often came from a hereditary priestly class. Individual deities would often have their own priesthood, and priests specializing in particular ritual tasks would perform them. Also, unlike the shaman, who tended to be concerned with all aspects of the sacred life of the tribe, the role of the priest increasingly became focused on formal rituals conducted at discrete times and places, which typically involved sacrifice. Finally, with literacy and the establishment of written texts, myths began to become standardized and no longer open to creative interpretations as was the case in primal, shamanistic cultures. Pantheons, priest-castes, and literacy did not, however, change the fundamental religious ecology of the cosmological community.

The sacred ground itself remained the same as it had always been: the natural world, the cosmos upon which human life depended entirely and without question. One's sacred duty remained the same as well: maintain the proper relationship with the mysterious and powerful forces of the natural world (whether as the manifestations of mana or in the personages of gods). Myths, of which creation myths most clearly expressed the meta-myth, disclosed the eternal cosmic context of the relationship; and rituals, of which seasonal rituals were the most wide-ranging and culturally extensive, allowed persons and whole cultures to reaffirm and literally reestablish that relationship. Nature, however it might be symbolized, was the ultimate concern, the sacred ground of being, and as Bellah reminds us: "the individual and his society are seen as merged in a natural-divine cosmos...[in which]...social structures and social practices are considered to be grounded in the divinely instituted cosmic order, and there is little tension between religious demand and social conformity. Indeed, social conformity is at every point reinforced with religious sanction."[5]

---

4. Using generally accepted dates for *Enuma Elish* and *Gilgamesh*.
5. Bellah, *Beyond Belief*, 31.

Postmodern culture

Although the concept of the sacred has changed in the postmodern world, what Bellah has said about ancient cosmological cultures holds equally true for contemporary culture. As explained earlier, if the economy has replaced nature as the sacred realm in the cosmological culture of post-modernity, the myths of this culture articulate the sacredness of the economy, and rituals of acquisition (or the process of acquisition, consumption, and disposal) relate its residents to the sacred realm. As the religious expression of a cosmological culture, postmodern religion is a culturally embedded pattern of mythico-ritual activity, rather than a discrete institution. It is an ongoing, ever-demanding, all-absorbing process of being in which one's self-understanding is developed in the context of the culture's mythic narratives and one's most significant activities are ritual performances.

This type of religion defines persons on the basis of not so much what they believe as what they are; not so much by what they profess to be their personal faith as what they actually do in order to be legitimate members of a collective sacred society; and not at all by what they may dream themselves to be but how they live religiously in the context of the sacred power that overshadows, enthralls, and dominates their world. Religion, thus, refers to the sacred stories in which persons find their identities and the actions they perform to confirm their identities as given in the stories. In the contemporary context, the order and process of the economy define the sacred, which is mediated religiously in and through mythic narratives and ritual activities of consumption. This ongoing process of mythico-ritual activity integrates persons with society and culture as a whole with the sacred realm. The lives of individuals thus become part of a grand dharmic drama in which the myths are the story line and the ritual performance is the play itself.

This version of cosmological religiosity thus presents a third type, and although separated by a considerable interim from the heyday of its ancient relatives, the primal and archaic, its fundamental religious ecology is little different. What is different, and markedly so, is the sacred ground, with the economy replacing nature. Aside from this difference, however, the general description of cosmological religions given here and in chapter 1 holds true of postmodern culture; and in practice, this species of cosmological culture syncretizes the religious practices of the two ancient systems described previously. In short, the religion of postmodern culture is a hybrid of primal and archaic religions, which reveals primary features of both. Mana is certainly part of this religion, but so too are gods; there are priests and also shamans; its myths tend to be communicated orally and visually as in primal cultures, but written and iconographic expressions of the myths also exist. The primal ritual activities of hunting and gathering are vital aspects of this religion, as are the priestly sacrifices and specialized rituals of archaic systems. Of course, the grand high rituals of seasonal transitions are remarkably similar to those of archaic cultures.

Above all, however, is the striking continuity of postmodern religious expressions with the general unifying and harmonial characteristics of all cosmological systems. The integrative function of postmodern myth and ritual remains consistent with their function in earlier cosmological systems; all serve to harmonize persons and society with the sacred order, stabilize society itself, and integrate individuals with the social system, which is itself an expression of the sacred order. As Berger explains, with regard to ancient cosmological systems of Egypt and Mesopotamia (but with equal validity for turn-of-the-millennium postmodern culture, substituting economic order for "cosmic order"), in these systems:

> [T]he human world (that is, everything that we today would call culture and society) is understood as being embedded in a cosmic order that embraces the entire universe. This order not only fails to make the sharp modern differentiation between the human and the non-human (or "natural") spheres of empirical reality, but, more importantly, it is an order that posits continuity between the empirical and the supra-empirical, between the world of men and the world of the gods. This continuity, which assumes an ongoing linkage of human events with sacred forces permeating the universe, is realized (not just reaffirmed but literally re-established) again and again in religious ritual.[6]

Our question now becomes just how the postmodern cosmic order posits its continuity between "men and gods" and how its assumption of an ongoing linkage of human events and sacred forces is ritually realized. To begin to answer this question, we can now turn our attention to the formal religious components of postmodern cosmological culture; by doing this, perhaps we can discover how the religious structures of antiquity are reembodied in our seemingly secular world.

---

6. Peter Berger, *The Sacred Canopy* (Garden City, N.Y.: Anchor Books, 1969), 113.

Part II

POSTMODERN MYTHS
AND RITUALS

— F O U R —

Postmodern Myths and Media

Up until now, the general affinities between postmodern culture and its ancient cosmological antecedents have been sketched in summary fashion. We can now consider more explicit elements, specifically our myths, ritual activities, and the roles and practices of our religious specialists (shamans and priests). This chapter specifies and analyzes the formal components of myth as they appear and function in postmodern, cosmological religiosity. Chapter 5 then focuses on rituals and religious specialists.

As outlined in chapter 1, myths are narratives about the sacred and humanity's relationship to the sacred. They are set in a sacred time and concern the actions and teachings of ancestors, heroes, saviors, and gods. These entities display and act out the proper activities of persons in the present world. They communicate truths of such profundity that, even in the face of falsifying material or contrary evidence, the believer continues to accept them and the reality they disclose. We receive them without question or with ritualized expressions of incredulity that mask our acceptance of a reality that exceeds our everyday commonsense world — "I can't believe that," "how could he make so much money?" "nobody lives like that."

Myths and the meta-myth

In the postmodern epoch the meta-myth of our culture is the sacred narrative of success and affluence, gained through a proper relationship with the economy, and revealed in the ever-expanding material prosperity of society and through the ever-increasing acquisition and consumption of products by individuals. As with our ancient cosmological forebears, the meta-myth is made accessible in secondary and tertiary myths. In our culture, these myths are communicated via the mass media (especially TV) and then repeated in countless individual narratives, as when persons talk with others about these media-transmitted narratives. The fundamental focus of these myths is economic success, and the great heroes of our myths are people

53

who have achieved this success. Unlike ancient cosmological myths, the sacred time of these contemporary myths is not a far distant point in the dim recesses of time (typically the time of creation), but rather the ever-recurring, ever-retuning primordial moment when the eternal truth of the meta-myth is vivified, usually in a secondary or tertiary form: as in interview shows with "stars," sitcoms and sitdrams, or TV commercials and print advertisements.

The stars of popular culture are often the focal point of our contemporary myths. Whether from the world of music, stage and screen, technology and science, TV, sports, industry, or even politics, these persons entertain, enthrall, and enchant us. Their narratives tell of persons who have made a name for themselves, garnered accolades from their peers, been judged to be masters in their fields of endeavor, and achieved positions of power and prestige that can be measured in terms of financial success and material prosperity. The media thrills and gushes over each new achievement: the multimillion-dollar contract, the acquisition of a palatial estate, the costly divorce settlement, the corporate takeover, the latest hit record or record-breaking movie release. Through the media, the rest of society learns about the new achievement and individuals seek to emulate it in their personal lives. We also talk about these figures, constructing living narratives of their success, involving ourselves with the myths, and seeking to replicate them in our own experiences. In this manner the mythic narrative is transmitted in our times.

Still we may grouch and complain about the baseball-basketball-football-tennis-golf stars who make millions of dollars for their prowess, but this only underscores how thoroughly they are entrenched in our mythic world as grand exemplars of the success and affluence we too desire to achieve — perhaps in other venues but still in ways that are large and memorable. We also go to the games (or more typically attend via TV) where the heroes perform or we read or hear about their exploits in reports received via the newspapers and the broadcast media. We may still grouse about how much they are making for "playing a game" or (on the other hand) cheer and sense guilt for our previous castigation of their failings or incredible earnings, but we are nonetheless drawn into the myth. In terms of the impact on society, whether the hero is Tiger Woods, Mark McGwire, Michael Jordan, the Williams sisters, or Mia Hamm matters little. We follow their stories and listen when they speak to us and tell us about what they consume, directly or indirectly, through media coverage of their lives.

In the same way, we may shake our head in disbelief at the cinema queen or king who receives a small fortune to perform in a movie. Still, we go to the movie. We watch them perform, become captured in the performance, the story; we become immersed. Again, the names of the figures are not as important as their fame, their success, their stardom. The mythic narratives spin out in much the same way whether the hero is Cameron Diaz, Tom Hanks, Brad Pitt, or Julia Roberts. Small-screen and music stars are no different, as are celebrity talk-show hosts, business magnates (Trump, Jobs, Gates), and even politicians. We are deluged with stories about these contemporary stars. They are vital elements of our cultural ecology, part of the very atmosphere of our times. We know these figures as well as we know our neighbors and friends — perhaps even better. Still, they are different from us; they stand apart from us, above us, superior to us, and yet representative of us, our goals, ambitions, and dreams. We accept the narratives of their success, accommodate them, internalize them, and recommunicate them to family members, neighbors, friends, and colleagues.

At one level, and in one sense, these persons are only celebrities of our consumer society, and to the degree that we read postmodern culture in strictly economic terms, they merely confirm the personification of economic success in such a culture — nothing more and nothing less. In a way, and following the old transcendental critique of cosmological religion, they are only idols. In another way, and I think a more profound way, they are the myth-bringers of our time; these stars communicate to us unending variations of the meta-myth of our culture — success, achievement, the high life of material prosperity, and the capacity to acquire-consume-dispose of material goods at a rate that exceeds the rest of society. In this regard they tell us about sacred time, not as a far-gone sometime, but as a self-evident "now" that is potentially accessible to all persons in some degree through individual and collective rituals.

In their lives and through the ceaseless reporting of their activities, the stars depict actions and supply social guidance, which in ancient cultures would have been vested in sacred beings — avatars, ancestors, heroes, saviors, and gods. The stories of our cultural stars have thus become the clearest expression of the meta-myth of our culture: success and affluence, gained through a proper relationship with the economy, and revealed in the ever-expanding material prosperity of society and through the ever-increasing acquisition and consumption of products by individuals. The stories of their lives are tales of economic achievement, financial advance, and social superiority. They are the models for how one properly relates to and engages the economy, and their narratives explicate the meta-myth of

our culture that the rest of us receive through all the media of our society —
newspapers, tabloids, radio, the Internet (most have Web sites and some
have many), movies, videos, and most fundamentally, television. In our
own ways we each also seek to embody the truth disclosed by the meta-
myth, but because the meta-myth is articulated in narratives of beings who
are far removed from us we must rely on other myths that domesticate it
and allow us more immediate access.

Ellul's discussion of the relationship between what he calls "essential"
or "basic" myths and other myths is helpful here.[1] As he says in his
analysis, what I am calling meta-myths (his "essential" or "basic myths")

> are composed of tertiary myths which have their own individuality
> but which exist only through their reference to the essential myth, of
> which they are really only facets, and to which they lend a brilliance,
> a color, and reality. They provide the basic myths with a resurgence
> of vitality, although dependent upon them for their force. (109)

In short, the meta-myth supplies the tableaux from which all the other
myths are derived. As noted in chapter 2, I believe Ellul errs in his designation of the meta-myths of contemporary society; his analysis, however,
of the relationship between meta-myth and secondary or "tertiary myths"
is very much on the mark and consistent with the work of others on the
interrelationship of mythic narratives.[2] As such, where might we find those
secondary and tertiary myths that bring brilliance, color, reality, and "a
resurgence of vitality" to the meta-myth of postmodern culture?

I believe the answer can be found in the process through which the
meta-myth is personalized, relativized, and essentially domesticated. Metaphorically, and in short, this process translates the meta-mythic narrative
of Michael Jordan, the hero and paradigmatic success, into the tertiary
myth that tells us just how we can "be like Mike." Rather than weakening the master narrative, this process revivifies and illumines it for culture.
Moreover, this very process takes the meta-myth from the realm of pure
narrative to the threshold of ritual embodiment, transmitting its meaning

---

1. Jacques Ellul, *The New Demons* (New York: Seabury Press, 1975), 88–121.
2. See, for example, Levi-Strauss's work in *Mythologiques* and Eliade generally. For a brief
summary of Levi-Strauss in this regard, see Marcel Detienne, "The Interpretation of Myths:
Nineteenth- and Twentieth-Century Theories," in *Asian Mythologies* (Chicago: University of
Chicago Press, 1993), 9–10. For Eliade, see, for example, "Sacred Time and Myths," in *The
Sacred and the Profane* (New York: Harcourt Brace Jovanovich, 1959), and Beane and Doty's
analysis of Eliade in "Myths — Sacred History, Time, and Intercommunication" in *Myths,
Rites, Symbols,* ed. Wendell Beane and William G. Doty (New York: Harper and Row, 1975),
esp. 2–10.

through highly accessible narratives that supply patterns and directions for proper ritual performance. In a very real sense, the process resembles how the meta-myth of Hinduism is translated into the Gita, when Krishna (an avatar of Vishnu) tells Arjuna about dharma, yoga, and samsara.

As noted previously, two carriers (or media) are primary in this process of personalization and domestication of the meta-myth. The first is TV, specifically talk shows, broadcast sports, sitcoms, and sitdrams. The second is advertising. In terms of their relationship with the meta-myth, TV narratives serve as secondary myths and advertising as tertiary myths.

Secondary myths

TV is the primary medium through which secondary expressions of the meta-myth are communicated. Television is the sacred text of our time, and its mythic narratives continue endlessly. Through TV we have much closer contact with the meta-myth and its sacred personages. We can actually watch and listen to Susan Sarandon talk to David Letterman, Jodie Foster chat with Rosie O'Donnell, Shaquille O'Neal visit with Jay Leno, or any other star engage in friendly conversation with any other talk-show host. Of course, we consume requisite clips of the celebrity's newest film or athletic achievement because this is what has made the person successful and is what really matters. But here, in this smaller, closer, more accessible environment, we gain more intimate details of the star's successes and details about her/his life. We already know about these celebrities, if we are at all engaged in culture; we know of their success, their wealth, their fame. They function as would a hero, an ancestor, a god in ancient cosmological myths, whose stories also would be known universally. Rather, though, than the story of their lives exemplifying the story of nature and the right relationship with it, as would be the case in antiquity, the stories of our sacred beings exemplify the right relationship with our concept of ultimate concern — the economy. We seek in some way to emulate these figures or some special one of our preference. After all, as with any cosmological culture, the deities of our pantheon each have their own stories; yet back of all the stories is the same meta-myth of which the secondary myths are only variations. Talk shows supply the variation, what Ellul would call the vitality, and with it the possibility of greater personal meaning.

The critical role of these secondary myths is to bring us into closer proximity with one or another sacred being whose life dramatizes the meta-myth. Still, we also know that who and what she or he is remains radically different from who and what we are. How, then, can we be like this celebrity? The TV-talk show host helps bridge the gap, shorten the distance between the sacred world of the mythic figure and the world of our immediate experience. Again, think of Krishna talking to Arjuna in the Gita; the moment is an epiphany, a theophany, the advent of an avatar — right in our own home, our living room itself. Today, the Bible may not be on the coffee table or the mantel of many homes, but the sacred text of our time is conspicuous, and its mythic narratives are ever-accessible because they never end. Turn on the TV, and there they are. All that changes is the appearance of the avatar.

As communicators with the sacred, talk-show hosts (like sports broadcasters, to be discussed later) might seem to serve the function of the shamans or priests of cosmological culture, the ones who mediate our relationship with the sacred, but this assessment would not be quite right. First, the talk-show host is too distant, closer indeed than the sacred being, but still removed from our world. The host is more like Arjuna (even Sanjaya) in the Gita, or the narrator of Gilgamesh, or Luke in the gospel that bears his name, or John in the book of Revelation. These figures are heroic in their own right; they are certainly more like us than the sacred beings, but also removed from us in space, time, and accessibility. Still, the hosts do make the sacred more immediate, more immanent — not as priests or shamans, but by virtue of being part of the mythic narrative itself. They are certainly different, but they are enough like us that they help us better understand the meaning of the myth in a new, more vivid manner. Second, the host is not a priest or shaman, for these religious specialists mediate our relationship through ritual, which may involve narrative elements but most fundamentally requires action on our part. At this, the secondary level of myth, we are still entirely in a narrative environment, which is certainly closer, more personal, and perhaps even more relevant to us, but still at the level of preritual, still part of the mythic realm.

Another well-known vehicle for our secondary myths are sitcoms and TV dramas. Like the talk show, these secondary myths function to domesticate the meta-myth, but sitcoms and sitdramas do so in a somewhat different manner than talk shows. Their heroes are very much stars in their own right, living in realms beyond our ken, in sanctified domains of power and prosperity, limned by the secondary myths in the striking hues of cultural success. At the rational level we know that Calista Flockhart, Ray Romano, Pamela Anderson Lee, or any other TV star lives an existence far removed from ours; myths, though, transcend all rational levels, and mythically (in the TV narrative), the stars inhabit worlds with clear similarities to the everyday world. Thus, the line between the sacred and the profane blurs, and beings from the sacred realm not only enter the world of our personal experience, they do so in guises that are familiar to us.

For the most part, sitcoms and TV dramas present stories of persons whose lives are heightened versions of our own, but they are stories whose protagonists are really from a higher, more sacred realm. Our knowledge of their true identities is suspended for the duration of the story, thus allowing us to identify with them, their challenges (which are typically resolved), their loves (which are typically intriguing and complex), and their attractiveness (which is typically greater than ours). We do not enter the world of the meta-myth, which is their home; but, like the gods of antiquity, they enter ours, and they do so in ways that are interesting, lively, and stimulating.

Moreover, in a mythic and virtual sense, these stories and the figures who embody them come alive for a short time in our homes on a regular and routine basis. In this way, these stars are domesticated versions of more powerful mythic figures like Denzel Washington, Drew Barrymore, or Nicholas Cage. Week in and week out, their characters remain constant, their dwelling spaces the same, their community of family and friends essentially consistent. They are, if you will, our household gods; not the grand high deities who are the stars of movies (changing their roles and appearance just like the grand high gods of archaic cultures), but gods to whom we can more closely relate, who are more dependable, and whose mythic lives are part of our routine domestic environment.

A similar narrative transaction occurs in sports broadcasts. The stars of these narratives can be analogized to seasonal gods of traditional cosmological cultures (e.g., Persephone, Tammuz). Like talk shows, broadcasts of professional sporting events function as secondary myths in that they present archetypical figures of the meta-myth in immediate and accessible narratives. Like the sitcom or sitdram, they are recurring narratives that transpire through a "season," which culminates in a final episode, a championship, which anticipates the next season.

In these "live" stories, the archetypical figures are removed from the sanctified realm of the meta-myth and, again, come into our homes via the dominant narrative medium of our age. Here they descend from their Olympian heights (their palatial estates), leave their mythic vehicles (BMWs, Hawker Siddeleys, and Lamborghinis), and shed the sacred trappings of their success (designer clothes, Blancpains, Montblancs). They are still the sacred beings they were before, but in the mythic narratives of their competition they reveal how and why they are entitled to their mythic status as the stars that they are. What's more, these revelations

occur in the context of an event with which all who view can identify —
a game. In fact, all the games in which our stars perform are those that
children in our culture can learn to play at an early age.

What makes these games different, and in fact, not so much games as
mythic narratives, are the participants. Here, we learn that at one level, we
really cannot be "like Mike," or Brett Favre, or Ken Griffey. In another
sense, and the most critical mythic sense, we find that these archetypical
beings are not entirely *unlike* us. They are not so far beyond us as they
seem when we only know of them in terms of their wealth, their invest-
ments, the size of their contracts, the money they give away (which only
suggests the vast amount that they have), and even the physical dimensions of their bodies when seen in the proximity of a person of average
size (as on a talk show or tabloid cover). When they play, they do just what
we do, only their skill is far greater and their mastery of the sport more
complete. Still, they are only exaggerated (greatly exaggerated, to be sure)
participants in a contest that we know, understand, and actually partici-
pate(d) in ourselves. What makes them different is what we know about
their lives and their engagement with the meta-myth of our culture. They
are mythic heroes and so we watch them and then renarrate the story of
their exploits throughout the following days, until the next mythic event
occurs. This relationship renders the games myths and not rituals. We do
not participate; we only watch, most often in our own homes.[3]

As with talk-show hosts, sports broadcasters (announcers and commentators) serve to narrow the distance between the listener/viewer and
the realm of the meta-myth. They too are part of the secondary myth
and exalted figures as well, either gifted in their knowledge and capacity to communicate the significance of the secondary myth or perhaps
persons who were themselves once participants (coaches or players). As
storytellers, they inform us about the mythic event with a rhetoric that is
at once appropriate (serious, profound, dramatic), accurate (statistics, previous feats), and relational (biographical insights, contract status, schools

---

3. My intent here is not to explore the ways in which sports might function as a symbolic
expression of capitalist culture, in which competition is an elemental reality. Suffice it to say
that sports certainly does function in this manner. As regards the function of sports as myth
or ritual, I am clearly classifying it as myth since the viewer (the consumer of the event) does
not participate directly in the event or in any way seek to replicate the actions being portrayed
by the participants. If ritual does occur in the context of spectator sports, it involves ritual
consumption, specifically of ritual foods, beverages, and team apparel. For a good collection of
articles on the religious dimension of sports, see Joseph L Price, ed., *Sports as American Religion*
(Macon, Ga.: Mercer University Press, 2001). See especially Price's "An American Apotheosis"
in this book and also in *Religion and Popular Culture in America,* ed. Bruce David Forbes and
Jeffrey H. Mahan (Berkeley: University of California Press, 2000), 201–18.

attended). In the course of the event, broadcasters surround us in a web of words to accompany the stream of images, telling of the successes and shortfalls of the sacred beings whose labors we celebrate or castigate.

What must be remembered here, especially, is that the games themselves are secondary, not primary, myths — except for all but a few, who would be called the "die-hard fans." For these diehards, the games may function as meta-myths, "live" narratives that disclose the realm of ultimate value and meaning, not just for the duration of the event, but for the whole of existence. At times whole communities may become caught up in such a reality (as when a local team goes to the World Series or the Super Bowl), but in the context of long-term social order and cultural practice, such a transposition (secondary myth for meta-myth) is rare and short-lived for all but the true diehard.

Announcers and commentators remind us of the relationship between the meta-myth and secondary myths by at once drawing us into the mythic experience of the secondary myth while also reminding us of its relationship to the meta-myth. This engagement occurs in several ways. First, broadcasters, as "close to the action" as they may be, are still removed from the event; they are not participants, only the narrators. In this function, announcers also remind us that we are not participants either, and even further removed from the event than the narrators. By watching and listening to the broadcast, our identity as observers is mythically established. We witness the sacred beings perform for the brief duration of the game and then disappear again into their higher, more rarefied, more mythic realms. Broadcasters not only tell us about what the sacred beings are doing during the event, they also narrate their arrivals from and departures for the world of the meta-myth, which is the world of their genuine existence. They make spectacular entrances, the greatest ones called by their names, and they disappear into tunnels. Like any good story, the mythic narrative of the sports broadcast has a beginning and an end, while the meta-myth is endless, timeless, and yet informative of the secondary myth.

Second, broadcasters may interview one of the players before, after, or at the halftime of a game. In these brief exchanges, interviewers play a role similar to the talk-show host, offering a more personal depiction of the mythic hero in the context of the secondary myth itself. They make the sacred beings more accessible, rendering them more like us (engaged in a competition and striving to succeed), but also reminding us of the distance between our world and the world of the sacred being, and even the world of the interviewers.

We are neither interviewers nor interviewees, as much as we might desire to be one or the other. They are part of our experience for a short time and then are off to their more important tasks, the tasks of the sport to be sure, but also the grander tasks of performing their roles in the meta-myth of culture — succeeding on a grand scale (whether the immediate game is won or lost), consuming the best and most precious commodities, and generally living large in ways we can hardly imagine. We can perform neither of the tasks of the sacred being for we cannot really be like the "Mikes" of sports and we cannot achieve the same level of cultural success. The sports interview tells us this as we watch and listen again and again to these brief conversations, and then witness the star's sudden disappearance out of the picture and out of our world.

Third, and finally, the broadcasters, who have so professionally performed their duty (appropriately, accurately, relationally), also professionally perform their duty to the meta-myth by revealing the secondary nature of the broadcast myth to the meta-myth. This revelation occurs when the game ceases for commercial narratives. At times, the intrusion is announced or signaled by a broadcaster, but whether the suspension of the game and its broadcast for the advent of the commercial narratives is recognized formally ("when we come back...," "with the score...," "and now a word from our sponsors..."), the broadcaster always pays homage to the ultimate power of the meta-myth by literally becoming silent so that the truth of the meta-myth can be expressed in the most personal and accessible way of all — advertisements. This homage of the broadcaster also reiterates the ultimate meaning and value of the secondary myth, as well as the ultimate meaning and value of the sacred beings, the broadcasters, and we who are watching and listening: success and affluence, gained through a proper relationship with the economy, and revealed in the ever-expanding material prosperity of society and through the ever-increasing acquisition and consumption of products by individuals. In short, the meta-myth takes priority, and the whole narrative assemblage of the secondary myth ceases completely so that entirely new versions of the myth can emerge.

This same operation occurs in all of our secondary myths (talk shows, sitcoms and sitdrams, and sports broadcasts); the secondary myth is interrupted for the even smaller-scale mythic narratives, which on TV are traditionally called commercials. These myths are not, of course, limited to TV. They occur in and are necessary parts of all the major media instruments of our age — radio, newspapers, magazines, tabloids, Web sites, and billboards along our highways and city streets (which also are media instruments today). In their general form, we call these myths "advertisements."

In advertisements, we find both the most pervasive and immediate mythic narratives — the tertiary myths of postmodern culture. In these myths the most sacred entities of all insert themselves into our world. These are the commodities of consumer culture, goods and products, the sacred objects and images of ritual consumption; and their stories are of supreme importance to us all. They silence Leno and Letterman, stop dramas in their tracks, and put Shaq and Kobe on the bench. Ads, after all, are not concerned with stars and celebrities or the games and shows they interrupt. They are concerned with commodities, and as tertiary myths they tell us about our presence in the meta-myth and how we too may experience its reality through sacred consumption.

Tertiary myths

The tertiary myths of advertisements are certainly the shortest of all mythic narratives. They could be called mini-myths and not just because they are so brief but precisely because they are miniaturizations of the meta-myth itself. As such, they tell us much and they do so with an incredible economy of language and images. They bring us each and all into closest proximity to the meta-myth, making it personal, least mediated, and most vital to our existence. In form and structure, they are also the most consistent of all the myths.

The characters in these narratives are the most like us. They are everyman and everywoman revealing the most personal dimension of the meta-myth for they present the ways in which we too can participate in the meta-myth, through engagement in the ritual of sacred consumption. Typically, the figures in the advertising myth are attractive people and sometimes, though seldom, stunningly so. Occasionally, they are strikingly unattractive, silly, and obnoxious. At times, a figure from a secondary myth appears, but these are exceptions, not the rule. Some tertiary myths have no human characters at all, only material objects embedded in a narrative of success and achievement. In every case, however, the advertising narratives seek to capture our attention, focus it on the products depicted in the narratives, and direct us to consume the products for the sake of our well-being. Here we learn the precise way that we can be like Mike, or like the figures in the tertiary (advertising) version of the myth, or achieve the well-being connoted by the material object: we can acquire the product depicted in the narrative. This ineluctable story line defines every tertiary myth.

The narratives themselves, of course, have numerous plot variations, and my intent here is not to enter into a detailed analysis of all these many variations, only to highlight several general structures and how each functions as a tertiary version of the meta-myth. The five most dominant tertiary myths are: (a) The Overcoming Difficulty Story, (b) The Living the Good Life Story, (c) The Funny Story, (d) The Heroic Emulation Story, and (e) The How-To Story (which makes fair claim to being a mythic genre all its own).

The Overcoming Difficulty Story tells how one can resolve challenges by consuming a specific product, which can range from a financial service to an airline flight to a nicotine transdermal patch to a cyberspace conveyance device — to just about anything. As is true of the other four variations, virtually any product can fit any model. The characters in these narratives are usually people of average appearance, wearing everyday clothes. Typically, the setting of the narrative is a home or work environment. Often an authority figure (sometimes a recognized sacred figure) in better clothing appears to give insight into the difficulty and its resolution; the same function is served by an off-camera authoritative narrator. In this model, the story develops around a problem, often involving brief narratives presenting its personal dimension (a middle-aged couple is discussing their concerns about not having enough money to retire on); the problem is resolved when the product is acquired (in this case, the retirement plan of a certain financial service). The couple is then depicted with relieved or confident expressions, presumably to live happily ever after.

Another variation of this same model follows the travels of a particular vehicle easily navigating frighteningly treacherous terrain and smoothly negotiating incredible hazards. Here the difficulty is simply avoided because of the vehicle, and the message is that the viewer can successfully avoid difficulties by acquiring the vehicle depicted. Usually these stories conclude with a person or a family group stepping out of the vehicle as though nothing out of the ordinary had occurred. The character(s) then go about some routine task or begin to engage in festive activity.

The Living the Good Life Story can be seen as picking up where The Overcoming Difficulty Story leaves off. In fact, when tertiary myths are experienced as part of a coherent mythic ecology, they seem remarkably integrated, with one story mythically leading to the next. Upon overcoming the challenge presented in The Difficulty Story, I can more fully enjoy the good life, in which no hint of difficulty exists whatsoever. The mini-world of this narrative is a pure postmodern paradise. Its inhabitants are happy, successful people, enjoying leisure activities or exciting adventures in clean and pleasant environments. Seldom do these stories involve recognized characters from the larger myths; they are very much about the world of possibilities for the average person. We already know that the sacred beings live this way; what we need to also know is that we can too. Sexuality and sensuality are hardly strangers in the plots of these narratives. No litter appears on the pristine beaches of these carnival realms, no poverty in the cities the good-life traveler visits, no dead animals by the side of the rural road as the sleek new roadster roars on to its mythic destination — only leaves swirling with its passing.

The message here is that the focal product of the minimyth is an elemental part of this good life: beer on the beach as beautiful people pass by, or throwing the cell phone into the ocean when it beeps and reaching for some other beer; the sleek new car speeding down the open road to freedom and the good life; the striking couple in sensual repose in the minimalist studio gazing at the new flatscreen TV; the high-end cosmetic product superimposed on the scene of twin skiers gliding down some alpine slope. An exceptional example of the good life narrative is a GUESS? clothing ad in the November 12, 1999, *Entertainment Weekly.*[4] A handsome young couple is depicted standing close together, man behind the woman. He is shirtless and she is wearing (one presumes) his shirt and no bra. She is smiling slightly, and he has a somewhat stern expression. Both are wearing new jeans and staring at the camera. A paradigmatic story of the good life is, thus, told in a single photograph. The message here, of course, is to get the date, you get the jeans; to attain the good life, acquire the product those living it possess. All other Good Life Stories replicate this same myth.

The Funny Story is a melding of The Difficulty Story and The Good Life Story, using the premise of the former as a pretext for humor to reach a conclusion that is similar to the latter. Where The Difficulty Story offers a solution to a serious problem The Funny Story presents a trivial or even ludicrous problem, which is resolved (or not) in silly, offbeat ways by equally silly and offbeat characters — and always in the context of a product of the characters' interest. Its humorous parody of The Difficulty Story leads to an association of the product with mirth and frivolity and perhaps ourselves with the funny characters in the story. Here, the narrative serves to free us from the notion of genuine difficulty through the humorous depiction of a weird or silly challenge. Breaking free of difficulty is elemental to the good life of success and achievement. Ultimately, these stories are all about fun and some of them are simply hilarious.

---

4. *Entertainment Weekly* no. 512, November 12, 1999, 9.

Neighborhood guys go to ludicrous extremes to deceive their wives so that they can watch sports on TV and drink beer (only to be found out by their wives); the new car owner nearly breaks his neck to stop a shopping cart from hitting his prized possession; a man needs money for a Valentine's Day gift and is counseled by an overweight Cupid with tiny wings to acquire Lotto tickets; the cat-herding cowboys in the popular Super Bowl (2000) commercial; and the characters who so delight in their new vehicles that they look for any excuse to drive them (even to the mailbox ten feet from their front door).

The Funny Story also includes characters from the animal kingdom. Some of the more well-known animal stars are the talking Chihuahua obsessed with Mexican fast food, the hand-puppet dog communicating with real animals as he delivers pet supplies from an e-commerce business (pets can't drive), the talking frogs and their colleagues who have humorous adventures and misadventures in a swamp adjacent to a bar serving Budweiser, and the monkeys who break out of their cages so they can take their captors' vehicles for a drive. Each of these anthropomorphized, totem-like beings plays the same mythic roles as their human counterparts. They make us laugh at dilemmas, associate the acquisition of their featured product with fun and funny experiences, and generally leave us with a sense of well-being.

The Heroic Emulation Story is the model for the classic "if I could be like Mike" narrative. This long-running and quite well-known commercial (actually a series of commercials) is typical of all Heroic Emulation tertiary myths. In these narratives, a widely recognized and revered figure functions as what is commonly called a "spokesperson." Here the hero or sacred being serves as a model for ritual behavior, specifically through use of a certain product. The mythic figure is well known in the culture as an exemplar of economic success and achievement, and his or her activities are thus appropriate models for emulation. But the emulation cannot extend into the sacred realms of the meta-myth or even those of the secondary myth where the hero is nearer to us; instead a more religiously appropriate and ritually correct form of emulation is substituted — consumption of products blessed by the mythic figure. This we can do and thus replicate the activity of the mythic figure. In this way, I can be like Mike, or some other star of our cultural firmament.

This version of the tertiary myth has its greatest exposure during sports broadcasts when narratives of the various heroes and sacred figures are presented in commercials that interrupt the secondary myths, often ones in which they themselves are appearing. Foods, beverages, apparel, and hygienic products are the primary objects depicted in these myths. A less common form of this type of myth depicts movie and TV stars in the context of specific products. The consequence is the same: an otherwise removed and distant being of mythic dimensions is depicted consuming a product that we also have the opportunity to consume. In the consumption we come closest to the being and the myth of success and achievement she or he embodies.

The How-To Story is the shortest and least developed, yet perhaps the most critical of all the tertiary myths. This myth appears most commonly in Sunday newspapers as tabloid inserts but is frequently supplemented by TV and radio narratives and even direct mailings sent to the homes of local residents. Of all our sacred narratives, this myth is the most mundane, but it is also the one that brings us closest to the threshold of ritual, serving as the final mythic narrative prior to our visit to the temple and our personal ritual response. Alone among the tertiary myths, The How-To Story tells us where and when it is most appropriate to engage in the ritual of acquisition. We also learn what is expected of us in the ritual, for in this particular myth, the sacrificial offering is always communicated explicitly.

No matter the media, The How-To Story celebrates the ritual objects themselves; if humans appear, they are always depicted in emphatic engagement with the objects — wearing a featured shirt or undergarment, interacting with a tool or appliance. If humans appear at all, they are invariably veiled in utter anonymity; not even the fairly well-known characters of the TV or magazine narratives appear in these stories, but instead, the most average of average persons — flat, plain, as one-dimensional as the tabloid page or "one-week-only sales event" TV or radio ad.

Certainly they are overcoming some difficulty, living the good life, having fun, or emulating a hero, but we already know this if we recognize the object they possess. In this regard, The How-To Story can be informed by any of the other myths; but in this narrative, the message of the other myths is understood, for here the object and our sacrificial relationship with it is all that matters. Persons are secondary, at best; in fact, the term we use for them (models) tells us that their primary role is to display the object. After all, these narratives are not about people who possess the objects and they do not aim to develop our identification with other people; they are about the objects themselves, the religious duty we have to acquire them, and (here, as in no other mythic genre) the precise dimensions of the sacrificial offering — what we call the "cost" of the objects. In a certain sense, then, this version of the tertiary myth can be thought of as the last installment in the mythic testament of our times, the final revelation of the myth of the economy, bringing the objects of success and achievement into our ken and stating emphatically our sacrificial obligations.

At their most fundamental level, all the tertiary myths are communicating the same story, which is the same story disclosed by the meta-myth and the secondary myths. Although these tertiary myths are the most extreme miniaturizations of the meta-myth, they nonetheless carry the same message, the same sacred theme. Whether in overcoming a difficulty, living the good life, having fun, emulating a hero, or learning how to acquire an object of our desire, these myths communicate most clearly and most directly the process through which we may enter the reality of the sacred realm of ultimate concern. In their unique and various ways, each reveals how we are to properly perform our religious duty (follow the imperative of our dharma) to consume and thus embody for ourselves the sacred imperative of material success and affluence. This embodiment is, of course, a ritual action; like the ritual actions of earlier cosmological cultures, it transpires at sacred sites under the immediate guidance and supervision of religious specialists.

— F I V E —

Postmodern Rituals, Shamans, and Priests

As described in chapter 1, rituals and myths are intertwined in such a way that rituals reenact myths and myths illuminate rituals. Having considered postmodern myths in the last chapter, our interest here is in how these myths are ritually embodied. Necessarily, this inquiry requires a careful consideration of the office and function of religious specialists, since they are the ones who guide and direct ritual activity, and their work itself helps to further our understanding of the ritual process. Because postmodern cosmological culture represents a synthesis of primal and archaic religiosity, that both the shaman of primal culture and the priest of archaic culture can be found here is not surprising, although the office and function of shamans are ritually secondary to the office and function of priests. For this reason, in addition to examining the office and function of each type of specialist, a short analysis of postmodern sacred sites is also included. This analysis serves as a segue from the section on shamans to the section on priests and reveals how the archaic character of the sites themselves largely accounts for the subsumption of the shamanistic duties in the larger priestly hierarchy. Before considering these specialists and their sites, however, we must first explicate the general features of postmodern cosmological ritual, for here the specialists and their patrons find their fundamental religious identity.

Rituals

As presented previously, postmodern religious rituals occur in the context of the myths (meta-, secondary, and tertiary) of postmodern culture. They are reenactments of the myths that allow participants to experience the sacred time of the mythic narratives and come into communion with the foundational reality they disclose. The rituals are of incredible significance for through them persons participate in or otherwise affirm their proper relationship with the sacred. Religious specialists (shamans and priests, in this instance) thus have an enormous responsibility. Remember, however, that the religious specialists are not participants in the myths themselves. They have no role in the sacred narratives, any more than a Brahmin priest in Hinduism has a personal role in one of the Vedas or a parish priest in Catholicism has a personal role in one of the Gospels. Instead, their role is to re-create the myth itself through ritual activity. Like their distant forebears in primal and archaic cultures (and to a certain extent their contemporary peers in Hinduism and Catholicism), they are the go-betweens for other individuals and the sacred realm with which they have a unique relationship and to which they have unique access. Like their ancient predecessors, they are the ones who know the mysteries of mana, the secrets of the gods, the right ritual activity to achieve harmony with the order and process of the sacred. In the postmodern context, they know the way to properly embody the sacred narrative of success and affluence and thus assist others in manifesting the proper relationship with the economy — specifically the consumption of products.

The professional religious activities of the postmodern shaman and priest differ from those of their historical precursors only because the locus of the sacred has changed (the economy replacing nature), and with it, the mythic narratives that must be ritually embodied (harmony with the economy replacing harmony with nature as the meta-myth). No longer do they facilitate ritual activities that establish a proper relationship with the forces of nature, but rather, the proper relationship with the forces of the economy. To do this, they must supply the ritual embodiment of the meta-myth (success and achievement, gained through a proper relationship with the economy), which is ritually revealed through the ever-expanding material prosperity of society and the ever-increasing acquisition and consumption of products by individuals. The shamans and priests of our culture thus facilitate the ritual activity of acquisition (which leads to attendant rituals of consumption and disposal).

How this happens is at once profoundly religious but also profoundly simple — as anyone who has had experience in the acquisition and consumption of commercial products knows. Religious specialists take care of the complex aspects of the ritual, for that is their necessary function. The most critical part of the process is the actual acquisition of the products themselves. Usually, we do not give much conscious attention to the narratives that are guiding our behavior. Why should we? They are all around us, and even more importantly, they are within us and we within them. We are not mindful of the cultural imperative to consume, we simply do so. We certainly do not consider our acquisition of products a *religious* activity — perish the thought! All the better, too, that we do not see acquisition as a religious activity, because in terms of the way cosmological religious logic works, religion is not a distinct institution and humans are defined, religiously, not apart from their social duty but rather in terms of what they do to be legitimate members of a collective sacred society.

Thus, in postmodern cosmological culture, that we acquire products incessantly is only natural; moreover, it is only religious that we do so. Suffice it to say, in our postmodern world, we do not give much thought to the sacred dimension of our rituals of acquisition, which is, after all, how the ritual process works in cosmological cultures — it is simply what we do at appointed times and places, and to achieve desired ends. We know the rituals and we dwell in the myths that illuminate the rituals, just as fully as the primal hunter knows the rituals of the hunt and the myths that illuminate them, just as fully as the archaic farmer knows the rituals of planting and the myths that illuminate them. If this activity was not ritualistic in a cosmological sense, we would reflect on the process, relate it to transcendental verities, and consider the eternal consequences of our actions. By and large, we do not. We acquire and consume; if we really do it right, we dispose of the outmoded item that our new product has replaced. We keep the economy's process running in perfect accord with the meta-myth of our culture. Here our postmodern religious specialists (shamans and priests) play their appropriate roles.

The climax of the ritual, from the standpoint of worshipers, occurs when the desired product is acquired and the process of consumption initiated. Shamans and priests facilitate the proper conduct of the ritual, although their roles vary, and in certain instances shamans play little or no role at all. As discussed later, priests are always necessary and some level of the priesthood generally performs the final phase in the ritual process — the sacred transaction. As with any cosmological system, a number of specific ritual performances must occur in order for the sacrifice to be successful. Each performance has a different performer. For this reason, the postmodern priesthood, like the archaic priesthood, is compartmentalized, with different offices tasked with different duties; and in an interesting departure (which is a real melding of primal and archaic systems), the office of shaman has been incorporated into the priestly organizational structure. Who, then, are the shamans and the priests of postmodern culture, and what do they do?

The specialists

As noted in chapter 3, the two types of ancient cosmological religions each had a unique type of religious specialist. In primal religions, the specialist was the shaman; in archaic religions, the specialist was the priest. The distinctions between the shaman and the priest, sketched previously, developed largely because of slight modifications in the concept of the sacred as well as (and perhaps resulting from) sociological changes brought on by urbanization and its accompanying class stratification and individuation. These alterations resulted in the compartmentalization of religious activity and the rise of a social class of priests — a priesthood.

Whereas in primal culture, the shaman tended to be the sole religious specialist for a tribe, in archaic cultures we find a significant increase in both the number of religious specialists and a corresponding decrease in the scope of duties for any single priest. As with the rest of archaic society, the priestly class was hierarchically structured, with the relative power and responsibility of each member based on the member's place in the hierarchy. The work of individual priests tended to be highly specialized; their service might be restricted to a single deity, a specific type of formal sacrifice, or certain managerial tasks related to the order and maintenance of a sacred site. Their shamanistic precursors, on the other hand, would have been responsible for the welfare of the entire tribe and expected to serve as a general mediator of the sacred realm for each and every one. Moreover, with the rise of literacy, the religious specialist was not allowed the same sort of creative latitude as the shaman in presentation and interpretation of the mythic narratives. In fact, with the rise of literacy, new types of religious specialists emerged: scribes, copyists, the Sopherim. To these people was entrusted the responsibility of maintaining the myths accurately and consistently.

Still, in spite of the differences in the specific activities of the shaman and the priest, their essential function remained the same: mediation between the sacred realm of nature and the human world. Both types of religious specialists served as the official intermediaries between the sacred realm and their communities. All others depended on their religious expertise in order to establish and maintain the proper relationship with the sacred realm. Here, in this common function of both the shaman and the priest, we find parallels with the religious specialists of our postmodern cosmological culture. Moreover, we find both shamans and priests in the religion of postmodern culture, with each specialist serving to mediate our relationship with the sacred realm of the economy. Both participate in the sacred ritual of acquisition, but each plays a different role.

Postmodern shamans

Like their primal ancestors, shamans of today are acutely sensitive to the sacred realm and the mysteries of mana. The sacred realm, of course, is articulated through the various myths, which were discussed in the previous chapter. But what of mana? Traditionally, and generically, mana is understood as a primal belief (specifically Melanesian, but found in various other primal cultures) that in one way or another affirms the presence of a sacred power and potency in selected elements and persons — more present in some than others.[1] Explaining the belief, Mircea Eliade observes: "Everything that *is* supremely, possesses *mana;* everything, in fact, that seems to man effective, dynamic, creative or perfect."[2] In our culture, mana is just as present as in primal cultures, and is most readily apparent and found in its highest concentrations in the products of our desired acquisition; the greater the desire for the product, the greater its mana.

Shamans are aware of the mysteries of mana, its presence in products, and the way to ritually expedite our right engagement with its power and potency. In short, shamans are the intermediaries between the ordinary commonsense world and the sacred realm where mana proliferates and where sacred acquisitions can occur. Our customary term for these religious specialists is "salesperson." We can now briefly explore the way in which mana relates to shamans of today and how their religious work vivifies and vitalizes postmodern religious activity.

Like the shamans of primal cultures, postmodern shamans are storytellers and retellers of sacred narratives, gifted with insight into the origins and order of the world, and aware of the relationship of human beings to the sacred realm. They are conversant with the myths and, unlike priests, they are free to improvise on them. The best are charismatic, even ecstatic, in style, yet knowledgeable of the mysteries of the products whose mana they control. Most of us have encountered excellent car salespersons — these are exemplars of the master shaman.

Not unlike the shamanistic "master of animals" in primal cultures, shamans of today are intimate with things we know little about and perhaps fear — technological devices (especially computers), cyber systems, investment portfolios, large appliances, automobiles. The greatest shamans are people tasked with harnessing the massive mana found in

---

1. For a brief discussion of the concept of mana in the context of my usage here, and related concepts such as the Sioux *wakan,* the Iroquois *orenda,* the Huron *oki,* the West Indian *zemi,* and the Bambuti *megbe,* see Mircea Eliade, *Patterns in Comparative Religion* (New York: New American Library, 1963), 19–23.

2. Ibid., 20.

these and other products deemed highly desirable — fine jewelry, elegant cosmetics, exotic perfumes, Louis Vuitton handbags or pens, Vizio watches by Movado. They understand their mystery and so they, like shamans of any time, are somewhat mysterious as well, for they too possess mana, and in the ritual environment, much more than those who visit them for ritual assistance.

In their ritual role shamans create the environment through which we can experience the reality expressed in the myths. Their gift and religious genius are perhaps most evident in their ability to draw us into the sacred world portrayed in the advertising myths. Through their words and actions we come to identify with the products portrayed in the myths and we sense something of the reality depicted in the myths. They allow us to "see ourselves owning it," whatever the product may be. Their ritual performance may include interaction with the product — something we cannot do, at least not yet, at least not until we achieve acquisition. Ever the master of the product and its mana, the shaman shows us how it works, reveals its internal mechanisms and unique features, takes it apart and puts it back together again, draws us close and closer still to the product and the power it possesses.

Through their ritual performance, the sacred importance of possession is reinforced. The product is transformed into what was in the advertisement myth, becoming the talisman for overcoming difficulty, living the good life, having fun, or emulating some hero; just as it (or something quite like it) did in the mini-myth of the commercial or print ad. The product is bigger, smaller, faster, easier to use, smarter, smoother, richer, deeper, and always better than anything like it that we currently possess. As Eliade might tell us, the object of desire seems to us to be effective, dynamic, creative, or perfect. The shamans tell us all of this and more through performance, narrative, and mythic reenactment. Thus are we drawn into the sacred reality disclosed by the myths. Only now, the sacred reality of the myth is drawing close to an actual experience for us. Still, proximity is not enough.

The shamans may take us further if the ritual has still not reached its climax, which is our decision to actually acquire the product. In this phase of the ritual, the shamans, in their wisdom, and with their mastery over the product and the ritual environment, may allow us to experience the reality of the product and its mana. We may be given an opportunity to try on the product, have a test drive, take a sample, or operate the device for ourselves. In doing this, we gain something of the shaman's power over the product, and even more importantly, we come closer to the reality of the

myth and the experience of our proper relationship with the economy —
our own acquisition of something new. After all of this activity, if the ritual
is still unsuccessful and we should continue to experience difficulty in acquisition, shamans may turn to another product and commence the ritual
process again. This, after all, is their sacred duty: to allow us (their tribe)
access to the sacred realm of acquisition — by any and all religious means.

Just as in primal shamanistic cultures, incredible variation exists among
shamans of today; although the postmodern religious environment more
closely resembles that of an archaic culture, the shaman's foundational
ritual activities remain the same. The major modification we see today is
that shamans tend to be more specialized relative to ritual practices. In the
past, shamans would differ based on the characteristics of their individual
tribes and their identities within their own tribes.

Today, their differences are related to the specific products over which
they have ritual power and dominion. This change is only cosmetic, however, resulting from the loss of tribal identity in postmodern culture, the
incredible proliferation of material goods with which we must establish
religious relationships, and changes in the ritual environment of our cosmological religion. No single shaman can have sole responsibility for a
"tribe" as large as ours or gain mastery over the incredibly vast array
of mana-bearing elements inhabiting our world; furthermore, because the
postmodern religious environment is more akin to that found in an archaic culture, the shaman's ritual function has become largely subsumed
within a system that is more compartmentalized and specialized than the
typical primal system. Thus, in today's postmodern cosmological culture,
our shamans tend to exercise ritual power over specific products or classes
of products rather than all aspects of religious life. Still, their ritual roles
remain consistent with those of their primal antecedents and their ritual
processes (described above) essentially consistent.

In contemporary culture different shamans exist for different products,
but the authentic ones, like those described by Robert Ellwood and Barbara McGraw as being "singled out by the divine to receive special ecstatic
powers for dealing with spiritual things,"[3] are still best thought of as gen-
eralists. True, their work tends to be focused on single products or classes
of products, but the genuine shamans are capable of properly exercising
ritual power over a wide range of products. What this means is that the
vehicle shaman may be an equally effective insurance shaman, the ap-

---

3. Robert S. Ellwood and Barbara A. McGraw, *Many Peoples, Many Faiths*, 6th ed. (Upper
Saddle River, N.J.: Prentice Hall, 1999), 36.

pliance shaman of today might be the investment portfolio shaman of tomorrow, the Mary Kay shaman could become a real estate shaman — and so on. Over time, shamans may settle into a comfortable relationship with a specific product but many move around from one type of product to another, perhaps changing ritual environments in the process. What remains consistent, however, is the shamanistic function and the point of the rituals they perform. For them, the sacred duty, their dharma, is to assist us in fulfilling ours — acquiring products. To fall short of this result is sacrilege, a violation of their sacred dharma and ours as well; and, more critically, falling short is a theft from the sacred ground of being itself — the economy.

Sacred sites[4]

The physical locations and material qualities of religious activity are of critical importance to the proper performance of any cosmological religious ritual, and a brief comment on them is necessary here. This will serve as a transition from the study of postmodern shamans to the study of the postmodern priesthood, since the form and structure of our sacred sites help to sharpen the contrast between shamans and priests while revealing the functional dominance of the latter specialists over the former.

To better understand the nature of our sacred sites and why priests play such a pivotal role in our rituals, let us again take a step back to primal times when sacred environments were typically locations in the natural world. Here, the sacred site would be a place where mana was significantly concentrated: high places, springs, caves, rock formations, sacred groves, locations where hierophanies occurred, places of tribal origins, totem centers, and burial grounds. Of course, in primal times, to a certain extent, all of nature was a sacred place because of the ubiquitous presence of mana. With the rise of archaic cultures and the emergence of large-scale urbanization, sacred places began to be constructed. The geographic locations of these new religious structures had religious significance, and the edifices themselves had exacting (sacred) design specifications related to astronomical cycles, celestial traffic, and mythic narratives based in nature. Like the sacred places in the natural world of primal peoples, the religious structures of archaic cultures were the sites of the communities' most important ritual activities. Perhaps the best known of these struc-

---

4. This term and the general understanding presented here are derived, with some modifications, from Eliade's discussion of "sacred places." See Eliade, *Patterns,* 367–85.

tures are from early archaic cultures, such as Stonehenge in England, the pyramid complexes of ancient Egypt and Mesoamerica, and the ziggurats of ancient Mesopotamia.

In later archaic times, specifically the Graeco-Roman period, these large-scale religious structures gave way to somewhat smaller ones, which today we refer to as temples. These structures were often dedicated to individual deities or families of gods. Perhaps the most well-known temple to an individual cosmological deity is the famous Parthenon in Athens, although the temples of popular gods (such as Isis and Asklepios) proliferated throughout the Hellenistic world. The best example of a temple for a family of gods in Western antiquity is the Pantheon in Rome; such temples are also typical of Hinduism, in which not only are families of gods accessible, but also the members of more than one family.[5]

As we consider the sacred places of postmodern culture, we find that archaic temples, specifically those of the pantheon type, are the ones that most closely parallel our own. Of all these sites, the most magnificent (and sacred) of all, our grand high temples, are what we call "malls," although a wide variety of other types of sacred sites exist also. The most significant of these other sites include department stores, specialty shops, professional (especially financial) offices, drugstores, restaurants, and grocery stores. What makes our malls so much like the ancient Roman Pantheon or the Hindu temple of today is that they feature a variety of sacred sites and ritual environments, each dedicated to a specific mythic narrative and sacred personage or family. As part of the mall-temple complex, the individual sites are best considered shrines within the larger temple; however, when they are independent structures, they are appropriately considered temples in their own right. In the mall as a whole, but in each of the more specialized temples or shrines, we find what Baudrillard calls the "systematic organization of ambience,"[6] which may be better understood as the sacred organization of ambience.

Baudrillard captures the notion of the temple's sacredness and ritual purity, perhaps inadvertently, in his discussion of the "phenomenology of consumption" in which he finds:

---

5. Typically, the Shiva and Vishnu families are present. See field-research notes of Bob Waller at Mylapore Temple, Madras; Vaikunta Perumal, Kanchipuram; Trivandrum Temple, Trivandrum, and several others in India; and Govinda Gardens, Zephyrhills, Fla.; Vaishnava Temple and Hindu Temple of Florida, Tampa, Fla.; Vaishnava Temple in Raleigh, N.C.; and several others in the United States. Report to the author, June 20, 2000.

6. Jean Baudrillard, *La société de consummation*, 23–24; as translated in *Jean Baudrillard: Selected Writings*, ed. Mark Poster (Cambridge: Polity Press; Stanford, Calif.: Stanford University Press, 1988), 33. Passage from Kellner, *Jean Baudrillard*, 13.

climatization of life, goods, objects, services, behaviors and social relations represents the perfected, "consummated" stage of evolution which, through articulated networks of objects, ascends from pure and simple abundance to complete conditioning of action and time and finally to the systematic organization of ambience, which is characteristic of drugstores, the shopping malls, or the modern airports in our futuristic cities.[7]

This articulated network of objects, which leads to the complete conditioning of action and time, and ultimately, the systematic organization of ambience, is the defining characteristic of the ritual center. In this analysis, this network is precisely what makes the temple sacred. While certainly apparent in drugstores, airports, and especially malls, this sacred quality is, however, found most commonly, even if not most vividly, in the ubiquitous chain stores of postmodern culture; there, the systematic organization of ambience is dedicated to one purpose, the highest purpose of our culture: the ritual of consumption.

Moreover, like the temples of antiquity, the geographic locations, specific designs, and construction requirements of our sacred sites have profound religious significance. Where the religious edifices of antiquity were constructed with regard to astronomical cycles, ours are constructed with equal regard to economic cycles, consumer (especially vehicular) traffic, and mythic narratives of success and affluence. Thus, like the temples and shrines of yore, our sacred sites of today are located at, and locate for us, the *axis mundi* (center of the world) of our culture; only today the *axis* is different, and so too is the *mundi*. The role and function of temples and shrines is addressed later in the book, but for now, let us examine the tasks of various members of the priesthood at a quintessential temple site, one of the seemingly infinite points of access to the *axis mundi* of our culture.

For purposes of clarity and ease of exposition, the focus here is on department stores, because these locations are perhaps the most representative and probably the most well-known sacred sites in our culture. They can function as major shrines within a mall or "standalone" temples, which are in fact miniature models of malls. In either case, they most fully reveal the various dimensions of the priestly system. Here shamans and priests both perform their sacred duties. Shamans have been discussed previously, so we can now introduce the priests, whose work commences when the work of the shaman has been successful — that is, when persons

---

7. Ibid.

have reached the requisite sense of the sacred to actually fulfill their desire to acquire and consume a product. Not all priestly duties require the previous activities of shamans. In some sacred venues (such as the grocery, convenience, or mass-market discount store), shamans play little or no role. In all venues, the role of the priesthood is imperative.

The postmodern priesthood

The contemporary priesthood functions very much as the priesthood in archaic cultures. What is notable about the postmodern priesthood is that it (unlike the ancient system) allows for and actually incorporates the religious activity of shamans. At sites where this dual function occurs (typically upscale department stores), the shamans would be those salespersons who have a technical or specialized knowledge of certain products and generally receive some sort of commission on the sales they make. In this regard, shamans at such sites might also perform certain priestly duties, as is described shortly. Aside from this difference, however, the religious system of postmodernity closely parallels that of archaic cultures, and the duties and responsibilities of its priests are essentially the same as those of their ancient predecessors. As noted earlier in this chapter and in chapter 3, while the specific activities of religious specialists (priests) in archaic cultures differed from those of the primal shaman, their essential purpose was the same — mediation between the sacred realm of nature and the human world.

Before explicating the unique structures and offices of the priesthood of our culture, we should first review the chief characteristics of the priesthood in archaic systems. First, in distinction to primal systems, we find a significant increase in both the number of religious specialists and a corresponding decrease in the scope of duties for any single specialist. Second, the priest class is hierarchically structured, with the relative power and responsibility of each member based on the member's place in the hierarchy. Third, the work of individual priests is usually highly specialized; their service is perhaps restricted to a single deity, a specific type of formal sacrifice, or certain managerial tasks related to the order and maintenance of a sacred site. Fourth, and finally, the priest, unlike the shaman, is not allowed the same sort of creative latitude in presentation and interpretation of the mythic narratives. In fact, with literacy, and today virtually universal literacy, the stability and uniformity of mythic narratives becomes a religious imperative. In the past, the sacred duty of maintaining this stability and uniformity of myths fell to scribes and copyists — and today we find analogous offices within the priestly caste of postmodern culture.

As with their ancient forebears a distinction exists, then, between the primary duties of the priest and the shaman in postmodern culture; nonetheless, and as noted before, their essential purpose is the same — mediation between the sacred realm (of the economy) and the human world. Moreover, the ritual activity of the shaman is integrated with (and sometimes overlaps with) the activities of the priesthood, and fundamentally, both types of religious specialist serve as intermediaries between the sacred realm and their communities. All others in society depend on their expertise in order to establish or maintain the proper relationship with the sacred realm.

How, then, does this work? Again, just as one would expect in an archaic, cosmological, temple-based system. Ritual activity transpires in the context of specific mythic ideals, with persons relying on members of the priesthood to properly perform their requisite ritual duties at distinct and distinctly sanctified locales. Remember, only the religious specialist can correctly perform the ritual. Laypersons certainly participate, and in fact they have a vital role, but the responsibility of the specialists is to guide, direct, and ultimately consummate the ritual.

The focal point of all priestly work — that is, the duties of all priests in a particular community — is the successful consummation of the ritual. In the postmodern context, this consummation is the acquisition of a product, which occurs after a ritual transaction (a sacrifice) involving the most precious commodity of our culture (money). Such transactions, when they are successful, allow laypersons to acquire products and thus fulfill their dharma (social/sacred duty) as consumers, thereby reestablishing their right relationship with the sacred ground of being — the economy. The priesthood facilitates this ritual activity.

As with any cosmological system, a number of specific ritual performances must occur in order for the sacrifice to be successful. For this reason, the priesthood is compartmentalized, with different offices tasked with different duties. In the context of this study, and again, following the department store model, we focus on the offices that are probably most familiar to most persons in our society.[8] Using this model, then, there are four major offices in the postmodern priesthood. Our more familiar terms for these priests are: (1) clerks and cashiers, (2) location

---

8. To reiterate, these offices and priestly activities are essentially generic and can be found in some form (albeit modified in certain instances) in "standalone" retail sales outlets, financial offices, drugstores, restaurants, and grocery stores.

managers (department, area, and assistant or associate), (3) store managers, and (4) corporate officials (with the president or CEO functioning as the high priest in any given complex). For purposes of this brief survey, we give attention to the first three offices, noting that the fourth office (the high priest-president-CEO), although certainly necessary to the overall religious environment, is of relatively little significance to the ritual activity occurring at specific temples.[9]

Clerks and cashiers are responsible for an especially important part of the ritual. In archaic times they would be the priests who actually conducted a specific sacrifice, typically the slaughter of an animal. For many worshipers, these performance-priests are the only members of the priesthood with whom they have any interaction. In certain ways, these offices can be seen as the lowest level of the priesthood. Nonetheless, these offices are properly considered the most crucial to the actual ritual process, because the priests who serve in these offices are responsible for consummating the sacrificial act. Without them, the final phase of the ritual cannot occur. So critical is this phase of the ritual that even higher-ranking priests and shamans are empowered to facilitate the process.

The act itself may be prefaced by a number of preliminary performances: prices may be checked and reported, desired products may be discounted, checks written and driver's license numbers transcribed onto checks, credit cards scanned and credit verified, checks approved, money exchanged, and so on. Ultimately, and most critically, the ritual transaction is completed and the sacred ritual finalized only when the performance-priest affirms its successful conclusion. This final act is signaled through four standard formulaic procedures: (1) a printed record of the transaction is generated from a mechanical device controlled by the performance-priest; (2) the priest places the acquired object(s) in a carrying bag or bags (and when larger objects are acquired, a decal is applied to the object, indicating legitimate acquisition); and (3) the priest places the printed record in the bag or presents it to the worshiper. The ritual is formally concluded when (4) the priest transfers the bag(s) of acquired goods to the layperson and pronounces a terminating utterance, often consisting of the words "thank you" or a statement expressing a positive hope for the immediate future: "have a nice day (night, weekend, or holiday)," as the case may

---

9. The roles and functions of the high priests are just as religious as the roles and functions of other members of the priesthood, and the work of high priests is worthy of a study in itself. Such a study, however, would take us away from the immediate religious environment (the temple) and the immediate experience of religion (myth and ritual) in our culture. See also n. 10, below.

be. With these words, the ritual act is successfully concluded and the worshiper assured that the sacrifice has been received. The performance-priest has thus served as the mediator between the source of ultimate concern (the economy) and the layperson; the layperson, in exchange, has acquired a product (or products) that reveals religious engagement with the order and process of the economy itself.

In their dealings with these lower-level offices of the priesthood, the laity is most likely to encounter ritual challenges. Questions may emerge about advertised prices ("but the ad said..."), how many of a certain product one may acquire at an advertised price ("limit three to a customer"), unavailability of a desired item (get a "rain-check"), lack of a "brand name" product (the "store brand" is just as good), challenges with credit cards or check approvals (cash [like animal flesh in ancient times] is always the better sacrifice!), and general incompetence in more technical aspects of the ritual— "I don't know how to change the receipt tape," "I've never done a debit card transaction before," *"they* [whoever 'they' may be] never told me about *this* [whatever 'this' may be]." In terms of traditional analyses of the economy, clerks and cashiers form the front line of capitalism. They are the most expendable, the lowest paid, the least likely to advance, and the ones who are working the hardest and most desperately to succeed. Still, they are vital members of the priesthood, for they allow others to legitimately fulfill the final stage of the ritual process. Without them, no ritual is complete.

Location managers (department, area, and *assistant or associate store manager)* occupy the next level above clerks and cashiers. These priestly offices are very fluid and transitional. In the argot of the caste, in these offices you meet persons on the way up when you are on the way down— and on the way down when you are on the way up (so, "cover your 'precious organs' "). For those in ascent, the next level in the hierarchy will afford them more power and prestige; for those in descent, a lower level will require a fuller commitment to the ritual practices.

Like clerks and cashiers, and even more so, the responsibility of this priestly office is to facilitate the religious process of ritual transference: "making the sale." If a clerk or cashier is having a challenge, representatives of this office expedite the ritual process. If we are at all involved in pop-culture consumer activities, we see this activity routinely. Much more so than the clerk or cashier, when ritual fulfillment is in question, the consummation of the process is a priority of the location manager, who will "make it right," within (ritual) reason, of course. The completion of the ritual process is of primary importance. Hence, when a ritual transaction is not proceeding according to canon and myth, clerks or cashiers will call for the intervention of an on-site location manager.

The most respected members of this branch of the priestly order actually do "make it right" — lowering the price if need be, going "by the ad" even if the ad is in error, allowing products to be acquired for the "marked price" even if the marked price is lower than it should be, accepting "what the [in-store] sign says" regardless of the loss, etc. Again, in terms of contemporary popular culture, these members of the priesthood are dedicated to such mythic ideals as "the customer is always right" or "customer satisfaction: guaranteed." The result, of course, is that laypersons are able to acquire the objects of their interest and hence satisfy their dharmic obligations. In short, just as with the archaic priesthood, the higher a person is in the system, the greater one's responsibility for ensuring that the ritual process functions in an orderly and coherent manner. This important consideration brings us to the next office of the postmodern priesthood, the store manager.

Store managers are the priests who exercise the greatest ritual responsibility at temple and shrine sites. These senior religious officials are ultimately responsible for not only the smooth and orderly conduct of all the ritual processes going on throughout the entire temple, but also for preserving the sacredness and ritual purity of the environment, evaluating the conduct of lower priests, and maintaining communication with the highest levels of the priesthood.

All the qualities of superior location managers are found in store managers. In large part, they have ascended to their positions because of their excellence in lower levels of the priesthood. They too will strive to "make it right" in individual ritual situations if and when necessary, but the focus of their office transcends individual ritual performances and concerns the greater issues of the temple as a whole. What they must do is "make it right" (or as right as possible) for all the persons who visit the religious center. Among the duties noted above, perhaps the most critical one for the senior local priest is preserving the sacredness and ritual purity of the temple — the systematic organization of ambience, referred to by Baudrillard.

Preserving sacred ambience

To the general managers falls the task of preserving the sacred ambience of the religious site. As the senior priests of the temple, their primary religious duty and distinct dharma is to maintain and safeguard the sacredness of the temple. Our interest in the explicitly religious tasks of the senior priests is not meant to minimize the other important operational and managerial responsibilities that they have, but rather to focus our study on their religious duties to the temple and the culture as a whole.[10]

To properly maintain the temple's sacred ambience, the store manager, as senior priest, must be attentive to a number of critical elements. Our focus here is on the three most important of these elements: (1) an abundance of quantity and variety of material objects; (2) the right integration of objects with the tertiary narratives about them; and, especially, (3) the right integration of specific objects that appear in versions of The How-To Story. Each of these elements requires precise coordination of ritual activity and the mythic narratives that they vivify.

First, the temple itself must manifest that "climatization of life, goods, objects, services, behaviors and social relations," which Baudrillard cites as elemental to the phenomenology of consumption. In the department store-temple an abundance of material goods and a multitude of styles, sizes, and colors must be available for each type of product. From undergarments to large appliances, it is not enough for the temple to simply have sufficient amounts of a certain product, it must have copious quantities and multiple versions of each product. Bras and exercise shoes are good examples of the way this sacred ambiance is created. There is not just a single type of bra for each bust size; there is a vast multitude of different styles, colors, and fabrics in every size range, and then, of course, there are different brands, each with its own multitude of variation. Exercise shoes are no different; unique shoes must be present for different exercises, and different colors, shapes, and styles of each unique type of shoe. And here, again, there are different brands, which further expand the range. This same proliferation of product variety can be seen in varying degrees in every class of object.

Of absolute importance is that this prodigious variety be communicated visually and aesthetically to the layperson, for this variety creates the sacredness of the temple. In practice, the various sectors of the temple must

---

10. There are certainly crucial personnel, financial, corporate, and general bureaucratic duties to which senior priests must give great attention. These duties, like those of the high priests (corporate executives), however important and religious they may be, are still appropriately seen as institutional management obligations, which doubtless are similar to those of priests in any cosmological system at any time; in fact, they are obligations of senior management officials in any institutional system, religious or secular. By virtue of these obligations being undertaken by religious officials and in service to a religious institution (a temple), they are explicitly religious in character although they are not functionally different than similar tasks performed by others. The store manager as senior religious official at the religious sites of our culture has a more critical and much more explicit religious obligation, however: keeping the temple sacred.

systematically deploy vast quantities of products on shelves, racks, tables, and massive standalone displays: ceiling-high stacks of flower pots, thirty-foot-long aisles of storage containers, twenty racks of shirts, and in larger stores, huge concentrations of washing machines and refrigerators. Whatever the product may be, if it is not amassed in enormous quantities, the sacred sense is diminished. If the range of sizes, styles, colors, and textures of a certain product is anything less than extensive and visually apparent, something of the sacred glamour of that area of the temple is lost. Loss of this sacred glamour could lead to diminution of ritual commitment on the part of worshipers and a corresponding reduction in ritual activity. If this occurs in several areas within the temple, the temple as a whole may fall into decline.

As noted earlier, each department has its own priest, but the senior priest is responsible for all departments and the overall temple environment. Each department must itself manifest the qualities of the sacred (abundance of quantity and variety of products) and all departments must work together synergistically to manifest the fullness of the sacred abundance at the temple site. This abundance is all the more critical in the case of products that have appeared in tertiary myths, especially popular commercials and local tabloid advertisements, for these items are the focal points of ritual activity for large numbers of worshipers.

The necessary relationship between tertiary myths and the temple environment is the second major element to which senior priests must give principal attention. In this instance, they must oversee the proper integration of the temple's ritual objects with the mythic narratives that sacralize them. Items featured in television and mass-market magazine tertiary myths are of special significance. The best known of these items are, of course, what we usually refer to as "name-brand" products. The more myths in which they appear or the greater the frequency when these myths are communicated (through TV commercials or print advertisements), the greater the religious significance of the objects. As a consequence, these objects possess heightened ritual significance and thus they must be available to worshipers. Not only are these objects well known to vast segments of the population simply because of media saturation, their religious significance is markedly greater since by their appearance in multiple or frequently communicated tertiary myths they allow greater identification with the meta-myth. In short, one is more fully engaged with the myth of success and achievement by acquiring a product that is associated with a name-brand than a similar object that is not mythically sacralized. Ritually acquiring Black and Decker tools, John Deere lawn tractors, Rubbermaid dish drainers, Sony TVs, Weber grills, or Nike athletic shoes does make a difference. For this reason, the senior priests (and their departmental subordinates) must remain ever vigilant to the easy availability of such objects at the temple.

Of equal, and perhaps even greater, importance to having easily obtainable name-brand objects is having an abundance of objects that are featured in The How-To Story discussed in chapter 4. Because this tertiary myth is by far the most likely to inspire persons to immediate ritual activity and ritual engagement with uniquely specified objects at local temples, senior priests must be keenly aware of both the narrative details and ritual implications of the local How-To Story. In practice, senior priests are responsible for knowing and communicating to subordinates the duration of the heightened ritual period (the time period covered by the ad), having abundant quantities of the objects depicted in the myths, and assuring that the designated sacrificial offering specified in the myth accords with the offering expected at the temple. In addition, senior priests must be certain that subordinate members of the priesthood are aware of how the specific How-To Story relates to them and their individual areas of ritual responsibility. For a high priest to fail in any of these areas is to risk impoverishment of the ritual, an erosion in the temple's status, an offense to worshipers, a violation of the priest's own dharma, and (ultimately) a sacrilege against the economy itself.

•

Thus far, the chapters of this section have explored the formal religious components of postmodern cosmological culture, focusing on the myths and rituals of today's world and designating their affinities with those of primal and archaic cultures. As helpful as the designation of such affinities may be, however, they alone do not adequately answer the question posed at the close of chapter 3: how is the postmodern cosmic order, which assumes an ongoing linkage of human events and sacred forces, ritually realized? What we have discovered is how the religious structures of antiquity are reembodied in what appears to be the secular culture of postmodernity, but these rather technical findings alone do not delineate the full range and depth of postmodern religious experience. They only hint at the extent of cultural enthrallment and only suggest the depth of personal enchantment with the sacred.

Missing in the foregoing analysis of forms and structures is the religious dynamic of postmodernity, which vivifies and validates the formal relationship of myths and rituals in the lives of individuals and culture.

The disclosure and analysis of this vitalizing process of contemporary religiosity is the subject of the remainder of the book. Building on our study of myths and rituals, we can now turn attention to the definitive nexus between them: the sacred acts and attitudes of individuals and the sacred times and climes of the culture as a whole.

The next chapter examines the personal dimension of ritual consumption: the way the mythico-ritual dynamic is experienced and expressed in the lives of individuals. This study of the sacred acts and attitudes of individuals serves as both the conclusion to this section and an introduction to part 3, which investigates the sacred times and climes of culture as a whole. Traditionally called "holidays," these times and climes are more accurately termed "holy days."

— S I X —

Consumption and
the Religious Imperative

The designation of holidays as the socioreligious nexus of myth and ritual is hardly novel. As long as human beings have structured time using a calendar (that is to say, since the archaic period), certain distinct days or specific spans of days have been recognized as more sacred than others. On these holy days (or holidays) a community's most important secondary myths are reaffirmed on a massive scale, and related ritual activities reach their highest levels of intensity and participation. While vestiges of these sorts of culturewide mythico-rituals still continue in transcendental religions, the definitive expression of this type of holy-day activity is found in the cosmological civilizations of antiquity. In these cultures, which bear a striking resemblance to our own, the grand holy days and religious festivals were times when the mythico-rituals of cosmic order and process reached paradigmatic expression. In the context of postmodernity, during our holy days the mythico-rituals of economic order and process reach their paradigmatic expression, and the spirit of acquisition and consumption enchants the entire culture.

But a culture is made up of individuals, and before considering the ways in which holidays function as holy days for the culture as a whole, the personal dimension of sacred consumption must be considered. After all, cosmological religious activity is necessarily contingent on individuals accepting the ultimate truth of the community's dominant myths and then participating in common rituals that vivify the myths. Before such participation can happen on a culturewide scale, which is characteristic of holiday/holy-day rituals, the necessity of those rituals must be known, accepted, and lived as a "felt" experience by each participant — not in a formal, abstract manner (much as has done been in this text up until now), but with the fullness of one's entire being.

Juliet B. Schor and the personal dimension of consumption

As discussed in previous chapters, for us, consumption is a religious obligation, a dharmic demand; and as our myths (meta-, secondary, and tertiary) tell us, we must also consume as often as possible. We are perpetually pursuing opportunities to engage in the sacred activity, ever seeking the sacred time and space in which we can live the myth through the ritual experience of acquisition-consumption-disposal. Unlike our prehistoric forebears, we are not satisfied after a good hunting or gathering expedition, the generosity of the Caribou spirit, or the abundance of berries found in the glen; we believe that what we have is not enough. Ritual consumption is not about food any longer.

Unlike our archaic forebears, we are not satisfied after a good harvest or successful transition into the planting season, the beneficence of Min or Persephone's fortuitous return from Hades; we desire more. Sustenance is not the sacred ideal. We want to "have it all" and have it as often as we can, in as many ways as we can, and in forms that are new, unique, and admired. Most of all, and in a manner quite unlike our more communal ancestors, we want it personally, since in the mythico-ritual logic of our culture, only personal rituals of acquisition, consumption, and disposal indicate our proper relationship with the sacred power of the economy. How and to what extent this sacred logic is actually reflected in the lives of average persons requires some insight into the buying habits of individual consumers, a task made considerably easier by Juliet B. Schor's groundbreaking study, *The Overspent American.*[1]

An economist by vocation and a thoughtful advocate of reduced consumption, Schor focuses her work on the socioeconomic contours of contemporary consumerism while keenly elucidating the personal dimensions of postmodern consumption. Not surprisingly, she supplies a wealth of empirical economic data and analysis supporting Baudrillard and Jameson's theoretic assertions about the consumerist dimension of postmodernity. Needless to say, her work also offers economic data confirming the thesis of this book. Of particular interest is her detailed analysis of the economic, social, and psychological behavior of individual consumers.

She refers to the "have it all" attitude as "upscaling," which she finds reflected in the dramatic expansion of middle-class desires and acquisi-

---

1. Juliet B. Schor, *The Overspent American: Upscaling, Downshifting, and the New Consumer* (New York: Basic Books, 1998). References to Schor's book in this chapter will be cited, parenthetically, in the text.

tions in the last two decades of the twentieth century. She reports, for example, that "throughout the 1980s and 1990s, most middle class Americans were acquiring at a greater rate than any previous generation of the middle-class. And their buying was more upscale" (11). I suspect, too, that the rate during the 1960s and 1970s was higher than in the postwar 1940s and 1950s, and the postwar period higher than any other previously. In other words, the postmodern period (as defined by Jameson, from the 1950s on) is properly characterized by a massive dilation of consumer spending, which is progressively more upscale. Included in her list of items required for a middle-class lifestyle are larger houses, second homes, personal computers, private college education for children, designer clothes, home and auto air conditioning, and "Michael Jordan's ubiquitous athletic shoes, about which children and adults both display near-obsession" (11). Importantly, Schor's analysis reveals that the upper-middle-class

> is the group that defines material success, luxury, and comfort for nearly every category below it. It is the visible lifestyle to which most aspiring Americans aspire.... The average American is now more likely to compare his or her income to the six-figure benchmark in the office down the corridor or displayed in Tuesday evening prime time.... Taken together, 85 percent [of a consumer sample] aspired to be in the top 18 percent of American households.... Only 15 percent would be satisfied ending up as middle-class. (13)

The vast majority of persons no longer consider middle-class existence a measure of success. Instead the upper-middle-class is the barometer, a group that Schor cites as the "top 20 percent of households, with the exclusion of the top few percent" and whose midpoint income she pegs at ninety-one thousand dollars (12–13).

Even more critically, Schor's work reveals that the buying habits of most people are predicated not on the basis of their actual income and available resources but a desire to acquire products associated with the lifestyle of the highest economic class. Citing the findings of one team of researchers, she reports: "Sixty percent of respondents reported that advertisements for prestige items motivated them to 'earn more money so that I can afford the things they show'" (71–72).[2] All of this leads to an intensification of consumerism and an acceleration of what I refer to as the process of acquisition-consumption-disposal.

---

2. Schor's citation of Susan Fournier and Michael Guiry, "A Look into the World of Consumption Dreams, Fantasies, and Aspirations," Research report, University of Florida (December 1991), 30.

Sounding a bit like Baudrillard and Jameson, Schor tells us that "consumerism as a way of life is so ingrained it's hard to recognize within us and around us. Like air, it's everywhere, we're dependent on it, and perhaps most important, until it's really dirty, it cannot be seen" (24). Schor very much wants us to see it, however, and she offers cogent economic and psychological explanations of its presence. She also paints a vivid picture of the personal dimension of consumerism.

As suggested in the selections above, a primary reason for accelerated personal consumption is the aspiration of the majority of the general population to share in the consumerist practices of the highest economic class. Schor goes on to tell us that personal consumption is further fueled by such well-known socioeconomic forces as marketing, advertising, technological advances, and product innovation. We are all, individually, influenced by these forces, and as a consequence, we all consume more than we might otherwise, and certainly more than other individuals did in previous cultural epochs. But these details form only part of the picture.

More importantly, Schor calls attention to those interior, psychological dispositions and habits that perhaps more accurately articulate the personal dimension of ritual consumption. These include an increased willingness to incur significant consumer (credit card) debt, a dysfunctional denial of one's actual indebtedness, a quest to satisfy the ever-escalating desires of one's children, competitive spending, an acceptance of higher costs for gifts, increases in "self gifting," individual spending fantasies, and a rejection of taboos against conspicuous consumption (see chapter 4, "When Spending Becomes You," 67–109). While these dispositions are fairly common in the population as a whole, what makes them significant here is their highly individualistic character. Individuals act on these dispositions on a routine basis, as a matter of course, and as a consequence, accelerated consumption serves to structure their personal identity. Commenting on the "identity-consumption relationship," Schor observes: "Who we are not only affects what we buy. What we buy also affects who we become. Recent research suggests that the more we have, the more powerful, confident, and socially validated we feel" (57).[3]

In addition to these and other more obvious factors (name-brand identification, status seeking, class expectations), Schor gives special attention

---

3. The recent research to which Schor refers is: Susan S. Kleine, Robert E. Kleine III, and Chris T. Allen, "How Is a Possession 'Me' or 'Not Me'?" *Journal of Consumer Research* 22 (December 1995): 327–43; and Robert E. Kleine III, Susan S. Kleine, and Jerome B. Kernan, "Mundane Consumption and the Self," *Journal of Consumer Psychology* 2, no. 3 (1993): 209–35.

to the role of television programming in accelerated personal consumption. Building on the work of O'Guinn and Shrum, the Merck Family Fund poll, and her own studies, Schor's thesis is that since television programs typically depict the lives of the most affluent persons in society, and since almost everyone watches TV, the lifestyle of these exceptionally prosperous characters becomes the model for countless individuals (79–83).[4] The result is an inevitable increase in consumption for those individuals and consumption of high-end products. In her interpretation, commercial advertisements do not inspire our consumption as much as our desire to emulate the lifestyle of the characters on the programs. No longer are we trying to keep up with the proverbial "Joneses"; now, our peers are the rich and successful characters depicted on television programs — *The Fresh Prince of Bel Air,* in one example (80), *Frasier* in another (13). As detailed shortly, I disagree with this particular conclusion and argue that rather than trying to emulate the lifestyle of the TV characters, we are instead trying to emulate the lifestyle of the actors themselves.

Schor reports that, to her knowledge, her study is "the first statistical evidence tying television to spending" — and the evidence is compelling: "each additional hour of television watched in a week led to an additional $208 of annual spending" (82). To her benefit, Schor does qualify her thesis, noting that her "results do not unravel what is undoubtedly a complex link between watching a program and ending up at the cash register" (82). Nonetheless, her findings are extremely important for revealing the correlation between television viewing and increased personal consumption. This effect would be expected on the basis of my theory concerning the relationship between postmodern myths and rituals of consumption; and since Schor's explanation is somewhat different from that advanced earlier in this book, some comment is called for here.

As discussed previously, I believe the reasons for the correlation between television viewing and increased consumption are religious and have more to do with the mythico-ritual structure of our culture than the specific content of television programs. In this regard, the characteristics of certain television programs may certainly serve to further vivify the meta-myth, especially if they focus on the lives of affluent persons, but this connection is incidental to the medium. As noted in chapter 3, the fundamental importance of television to the mythico-ritual structure of postmodern cul-

---

4. For Schor's reference to O'Guinn and Shrum see Thomas C. O'Guinn and L. J. Shrum, "The Role of Television in the Construction of Consumer Reality," *Journal of Consumer Research* 24 (March 1997): 278–94. The Merck Family Fund poll Schor cites was conducted in 1995 by the Harwood Group; details appear in *The Overspent American,* 208.

ture is not the content of its various narratives but rather its function as the culture's primary sacred text, which personalizes and domesticates the meta-myth in a vast assortment of secondary myths. Television also is a major textual carrier for tertiary myths. Finally, the lifestyle depicted on the programs (of which, after all, only a select number actually depict excessive affluence) is not as much of an influence as the affluent lifestyle of the actors who appear and play roles on the programs.

Contra Schor, I would argue that we more likely strive to emulate the lifestyle of Will Smith than that of the Fresh Prince of Bel Air, Kelsey Grammer more than that of the Frasier character, Jennifer Aniston more than her character (Rachel) in *Friends,* and Ray Romano more than Raymond in the offbeat *Everybody Loves Raymond.* Suffice it to say, Schor's findings on the relationship between television viewing and increases in personal consumption offer clear support for the function of television as the mythic text of our time, although they do so most compellingly when television programming as a whole is considered and when the medium itself is understood in the mythico-ritual structure of our culture. Aside from this relatively minor modification, Schor's analysis of the impact of television on personal consumption is in virtual agreement with my own.

So too are her general findings. Where we decidedly differ, of course, is in the presuppositions of our respective inquiries — hers being that the phenomena of our interest is primarily economic while mine is that it is primarily religious. In any event, her work reveals that in the latter part of the twentieth century, the vast majority of Americans are personally engaged in the process of consumption at a rate far exceeding any ever seen before in our history, and indeed, in the history of the world.

The religious imperative of consumption

Schor's inquiry into this unprecedented cultural situation is developed on the basis of economic, sociological, and psychological analyses, and her conclusion is that the current situation is unhealthy to individuals, society, and the global environment. Hence, she advocates a significant change in our consumerist behavior, a modification she calls "downshifting." While her proposal is laudable, and certainly well argued, this behavioral change is reasonable (not to say achievable) only if her general presupposition is correct; that is, if what we are wrestling with is merely an economic process, undergirded by certain sociological and psychological forces. If this is the case, then some reasonable chance exists of changing the cultural situation through rational means, such as those utilized by Schor. If, however, we are dealing with a religious phenomenon, especially one of a cosmological type, then we are confronted with a wholly different order of experience and one beyond the reach of traditional secular strategies of persuasion.

What we are dealing with, in this case, is not a relative economic, sociological, or psychological condition but the fundamental reality of existence itself, and more critically, one's personal existence in the context of this reality. We are up against gods and sacred forces, dharmic duties and religious energies as inevitable as the seasons and the coming of night. In short, if the personal dimension of consumption, which Schor so masterfully depicts, transpires in a religious context, then we are dealing with a situation that defies rational mediation, as this book contends.

Thus, while Schor's research supplies empirical data on the personal dimension of consumption, which is consistent with the expectations of my thesis, when that data is considered in terms of the thesis itself, her findings indicate that rituals of consumption hold a far greater power over individuals than that which she suggests. Looking at her findings, then, in the context of my thesis, reveals that the contemporary desire to have it all differs not only from our communal ancestors' desire by being far more personal in character, the desire also differs from our more recent secular forebears' desire by being far more religious in expression.

From a cosmological religious perspective, personal consumption becomes less of a socially constructed behavior and a much more elemental imperative. Rather than simply consuming objects in conformity to social demands or even psychological motivations, the activity becomes a binding obligation. Schor tells us that "we experience consumer society as something natural. But it's not" (24). But if consumer society (and our social role as consumers) is predicated on the sacred logic of a fundamentally religious culture, and especially a cosmological one, then consuming is certainly experienced as though it were something natural. Thus, the demand to consume is functionally no different than any other natural demand to which we respond, and all the personal dispositions and habits that define the contemporary consumer become less like social and psychological motivations and more like hard-wired, instinctual behaviors — ritual activities performed without reflection and without doubt.

The process of disposal

Included in our personal ritual performance is the necessity of disposing of objects. Not only must we acquire and consume for the sacred to be fully experienced and our place in the order and process of the economy properly established, we must also dispose of previously possessed objects. The quicker the process can be completed and then reinitiated, the greater is one's engagement with the sacral realm, and hence, the greater one's personal sanctity in the mythico-ritual system. In actual practice, some products more readily reveal the importance of this part of the ritual process than others — clothing, automobiles, houses, major appliances, and cutting-edge technological devices, for example. For this reason, popular culture venerates the person who is able to keep up with the trends in fashion, obtain a new car every year (perhaps also explaining the recent popularity of automobile leasing), buy a *new* house, replace appliances on a routine basis, acquire the most innovative type of computer, and so on. What must be remembered, however, is that while these and other fashion- and technology-related items are perhaps the best examples of the disposal phase of the consumption ritual, all or nearly all other objects serve a similar ritual function. Whether the product is a new seasonal wardrobe or a new hair dryer, one must dispose of its predecessor to confirm that one has consumed it in a sacred sense.

Of course, we do not have to dispose of old products when acquiring new ones. We can keep the old washing machine if we like, or the clock radio, or the desk lamp, lounge chair, house slippers, hair dryer, cooking utensils, blouse, or lawn mower. But if we keep all the old products when we acquire their newer versions, we will eventually have to acquire a new, larger house; in itself this act would represent a legitimate ritual because we would have presumably disposed of the previous house, which, in a sacred sense, had been consumed. Moreover, when we acquired the new house, we most likely would also acquire new objects for it, even if we kept much of all the old stuff we had accumulated.

On the other hand, we could take several decidedly inappropriate actions in order to continue collecting old products. In ascending order of sacrilege, they are as follows: adding on to an existing house or renting a storage shed, letting old stuff accumulate inside the home, and finally having stuff pile up on the porch or in the yard. While these actions are certainly necessary if one desires to avoid the ritual obligation of disposal, they are clearly violations of the sacred order. In each instance, they indicate a failure to fully consume a large collection of objects, thus failing to properly complete the ritual cycle. In the cases of the home addition or the storage shed, they also inhibit individuals from further ritual activity since a sacrificial resource (money) is being used for nonsacrificial purposes — rather than being used in a ritual performance, the sacrifice itself is being consumed. This act would be analogous to a citizen in an archaic culture eating a sacrificial animal on the way to a temple on a holy day. Instances of piling are even more profane for obvious reasons. In such cases, individuals may be atheists or agnostics, and they are generally social outcasts. More generously, they may simply have been unable to convert to the new mythico-ritual paradigm, clinging to antiquated beliefs about use value and material limitation, just as they cling to the objects themselves.

One way or another, the ritual cycle must reach its appropriate conclusion in disposal — even if it means disposal of a house. We must dispose of a product to confirm that we have consumed it in a sacred sense, but we cannot actually dispose of the product until we have acquired another version of the same product. The ritual trigger, then, is not consumption, but rather acquisition; and the ritual is concluded not when an object has been consumed, but only when we dispose of it.

Disposal processes have ritual patterns all their own, but their primary function is in their symbolic signaling that the entire ritual process has been completed and (in the cyclical manner that is elemental to cosmological systems) that we can reinitiate the sacred cycle of existence once again. Old, consumed objects are removed from our dwellings to make space for new ones, or, in the case of houses, we ourselves vacate the old dwelling. With large appliances, delivery persons perform a ritual of removal: a truck arrives, laborers enter our house or garage, examine the old appliance, attach it to a dolly, transport it out of our structure, and then reenter with the new appliance. Often, this process is accompanied by some degree of ritual chaos, especially if children, pets, or carpeting are involved. In the case of automobiles, used cars are traded in when new models are acquired. Routinely, this process involves the mediation of a shaman and ritual struggle (another form of ritual chaos) between the shaman and the layperson. When successful, the ritual concludes with the old vehicle and a significant personal sacrifice left at the sacred site where the new vehicle has been acquired.

With other objects, the ritual process of disposal allows for some variation. Consumed items may be given to charitable organizations for resale, passed along to friends and family members, simply thrown away, or resold at yard or garage sales. In any event, the consumed object must be disposed of. While some objects are retained for sentimental reasons or moved to another area in a dwelling space (as with older televisions), the normative ritual is to divest oneself of a consumed object prior to or immediately upon acquiring a new one. Ideally, the consumed object is still entirely functional. As Schor reports in her study of accelerated "product divestment" in contemporary culture, not only is the quantity of disposed items increasing but the products found at yard sales, charitable groups' drop-off centers, and even public garbage dumps are in remarkably good condition (104–6).

The experience is not restricted to objects, and for this reason, contemporary culture also witnesses the proliferation of audio and video commodities and ever more novel, innovative, and sophisticated instruments for their consumption. As Jameson points out, we are constantly seeking out the new visual image or aural sensation to consume, resulting in the seemingly obsessive interest in television, films and video versions of films, popular music and videos of popular music. I would add to this list the equally vital quest to acquire the material instruments to consume the visual images and aural sensations: TVs, computers, VCRs, CD players, entertainment systems, cell phones, computer scanners, digital cameras, DVDs, laser disc players, palm pilots, and whatever is next. As is true of the more conventional objects discussed previously, we do not simply consume these items, we engage ourselves with them religiously through a sacred process of acquisition-consumption-disposal. With these objects, the process is rendered even more sacred because of the sheer velocity of their creation and re-creation, allowing those whose ritual activity is focused on these objects far greater engagement with the sacral realm, and hence, greater personal sanctity in the mythico-ritual system.

Sacred roles

Such heightened sanctity is to be expected in a cosmological system, which after all is quite hierarchical in its socioreligious structure. But cosmological cultures are also strongly unified for the same reason. While some certainly possess greater sanctity than others, all persons have a sacred role to play, and all may fully participate in the religious legitimation of society, thus fulfilling their own dharma while also affirming the sacred order of the culture. As suggested above, we make this affirmation whenever we engage in the sacred ritual of acquisition-consumption-disposal. While I may not be able to worship at an elite shrine, I nonetheless can worship. I may not be able to sacrifice to acquire a new computer, but I may sacrifice to acquire a new phone answering machine. I may not acquire, consume, and dispose of cars routinely, but I do acquire, consume, and dispose of athletic shoes, garden tools, and video game discs.

From toasters to gel pens, Gap jeans to Apple iMac G4s, Violent Femmes CDs to Barbie doll apparel, Lamborghinis to Gillette Mach 3 shavers, we all have individual roles to play in the never-ending sacred cycle. Moreover, what would happen if we abandoned the ritual or were unable to perform it properly and on a large scale, stopping or even slowing down our participation in the sacred cycle of acquisition-consumption-disposal? I suspect that the answer is obvious and doubtless well known (even if subconsciously) to most of us. Worlds would end, societies implode, whole continents would "melt down" — as occurred in much of East Asia in the mid-1990s. The catastrophic consequences of nonconsumption, in fact, function as subplots in the sacred story of our postmodern culture, as conveyed through the myth of the Great Depression of the 1930s and the more recent Asian meltdown. The narratives of these events are components of the meta-myth (or more accurately, eschatological inversions of the meta-myth) for they communicate a sacred truth about the ultimate power of the economy as well as our dependence and our obligations to it.

Of course, to fully satisfy these obligations, the items we acquire must themselves not be "used" before we possess them, and to most fully experience the sacred, the items acquired must be those deemed most desirable by culture as a whole or the socially determined "tastes" of our particular class (29).[5] In practice, our legitimate desires direct us not to a car, per se, but a new car, and not just any car, but preferably a BMW, a Mercedes, a Miata, perhaps a new 4x4 or SUV, the right minivan or station wagon for our family; not a pen but a Montblanc or a Classique; not any sort of sweet-smelling personal fragrance but one created by Ralph Lauren, Estée Lauder, Lancome, or Boucheron; not a watch but a Rolex, Bertolucci, a Raymond Weil, a Franck Muller, a Blancpain. These items are the achievable desires of the highest economic class, but as Schor has noted, they are the ideals of 85 percent of the population (13). Even more fundamentally, what is communicated is the sacred necessity of acquiring something new and better. Perhaps it is only a Ford or a Toyota; a Cross or a nice Parker pen; a Mary Kay or Avon fragrance; a digital Timex or Grunen. What matters is that it is new, novel, innovative, something better than what we have now, which we can now dispense with; an object legitimated by the myths of the culture; something that integrates us with the sacred order and process of the economy.

As is doubtless quite evident, critics, such as Schor, view the impact of this process as having decidedly negative consequences. The process

---

5. Schor follows Pierre Bourdieu in classifying normative categories of consumption by social classes ("legitimate [highbrow]," "middlebrow," and "popular"). See also Bourdieu, *Distinction: A Social Critique of the Judgment of Taste* (Cambridge, Mass.: Harvard University Press, 1984).

leads to waste, the destruction of the natural environment, personal debt, alienation (in all the old Marxist senses of the word), and the dehumanization of others (who themselves may be unfortunate [or perhaps, in the context of our times, *fortunate*] enough for one reason or another to have become commodities). This same process also helps account for and perhaps best explains the proliferation of addictive "diseases" related to consumption. Alcoholism, drug addiction, food addiction, sex addiction, shopaholism, and so on are revealed as not only diseases of consumption, as they are often classified, but perhaps most accurately as challenges related to the proper relationship with the acquisition-consumption-disposal process. Perhaps, then, they are expressions of a religious addiction.

Having made that point, and not to delve too far into the sacred-profane dichotomy discussion, if we can specify the religious through distinction from the nonreligious (or locate the sacred apart from the profane), then we can speak of it more explicitly. Thus, since the sacred is acquisition-consumption-disposal, and religion is the experience that fully engages us with this process (through myth and ritual), then the nonreligious would be that which disengages us from the process. This would be production. Although this note seems rather rudimentary and perhaps inconsequential, recognizing the distinction is necessary because, in this context, it allows for the isolation of the religious experience itself. The distinction also represents an inversion of the old Protestant work ethic, which vested religious merit in economic production, thereby fueling early and middle capitalism.

Today, the cultural logic is reversed. The approach is no less religious, but the religious basis is different; rather than transcendental and production-validating, the basis is cosmological and consumption-validating. Because labor and work prevent one from acquisition-consumption-disposal, production is the antithesis of the sacred. Production has thus become functionally profane, where in earlier times, it was functionally sacred; on the other hand, acquisition and consumption, which were once religiously restricted, if not actually profane, have become sacred. When I am working, I am not consuming, yet my working (profane) endeavors bring me the substance necessary for me to consume. I thus sacrifice time and energy in the profane realm for the sake of the economy; not because I find any particular satisfaction in contributing to production (and certainly not because of any religious merit, per se) but because I am equipping myself to better perform my religious duty. My sacrifice of time and energy in profane endeavors (labor) rewards me with ritual resources (money), which then allows me to participate in the sacred process of acquisition-consumption-disposal.

This threefold process, as opposed to production (the ideal of early and middle capitalism), defines one's primary religious duty (dharma) in the late-capitalist, postmodern world. As a result, we sacralize those times and places where we can maximize the experience of acquisition-consumption-disposal, thus motivating us to reduce the realm in which we are engaged in acts of production. From this motivation spin off popular ideals (and I would say mythic narratives) embodied in concepts such as the "golden years" of retirement, "extended vacations," "saving up 'comp' or sick time to use all at once," and a whole class of ideals related specifically to weekends: "T.G.I.F.," "living for the weekend," midweek "hump-day," the "three-day weekend," and certainly, for some, the "lost weekend." All of these richly evocative concepts express a resistance to activities of production and an idealization of leisure periods when we can fully immerse ourselves in sacred time and space — times when acquisition-consumption-disposal may be fully experienced and spaces entirely divorced from the profane sphere of work and production. What, after all, do most persons in our culture do in leisure spaces, places, and times? While relaxing activities or visits with family and friends might once have prevailed, every indication is that today we acquire, consume, and dispose. In this regard our holidays manifest a genuine sacredness, becoming true holy days when individuals and entire communities can escape the profane realm and reaffirm the sacred truth of their personal and collective existence.

The annual cycle of our holidays thus comes into correspondence with a typical cosmological cycle of ritual celebrations: fixed calendric periods that are recognized as particularly sacred and specifically dedicated to mythico-ritual activity. For postmodern culture, these holidays are holy because they liberate us from the profane realm of work and production, ushering us into the sacred times and climes of uninhibited acquisition-consumption-disposal and supplying the religious dynamic of postmodernity. As we turn our attention to these holidays we will find, using the title of Jack Santino's wonderful book, they take us "all around the year" and really are (adding his subtitle) "celebrations in American life."[6] We may also discover that they are celebrations *of* American life and its cosmological essence, celebrations that uniquely reveal the religious dynamic of postmodernity, and celebrations that are more profoundly sacred than their secular guise suggests.

---

6. Jack Santino, *All Around the Year: Holidays and Celebrations in American Life* (Urbana: University of Illinois Press, 1994).

Part III

HOLIDAYS, HOLY DAYS, AND THE POSTMODERN LITURGICAL YEAR

— S E V E N —

Primary Religious Elements of Postmodern Holy Days

Our understanding of the nature and function of holidays in contemporary culture has been advanced in a number of recent texts.[1] Each of these works contributes to the argument of this book, although few do so explicitly. Of special importance to this study is their delineation of the cultural history of major holidays and their deployment and analysis of data revealing the increasing commercialization of these holidays over the past century. Given the presence of these previous works, the massive commercial exploitation of holidays and associated increases in consumption during holiday periods seems firmly established, as well as being a fairly self-evident cultural fact, as most persons would acknowledge who have done any shopping during holiday seasons. Jack Santino summarizes the situation nicely in this short passage, which also references three other authors who have described it:

> Most of us are unaware of the ways our social values and behaviors validate the capitalist ethos. Only when these activities are exaggerated during festival periods are they recognized, and usually condemned as crass. Still, even a cursory examination of holidays

---

1. See, for example: Jack Santino, *New Old-Fashioned Ways: Holidays and Popular Culture* (Knoxville: University of Tennessee Press, 1996) and *All Around the Year* (Urbana: University of Illinois Press, 1994); Leigh Eric Schmidt, *Consumer Rites* (Princeton, N.J.: Princeton University Press, 1995); and "The Commercialization of the Calendar: American Holidays and the Culture of Consumption, 1870–1930," in *Journal of American History* (December 1991): 887–916; Richard Horsley and James Tracy, eds., *Christmas Unwrapped: Consumerism, Christ, and Culture* (Harrisburg, Pa.: Trinity Press International, 2001); Karal Ann Marling, *Merry Christmas! Celebrating America's Greatest Holiday* (Cambridge, Mass.: Harvard University Press, 2000); Stephen Nissenbaum, *The Battle for Christmas* (New York: Alfred A. Knopf, 1996); Penne L. Restad, *Christmas in America* (Oxford: Oxford University Press, 1995); William B. Waits, *The Modern Christmas in America* (New York: New York University Press, 1993); and Daniel Miller, ed., *Unwrapping Christmas* (Oxford: Oxford University Press, 1993). And, earlier, see Russell W. Belk, "A Child's Christmas in America," in *Journal of American Culture* 10 (1987): 87–100.

and popular culture reveals capitalism and commercialism at almost every turn. The holidays are used to sell merchandise (see, for instance, Schmidt 1991; Waits 1993; Miller 1993). Not only are holidays created and elaborated for commercial purposes, and not only are holiday symbols related to commercial products, but even the historical, legendary, and mythic figures that in reality belong to all of us are seen endorsing various goods. Our capitalist Santa Claus holds a bottle of Coke in his hand.[2]

Clearly, this book shares a similar interest in these phenomena, and this chapter considers many of the same holidays and utilizes some of the same data presented in the other texts. However, as indicated in the previous chapters, the basis of my analysis and the purpose of this book are entirely different from these other works. My interest is in the religious meaning of the holidays, while the primary interest of the other texts is historical, sociological, economic, and to some extent, psychological. The one exception is *Christmas Unwrapped*,[3] which takes a hostile theological approach and is discussed below. Religion is not overlooked in the other studies, and several give prominent attention to its relationship with the holidays. Aside from *Christmas Unwrapped*, however, the religion that shows up is typically traditional, transcendental religion — especially Christianity. Thus, studies of holidays frequently describe the often quite public religious condemnation of the secularization of holy days and the widespread commercialization of holidays in general.

The only recent text on the holidays that analyzes aspects of consumer culture in religious categories is *Christmas Unwrapped*, an anthology that shares the same basic premise as this book — that is, that America's contemporary Christmas celebration resembles archaic religious festivals. Besides this general premise, few similarities and several important differences exist between the approach of *Christmas Unwrapped* and the one taken here. These features are worth noting in the context of this chapter and the rest of the book.

In addition to the general premise, probably the most notable similarity is found in Richard Horsley's comparison of the Babylonian New Year's festival (the *akîtu*) with America's Christmas celebration.[4] Although I study the same festival, my analysis differs in a number of ways.

---

2. Santino, *New Old-Fashioned Ways*, 22.
3. See n. 1 for citation.
4. Richard Horsley, "Christmas: The Religion of Consumer Capitalism," in *Christmas Unwrapped*.

Without going into too much detail, four major distinctions can be cited: First, Horsley's use of the *akîtu* is restricted to a study of Christmas, while in my deployment *akîtu* functions as a model for all postmodern holy days. Second, Horsley focuses his comparative analysis on processes in the socioreligious institutional superstructure of culture while this analysis focuses on a wide range of phenomena related to the personal dimension of ritual acquisition. Third, Horsley's study tends to accentuate what might be called the manipulative or coercive dimension of both the *akîtu* and the Christmas celebration. In contrast, my analysis seeks to disclose the actual experience of sacred reality that occurs during holy days, using characteristic elements of the *akîtu* as a template.

The third distinction relates directly to the fourth, and here perhaps is the most important difference between Horsley's chapter (and indeed all of *Christmas Unwrapped*) and *The Sacred Santa*. Horsley's study is clearly antagonistic to the way Christmas is celebrated today. Like other authors in the anthology, his presentation is predicated on a negative evaluation of Christmas as a religious expression of consumer capitalism. An endorsement by Robert N. Bellah is illuminating in this regard. He writes:

> *Christmas Unwrapped* goes far beyond the traditional call to "put Christ back into Christmas," by showing how Christmas has become the greatest bacchanalia of consumerism in human history.... The contributors use this bloated misunderstanding of Christmas as an indicator of serious problems in our society that should wake up even the most complacent.[5]

I think Bellah is right in his interpretation. *Christmas Unwrapped* is certainly a valuable contribution to what Leigh Eric Schmidt calls "The Piety of Protest" — that venerable body of Christian cultural criticism that stridently opposes the rise of non-Christian institutions in the contemporary world. As such, *Christmas Unwrapped* is a powerful text and a real masterpiece of the genre.

As should be obvious at this point, however, *The Sacred Santa* is not part of this genre and does not share the same agenda as *Christmas Unwrapped*. In fact, contra Bellah, I am not even sure that "the greatest bacchanalia of consumerism in human history" is "a bloated misunderstanding of Christmas." Readers can decide that for themselves. If it is, so be it. The contributors to *Christmas Unwrapped* certainly tell you that this is the case. In contrast, *The Sacred Santa* is not intended as a

---

5. See back cover, *Christmas Unwrapped*.

hostile critique of Christmas. Instead, this book seeks to present a neutral and straightforward analysis of the religious dimension of Christmas and the other holy days of postmodern culture. Perhaps, then, *Christmas Unwrapped* can be seen as a counterpoint to *The Sacred Santa,* another way of looking at the same phenomena, the same cultural battle, and the same combatants. I think the field of the struggle is larger than Christmas, however; just as a "battle" is on for Christmas, as Stephen Nissenbaum reminds us, so too is there a battle for every other holiday and postmodern culture as a whole.

•

To introduce my examination of postmodern holidays, let me put the investigation into the context of my overall argument. As discussed earlier, my contention is that holidays in the postmodern world have not lost their religious or cultural significance but only their *transcendental* religious significance and their *traditional* cultural significance. Thus, the initial presupposition that our holidays have become secular events overlooks the ways and occasions (myths and rituals) by which the seemingly secular may actually be profoundly religious. Christianity's loss of the holidays (and, in principle, significant segments of culture as a whole) has not been to commercialism, consumerism, late capitalism, or some other manifestation of postmodern secularization. Those elements are certainly significant, but their greatest significance is in their role as what Peter Berger calls "carriers."[6] In this case, they are carriers of religion. Christianity has not lost out to secularization or one of its recognized institutions; instead, Christianity has lost out to another type of religion. I believe this other type of religion is more suited to twenty-first-century America and better equipped for success in the world's emerging postmodern culture. Ironically, this type of religion, the cosmological, essentially disappeared in the West over a millennium ago, largely because of the success of Christianity. What makes the neocosmological religion of postmodernity especially well-equipped for success is its capacity to vivify (via myths) and allow engagement with (via rituals) the ultimate (sacred) power of contemporary culture (the economy). The general theory and the principles behind my argument that the religious character of our culture is cosmological was outlined in part 1 of the book. Part 2 analyzed the character and function of postmodern myths and rituals and considered personal dimensions of

---

6. For example, see Berger, *The Homeless Mind* (New York: Vintage Books, 1974), esp. 9, 16, 40. In brief, Berger defines carriers as those institutions that are the "primary agents of social change" (9). Berger follows and expands on Weber's usage of the term.

ritual acquisition and consumption. How these various religious features relate to our holidays and transform them into postmodern holy days, however, has thus far only been suggested. The following chapters make this transformation process more explicit.

This chapter outlines characteristic elements of postmodern holy days, using cosmological New Year's celebrations as a model. Building on the various elements of holy days given in this chapter, chapter 8 analyzes the way myths and rituals function to define holy days apart from other holidays. Chapter 9 then offers an analysis of the postmodern liturgical year (through Halloween), focusing on the function of holy days and other observances in the annual religious cycle.

The eternal return: an ancient holy-day template

The relative sacredness of holidays in contemporary (and any other) cosmological culture is measured specifically by the degree of their culture-wide scope. On any given holiday (holy day) in our culture, work and production cease and persons are allowed to engage in acquisition-consumption-disposition. The extent to which work and production cease (in both time [calendar duration] and space [sectors of the productive economy]) defines the relative sacredness of the holiday. When holidays are longer in time and larger in productive interruption, they allow for greater experiences of ritual activity. They also allow for longer and more intense exposure to the mythic narratives that legitimate and inspire the consumption rituals.

As noted in the previous chapter, the role of holidays as dynamic focal points of the nexus of myth and ritual can be traced to archaic times. The sacred festivals of these ancient cultures were typically related to the transition of seasons, solar cycles and other celestially relevant events, and agricultural exigencies. At these times, entire communities erupted in paroxysms of devotion. Myths were widely communicated and fervently reaffirmed, and entire communities were swept up in intense and prolonged ritual celebrations, rehearsing and vivifying the myths, drawing all closer to the primordial ground of the archaic meta-myth — invariably, the myth of nature and its power.

The transcendental religions of today continue to reflect this characteristic of holy days, as can be seen in the activities of devout (and even the not-so-devout) religionists of various monotheistic traditions on their holiest days: Jews during Passover and Rosh Hashanah, Christians at Easter and Christmas, and Muslims during Ramadan and Id al-Adha. In celebration of these holy days or sacred periods, members of these communities follow an ancient religious pattern, one far more ancient than their respective religions: a reaffirmation of their foundational myths and a communitywide participation in related rituals. Not surprisingly, these foundational mythico-ritual occurrences coincide with the respective new years or decisive events in the religions' mythic history. Other holy days follow a similar pattern. Myths are reaffirmed with greater clarity, precision, and attention; rituals take on a more heightened significance and are performed with greater than normal devotion; and the truth of the meta-myth (related to a supernatural being, principle, or power) is vivified in the world of human meaning — at least to the degree that persons believe in the truth of the myth and the power of the ritual. Aside from the transcendental character of their ultimate reality, in their holiday rituals, the more recent transcendental religions are simply following the standard of their ancient archaic precursors with regard to myth and ritual. The holier the day, the longer and larger the mythico-ritual celebration; for archaic cosmological cultures, the greatest of all the mythico-ritual celebrations was the New Year's festival.

Peter Berger nicely summarizes the significance of the New Year mythico-ritual in archaic cultures in a brief passage from *The Sacred Canopy*. In his analysis of the processes through which ancient societies reaffirmed continuity with the sacred cosmos, Berger, following Mircea Eliade's study in *Cosmos and History*, concentrates on the interplay of myth and ritual in the New Year festival of ancient Mesopotamia. During this celebration, called the *akîtu,* he observes:

> the creation of the world is not only represented (as we today might understand it in terms of some sort of symbolism) but once more realized, made a reality, as human life is brought back again to its divine source. Thus, everything that happens "here below" on the human plane has its analogue "up above" on the plane of the gods, and everything that happens "now" is linked with the cosmic events that occurred "in the beginning."[7]

Berger's description of the Mesopotamian *akîtu* ritual, based on the mythic narrative of creation, the *Enuma Elish,* suggests the general char-

---

7. Peter Berger, *The Sacred Canopy* (New York: Anchor Books, 1969), 113–14. Berger cites Eliade's *Cosmos and History* as a source for his analysis. For Eliade's more detailed and comparative study of New Year rituals in archaic cultures, see *Cosmos and History: The Myth of the Eternal Return* (New York: Harper Torchbooks, 1959), "The Regeneration of Time," 51–92, esp. 51–62.

acter of the religious dynamic at work in all New Year mythico-rituals. Moreover, this dynamic is something of a theoretic template for all holiday activities, especially cosmological holidays but also including those of transcendental religions and most notably when a transcendental religion is culturally dominant. Building on Berger's summary description, we can add a number of more specific elements that further reveal common features of cosmological holidays. These elements, adapted from Eliade,[8] not only appear to be relatively consistent cross-culturally, but they also serve to further delineate how the religious dynamic of cosmological cultures is disclosed in their holiday mythico-rituals. Following Eliade, and remembering initially that rituals necessarily are reenactments of myths, the more revealing elements are:

1. The ritualistic return to sacred origins (as described in creation myths), through which "man participates directly...in [the] cosmogonic work...making him contemporary with the cosmogony."[9] To a certain extent this is a feature of all rituals when fully experienced. In short, every creation partakes of original creation; everything done now has its pattern in the primordial myth of origins, and when actions are properly (ritually) performed they link the performer with the ultimate power and ground of being.

2. Simultaneous with the return to the original creation, a ritualistic re-creation of the immediate socio-sacred world of the believing community and a reaffirmation of one's place in the community and the greater cosmic order that it embodies.

3. Large-scale experiences of ritual chaos followed by the establishment of ritual order.

4. Extended periods of ritual activity, often twelve days, coinciding annually with calendrically determined cosmic and solar events, typically winter solstices and spring or autumn equinoxes, which were seen as the periods of primordial creation.

5. Coincidence with rituals of initiation.

6. Specific rituals designed to expel evils.

7. The abolition of time.

---

8. These elements are derived from Eliade in *Cosmos and History*, 51–92, and elsewhere, esp. his *Patterns in Comparative Religion* (New York: New American Library/Meridian, 1958), "Sacred Time and the Myth of the Eternal Return," 388–409.

9. Eliade, *Cosmos and History*, 58.

As these seven elements suggest, there are indeed striking parallels between the Mesopotamian *akîtu* and the New Year (or foundational) mythico-ritual events of other cultures and religious traditions, our own included. Eliade describes these parallels in considerable depth, elaborating on the elements noted above and detailing additional points of affinity between the *akîtu* and similar mythico-rituals in archaic Semitic cultures, ancient Egypt and Rome, Vedic Hinduism, even in Judaism, Christianity, and Islam — to cite just a sampling.[10] Like Voegelin and Ellul, however, Eliade stops short of diagnosing the cosmological character of the contemporary world — in his case, overlooking clear parallels between archaic holiday mythico-rituals and those of the contemporary era. The one text in which he would have been most likely to explore these parallels, *Myths, Dreams, and Mysteries,* offers only a passing comment on the relationship of "certain festivals observed in the modern world" to those of ancient times. He includes "rejoicings over the New Year" among these festivals but concludes: "There are no means of estimating how far modern man is still aware of any mythological implications of his festivities; what matters to us is that such celebrations still have a resonance, obscure but profound, throughout his being."[11]

My contention is that the profound resonance Eliade speaks of is not quite as obscure as he suggests. In fact, I suspect that this resonance is no less obscure today than it was in ancient Babylon, India, or Rome; that modern persons are just as aware as their primal and archaic precursors of the mythological implications of their sacred activities; and, most of all, that the nexus of myth and ritual, which reaffirms continuity with the sacred cosmos, is just as vivid and discernible as it ever was. In short, Eliade, like Voegelin and Ellul, erred not in his recognition of some sort of affinity between today's world and the cultures of antiquity but rather in not recognizing the full range and character of the religious dynamic of contemporary culture. Like Voegelin, he erred in underestimating the extent to which contemporary culture is cosmological; like Ellul, he erred in misdiagnosing the definitive structures of contemporary cosmological religiosity. Yet he could have avoided these oversights, especially since he was so obviously familiar with the holiday rituals of archaic culture and had isolated at least seven common elements in these rituals across

---

10. See ibid., 51–92.

11. See Eliade, *Myths, Dreams, and Mysteries: The Encounter between Contemporary Faiths and Archaic Realities* (New York: Harper and Row, 1967), 28. He also offers passing references to affinities between ancient religious practices and contemporary cultural phenomena in other works, e.g., *Myth and Reality* (New York: Harper Colophon, 1963), 181–93.

a wide range of cosmological cultures. What he failed to do was draw the connection between the holiday festivals of antiquity and those of today. Let us, however, see if we can make this connection by considering postmodern holy-day rituals in the context of these seven elements, and perhaps we can make the resonance of their mythological implications a little less obscure.

The holiday nexus of myth and ritual

As a preface to this comparison, a brief analysis of the relationship of myths and rituals during sacred celebrations is needed, since this relationship supplies the foundation for the function of the seven cosmological holiday elements in contemporary culture. As noted in chapter 1, rituals allow persons to participate in or otherwise affirm their proper relationship to the sacred. They are intertwined with myths insofar as rituals reenact myths and myths illuminate rituals. Through rituals, believers experience the sacred time of the myth and are brought into communion with the foundational reality of life. As noted above, on holy days in ancient cosmological cultures, myths were widely communicated and fervently reaffirmed, and entire communities participated in intense and prolonged ritual celebrations of mythic reenactment — drawing all closer to the primordial reality of the meta-myth, which in archaic cultures focused on nature and its power.

Consistent with archaic holiday festivals, the key to the kinetic intensity of contemporary holy days is their capacity to energize the sacred nexus between myth and ritual. Like those of our archaic ancestors, the holy-day celebrations of postmodern culture vivify the critical sacred linkage of myth and ritual, in our case, drawing all who participate into closer contact with the primordial power of the economy. This distinctive feature of holy days, which accounts for the other characteristic holy-day elements, is revealed most strikingly in the proliferation of tertiary myths (advertisements) directly related to a given holy day. Although these are the shortest of all the mythic narratives of our culture, as noted in chapter 4, they offer powerful and compelling renditions of the meta-myth: success and affluence is gained through a proper relationship with the economy and revealed in the ever-expanding material prosperity of society and the ever-increasing acquisition and consumption of products by individuals. They also bring us into closest proximity with the reality of the meta-myth and the threshold of ritual itself.

During holy-day cycles, tertiary myths (advertisements) are widely communicated and fervently reaffirmed. One needs only consider the increased number and size of newspaper inserts on weekends preceding holidays or the greater number of ads in the holiday issues of magazines. Additionally, holy-day myths are acutely focused on the sacred concerns of specific holy days. As is discussed in more detail in chapter 8, in these ads we are given instructions about objects appropriate or simply available for purchase on specific holy days. We respond in kind by "going shopping," acquiring the objects featured in the myths, fulfilling our dharma as consumers, and reaffirming our primordial relationship with the economy's sacred power.

The nexus of myth and ritual glistens in these times; the connection between mythic narratives and ritual performances becomes more immediate, vigorous, deeply felt, and religiously significant. The connection is also experienced by more of us during holy-day cycles, drawing all closer to the primordial power of the economy. Taken as a whole, holy-day ads keenly remind us of the sacred significance of shopping and the necessity of doing so in the sanctified holy-day period. Thus, when one performs a ritual acquisition of objects found in a holy-day myth, the performance is more purposeful and the dynamic connection between myth and ritual is clearer, more vivid, and more vital for the participant.

The sacredness of holy days may also be communicated through secondary myths, as with holy-day shopping reports on television news programs, holy-day themes on sitcoms and sitdrams, and holy-day jokes and banter on late-night talk shows. Even when holy-day consumption rituals are not included in these narratives (although often they are), the mythic medium communicates the importance of the day. This importance is then sacralized (again) through the advent of tertiary myths, which typically carry primordial holy-day messages in advance of the holiday they sanctify. (I take this point up later in the book.)

Now, let us turn directly to the seven elements of cosmological holiday festivals, bearing in mind, of course, that their significance is predicated on the nexus of myth and ritual, which during our holy-day festivals is more immediate, more dynamic, and more likely to be experienced. Following an analysis of the first five elements, special attention is given to the last two — rituals designed to eliminate evil and the atemporal quality of the holy-day experience.

Returning to the eternal return: the ancient template today

The first element of archaic religious festivals is the ritualistic return to mythic origins. This psychospiritual experience is the definitive quality of all rituals when fully experienced. For postmodern persons, this experience would mean a return to our primary or primordial existence as consumers. Such a return occurs whenever rituals are properly performed, resulting in some variety of religious experience for the participant, which, after all, is the point of the ritual. Often, however, the sacredness of the act is vague or only dimly sensed, and the psychospiritual experience is muted or below the level of conscious awareness.

During holy days, however, the dynamic connection between myth and ritual (outlined above) brings heightened intensity and meaning to the ritual, revealing both the sacredness of consumption and the elemental sacredness of the person who consumes. Analogies could be made here between the grace that might be spoken at regular meals and the grace spoken at a Passover seder, the experience of mass on a typical Sunday and at a sunrise service on Easter, or daily prayers on normal days and special prayers recited at mosques only during Ramadan. At these times, the rituals, which otherwise might be routine, take on their full glamour and participants experience a sense of the sacred essence of the act in ways that are more vivid, vital, and personally validating.

Rituals at especially sacred times thus allow believers greater access to mythic meanings and sacred origins. Consistent with this, rituals performed during postmodern holy days return participants to their mythic origins as consumers, reestablishing harmony with the economy's timeless primordial essence by fulfilling the sacred duty to consume. In this way, individual rituals serve to reestablish the sacred order and process of the economy in the immediate world of personal existence while simultaneously affirming one's direct participation in the cosmogonic work of the economy as a whole. While we perform such rituals routinely, holy days bring their sacred meaning into sharper focus, lengthening, deepening, and enriching the ritual experience and its sacred cosmogonic meaning. This deeper penetration into the mythico-ritual world during holy days is directly related to the second element, which speaks of a reaffirmation of the immediate social world of the believing community.

For us, this second element is revealed through the way in which our personal reestablishment of harmony with the economy is linked with the general holy-day rituals of our community. Not only do we reaffirm our harmony with the economy by shopping, we also confirm the legitimacy of our place and often our family's place in the social order. Because so many of us are doing it during holy-day festivities, we collectively reestablish our community's right relationship with the economy. At these times, we are aware of others joining with us in the performance of ritual acts.

More of us are at shopping centers and malls, queuing up before the sacrificial altar of the cash register, engaging in ritual exchange with clerks, listening to the shamanistic tales of salespersons, strolling through shrines of consumption as we carry our purchases like the sacred objects that they are. Whole families may join together on holidays, collectively performing consumption rituals. We see neighbors, friends, coworkers, our subordinates, and our masters. We find parking lots more occupied with cars, fewer shopping carts, perhaps greater challenges in performing the rituals — but we persist. We have done all this before, on other holy days, and we will do it all again when other holy days come around — individually, to be sure, but collectively to be certain. Taken as a whole, then, holy days re-create the immediate world of the believing community. As it was in the beginning, so it is again on each and every holy day.

The third element, ritual chaos, is a fairly common feature of contemporary religious rituals. Importantly, to be genuinely ritualistic, and not simply some sort of mundane turmoil, ritual chaos must be a uniquely patterned activity (something that follows a clearly established and repeatable form), and the evil that it represents must be eliminated so that harmony with the sacred order can be properly established. With this caveat in mind, we can observe ritual chaos to be particularly present in rituals required for the acquisition of highly sacred objects (houses, automobiles, computers, and televisions) but it can be a part of nearly any acquisition ritual, and is especially pronounced during holy-day festivals. Although ritual chaos takes a vast array of forms, several expressions are quite common and serve to typify the role of chaos in various ritual processes.

First, and most generally, ritual chaos occurs when the sacred order-process of the economy and our relationship with it is interrupted. Chaos, in this regard, is an expression of evil (such as lack or limitation), which receives separate treatment later in this chapter. For now, the focus on ritual chaos reveals that it often occurs in the context of rituals pertaining to the acquisition of particularly sacred objects. I noted previously the type of chaos that can surround the ritual of acquisition-consumption-disposition of major appliances and automobiles. Besides these, ritual chaos may occur when an object (most commonly a technologically sophisticated device) does not perform properly immediately after acquisition. It also occurs when even nonsophisticated objects malfunction, are damaged, or simply disappoint us for some reason. When this happens, the ritual seems to have failed, and the evil of lack, coupled with a loss of personal sanctity, threatens the sacred harmony of existence. In such instances, the chaos is subdued by telephoning technical support personnel, who supply a remedy, or by performing yet another ritual — the product exchange.

During holy days any of the above-noted eruptions of ritual chaos can occur, and since we are more ritually active during holy days and our rituals more often focused on the acquisition of objects of greater sanctity, ritual chaos is more common. In addition to the increase in opportunities for ritual chaos, by their very nature, holy days are times when performing rituals is simply more challenging. These are typically chaotic times and ritual chaos takes many forms. More people are trying to participate in the ritualistic activity of shopping. There is a rush and crush at malls, our culture's sacred sites, and we all must wait longer to participate in the ritual of acquisition, postpone it, or in some cases give it up altogether. During these times, worshipers often peregrinate from site to sacred site; trying to "avoid crowds," "beat the rush," or simply because a certain shrine may suddenly seem like an especially sacred locale. This phenomenon is most pronounced during the annual pilgrimages of the Christmas festival. But, then, Christmas is the paradigm for all of these holy-day elements. Additionally, during any holy-day cycle tension and even conflict may arise between worshipers and priests, between worshipers, and even within the priesthood itself.

Each of these forms of chaos are ritualistic in character insofar as they follow standard patterns of unfoldment and resolution. They are all to be expected, especially at major holy-day celebrations, with Christmas (as it so often is) being the paradigm. Although ritual chaos can transform into actual chaos, especially when it is not surmounted, chaos retains its ritual character when one is first engulfed by it but then overcomes it through the successful completion of a ritual acquisition. Generally, this is exactly what happens. In fact, it must happen for the chaos to be properly ritualistic. Worshipers persist in the overall process and remain committed to the performance of the sacred ritual, no matter the chaos that envelopes them: colliding with other shoppers, moving forward in interminable lines, grumbling about delays, losing track of family members (often children or parents but sometimes spouses), checking one's watch, asking to see a supervisor, searching for misplaced tabloids to find the name of some as-yet-unacquired sanctified object or the shrine where it may be discovered, rushing to turn onto congested streets, cursing at people driving too slowly in cars ahead of us, receiving parking tickets, forgetting the object of our quest. But we always remember, or we call a friend or relative on our cell phone, who reminds us. Moreover, we always remember the purpose of the experience, the ritual event; and we remember our dharma, our duty to consume — no matter the greatness of the chaotic obstacles we must overcome to do so. Finally, and perhaps most importantly, we remember the distinct and definite end to the entire experience — the holiday itself.

Inspired by these various types of recollection, the chaos is not only subdued but also incorporated into the mythico-ritual order of the holy day. While not always welcomed by holy-day worshipers, the chaos is usually expected; as long as the chaos is overcome, it too becomes a vital element of the overall mythico-ritual process of the holy day. The role of chaos in the process, then, is threefold: it must be genuinely experienced, responded to ritually, and ultimately overcome. Once chaos is vanquished, holy-day rituals of acquisition become more satisfying and sanctifying, and one's rightful place in the grand scheme of the economy is even more firmly established.

In keeping with the fourth element, our holy days often cover extended periods of time. Eliade cites twelve days as typical, and while our greatest religious celebration (Christmas) covers a full month, most of our holy-day cycles are of shorter duration — two weeks at the most. In a number of instances, our holy days occur on Mondays following weekends, which are themselves essentially mini-holy days. While three-day weekend holy days are obviously important examples of the extended time feature of ritual celebrations, Sunday holy days are also important in the annual cycle. Buttressed by the richer mythico-ritual environment of the specific holy day and the sacred quality of weekends generally, weekend holy days afford greater time and more occasions for ritual activity, increasing opportunities for multiple performances and pilgrimages to many shrines and temples. The overall impact is a lengthening and deepening of the weekend's already highly sacred character.

The fifth element reminds us that holiday celebrations often coincide with rituals of initiation in cosmological religions. As we consider how such rituals function in postmodern cosmological holy-day festivals, we must first note that in transcendental religions, rituals of initiation are distinct events, which are set apart from other rituals. A Bar or Bat Mitzvah, for example, is a unique ritual event in Judaism; so too is a confirmation in Christianity or the monastic year in Theravada Buddhism. While these rituals allow a young person to become a fully vested member of the community and then participate in other rituals, in postmodern culture having rituals of initiation happen simultaneously with major holy-day festivals is not uncommon. Specific initiation rituals occur when a child, usually at a very young age (far younger than children in traditional transcendental initiations) is first given the privilege of making a personal purchase.

While initiations may take place any time during the year, three factors related to elements previously discussed suggest general reasons for holy days being especially appropriate for initiations: (1) the greater focus on the sanctity of acquisition rituals during holy days, (2) expanded community involvement in ritual activity, and (3) parental modeling. Collectively, these factors make holy days especially opportune settings for a child's introduction to the shopping ritual; they also make the child's first shopping experience more meaningful and memorable.

In addition, a number of annual observances have distinct relevance to children: Valentine's Day, Easter, Mother's Day and Father's Day, the Fourth of July, Back-to-School, Halloween, and, of course, Christmas. Although each of these celebrations is hardly exclusive to children (as a birthday party might be) and each involves the entire community, what makes them especially appropriate settings for initiation is that they all include opportunities for children to participate in rituals in the company of adults and in the context of a general culturewide celebration. Examples include: acquiring cards or candy for friends and classmates in the Valentine's Day cycle, spring clothes and holiday paraphernalia at Easter, gifts for mother or father on their respective days (but only if a child is allowed to also acquire "a little something" for herself or himself), fireworks for the Fourth, school supplies during the Back-to-School cycle, costumes and "treats" at Halloween, and various items at Christmas.

A survey of tertiary myths (advertisements) from Halloween, Back-to-School, and Christmas also reveals a significant number of images of children in association with ritual objects. Including images of children in these already highly evocative myths clearly invites the child into participation in the associated ritual and also signals parents that the particular celebration is a favorable time for the child's ritual initiation. With some modifications, Russell W. Belk offers support for the coincidence of initiation rituals with holy-day celebrations. In an excellent article on Christmas consumption and the impact of Santa Claus, Belk tells us that the Christmas tableau "prepares children to assume their roles as American consumers, perpetually hoping that happiness is the next purchase away.... Then as we learn that *we* are Santa (parallel to believing that God is in us), we realize that we should reward ourselves for doing well by buying ourselves things."[12]

While granting that Christmas is by far the greatest celebration of con-

---

12. Russell W. Belk, "A Child's Christmas in America: Santa Claus as Deity, Consumption as Religion," in *Journal of American Culture* 10 (1987): 95.

sumption, and thus by far the best time for initiation rituals, I would take Belk's analysis a step further and observe that other holidays are also quite well suited for initiations into the religion of consumption. For young and old alike, holidays may engender or heighten hopes that happiness is the next purchase away. Perhaps more profoundly, however, what they engender are not hopes but recollections and realizations of the primordial reality that personal sanctity is reestablished through the next ritual of acquisition. More commonly called a *purchase,* for many, this ritual was first performed during a holy-day celebration; and if not first performed at such a time, first performed as a ritual of community initiation. After all, during holy days children are most likely to first make purchases while being observed by parents and other elders, first harmonize their personal shopping with that being done by the entire community, and first sense the mythico-ritual significance of the ritual act — for themselves and for all others. Most of all, perhaps, at such times, the child first receives the all-important and greatly treasured confirmation that the ritual has been performed properly: "Thank you and happy holidays."

Evil, time, and the holy day's time out of time

Besides rituals of initiation, Eliade also observes that during cosmological holidays, rituals to dispel evil are performed. Some of these rituals relate to ritual chaos, discussed above, for chaos in cosmological systems is always an evil since it serves to interrupt the order and process of the ultimate power (nature in archaic times, the economy today). Examples of ritual chaos discussed earlier are evil enough because they interfere with individuals' immediate experience of the order and process of the economy by interfering with their shopping. What whirs about in the winds of ritual chaos is the threat of actual evil, which manifests its malevolence through lack and limitation — the inversions of success and affluence. The various forms of ritual chaos considered previously suggest the potential appearance of lack and limitation insofar as they may temporarily prevent one from shopping (lack) or restrict the range of objects available for purchase (limitation). Ritual chaos, however, only hints at the full power of evil, which, in its more daunting expressions, requires special attention and specialized rituals of exorcism. Holy days are times when we often engage in such exorcisms since, paradoxically, at these most sacred times the shadow of evil seems closer than ever and so too does the need for it to be dispelled.

By far the most general and widespread manifestation of evil occurs in the context of sacrificial resources (money). Such lack is the very essence of evil because it severs one's relationship with the believing community, and ultimately from the economy itself. Now, persons who experience such lack are not in themselves evil, but evil can be said to have overtaken them — in varying degrees to be sure, but evil in any degree is alarming. In the cases of extreme evil, the sacred truth of existence (success and affluence) seems beyond realization. Although the extreme cases are indeed tragic and worthy of study, our interest here is in the less extreme cases of evil, which are far more common and for which specific rituals of expulsion are available.

In these less extreme cases, evil typically manifests when persons find themselves lacking requisite sacrificial resources to participate in a particular object's acquisition ritual. This lack may cause them to feel cut off from the realm of ritual performance and unable to fulfill their dharmic obligations — especially during holy-day periods. Like persons who refuse to dispose of consumed objects, persons shackled by the evils of lack may be seen as sacrilegious and social outcasts by others and even themselves. Unlike the nondisposers (who may be atheists or agnostics and also nonconsumers), persons who feel entrapped by lack cannot acquire and consume, even though they desire to do so — often quite intently. While not as tragic as having no sacrificial resources at all, this plight certainly seems dismal to them and is by this account evil. The myths still resonate in their minds and hearts, most prominently those pertaining to the object of their particular desire; they still recognize their dharma, they desire to participate in the ritual, but the power of evil is blocking them. Fortunately, however, specific remedies and rituals are designed to expel the lack. The two most common are (1) ritual acquisition of an object appropriate for the available sacrifice, or more typically, (2) the acquisition of the desired object through the invocation of sacrificial credit. With the latter ritual, one is swiftly transported out of the dungeon of lack and into the sacred realm of affluence. Both of these rituals are frequently performed during holy-day celebrations. But another form of evil that is more frequently encountered during holidays is limitation, and with it comes still other expulsion rituals.

Limitation is the second of the two great evils of postmodern cosmological culture. While not as frightening as the evil of lack, limitation is still profoundly malevolent. In practice, this type of evil materializes when a desired object cannot be located at a shrine or temple. The evil of limitation assumes many guises. Perhaps there is a shortage of a desired product or what was once abundant now no longer can be found. Other manifestations of limitation are when we are sent elsewhere to acquire what we desire immediately or something we ordered does not arrive on time; or when the size, color, or texture we seek cannot be found or is found not to exist; when the brand we must possess is not obtainable at a local shrine or whatever-it-may-be is on back order. Like the evil of lack, the evil of limitation prevents ritual performance, causing us to be unable to fulfill our dharmic obligations. In a way, limitation can be even more pernicious because it even affects people who have more than sufficient sacrificial resources.

As with the other holy-day features considered here, the Christmas cycle best exemplifies the evil of limitation, notoriously in association with the most sought-after children's toys and games of particular years: Rescue-worker dolls and action figures in the 2001 season, Playstations in 2000, and Furbys, Tickle Me Elmos, Power Rangers, and Cabbage Patch dolls in previous years. The evil of limitation also manifests during other holi-day cycles as evidenced in the days before Thanksgiving when a certain sized turkey cannot be found, in the Valentine Day cycle with specialized jewelry, Father's Day with brand-name golf balls, Back-to-School with a vast array of products, and at Halloween with costumes — such as Fireman costumes in 2001 in the wake of the September 11 terrorist attack on New York City.

Although the evil of limitation can often become just as powerful as the evil of lack, especially when children are involved or the desired object is unique in its sacred significance, more often than not limitation is exorcised by the acquisition of an object in the same class as the desired object with similar or greater sacred significance. Here again, such exorcisms are common practices during holidays; in fact, they are virtually routine.

The seventh element, the abolition of time, has a deep connection with the exorcism rituals, for the passing of time is perhaps the greatest evil of all in a cosmological culture. The sacred festival itself abolishes this evil. In this conception of time we find an especially important point of affin-ity between ancient cosmological religious celebrations and contemporary holy days; nowhere does the religious dynamic of postmodern cosmolog-ical culture seem to harmonize more with that of antiquity than in the quest to escape from time. For us, as for the ancients, the holy day is an exorcism of time itself — literally a time out of time. Eliade's reflections on this matter offer exceptional insight into this aspect of the holiday dy-namic *then* and *now.* They also serve to underscore the religious character of contemporary holy days and our personal engagements with the rituals of sacred consumption. Eliade writes:

Collective or individual, periodic or spontaneous, regeneration rites [typical of holy days] always comprise, in their structure and meaning, an element of regeneration through repetition of an archetypical act, usually the cosmogonic myth. What is of chief importance to us in these archaic systems is the abolition of concrete time, and hence their antihistorical intent.... We refer to archaic man's refusal to accept himself as a historical being, his refusal to grant value to memory and hence to the unusual events (i.e., events without an archetypal model) that in fact constitute concrete duration.... Basically, if viewed in its proper perspective, the life of archaic man (a life reduced to the repetition of archetypal acts, that is to categories and not to events, to the unceasing rehearsal of the same primordial myths), although it takes place in time, does not bear the burden of time, does not record time's irreversibility.... Like the mystic, like the religious man in general, the primitive lives in a continual present... an atemporal present.[13]

And so do men and women of postmodern culture, as pointed out by a number of postmodern theorists, especially Baudrillard and Jameson, both of whom, not surprisingly, are particularly interested in the consumerist dimension of postmodernity. As Jameson observes: "our entire contemporary social system has little by little begun to lose its capacity to retain its own past, has begun to live in a perpetual present and in a perpetual change that obliterates traditions."[14] Baudrillard makes much the same observation, and both agree that this condition, rather than being a cause for alarm among postmoderns, is accepted and celebrated — especially through the acquisition and consumption of consumer products. In short, whatever identity we may have is given to us in and through the items we acquire and consume, or (using terms introduced in this book) through our dharmic engagement with the rituals of acquisition and consumption, which are inspired by the dominant myths of our culture.

As delineated here and in the next two chapters, these rituals find their dynamic and definitive expression in postmodern holy-day celebrations, what Eliade would call our regeneration rites. Importantly, these celebrations are ahistorical in precisely the same way that the regeneration rites of ancient cosmological cultures were ahistorical. They are experiences of the eternal return of the sacred and our return to community with it. In

---

13. Eliade, *Cosmos,* 85–86.
14. Fredric Jameson, "Postmodernism and Consumer Culture," in *Postmodern Culture,* ed. Hal Foster (Seattle: Bay Press, 1985), 125.

our annual celebration of various holy days, we too escape time, returning to our own primordial origins. We are "like a kid again," or as Eliade
would say, like a "primitive" again, who "by conferring a cyclic direction
upon time, annuls its irreversibility. Everything begins over again at its
commencement every instant."[15] Additionally, they allow us to fulfill our
dharma and solidify our right relationship with our immediate world.

Today, just as in archaic times, the rituals/rites are archetypical, a category of experience, not a unique event, and profoundly atemporal in
character. In the contemporary world, they free us from time, labor,
production, and the profane realm as a whole, giving us access to the
economy's timeless primordial reality, an eternal present where we reaffirm our true identity and ultimate purpose. Thus, in the mythico-rituals
of our holy days, we are at once most truly ourselves and also (necessarily) most fully disengaged from time through our participation in a
ritual that repeats an archetypical act of our culture — the acquisition and
consumption of consumer products.

While the ahistorical character of our holy-day rituals appears to me
to be the most significant connection between the religious dynamic of
postmodernity and ancient cosmological cultures, the other elements in the
mythico-ritual complex of archaic holiday celebrations are also strikingly
evident in our contemporary holy days. Each of these elements is revealed
with particular vividness in the explosion of mythico-ritual activity that
transpires during our New Year festival, which we call Christmas; but like
cosmological cultures of the past, Christmas is only one of many holy days
that intensify our engagement with the sacred realm. Most notably, and
most dynamically, the central feature of these celebrations is intensified
consumption — thus making them the most sacred times of the year.

•

Consumption is, of course, ubiquitous in our culture, and at its most basic
level this is no different in principle than the process of consumption in
any culture at any time. Human beings have always had to consume, for
consumption is the principle of survival. We have to eat, after all. As argued here, however, unique in our culture is our practice of consumption,
the ways in which we individually engage in the process of consumption.

As Juliet B. Schor reminds us, "consumerism as a way of life is so
ingrained it's hard to recognize within us and around us. Like air, it's
everywhere, we're dependent on it, and perhaps most important, until it's

---

15. Eliade, *Cosmos,* 89.

really dirty, it cannot be seen."[16] Even dirty, however, like air, we are still dependent on it, for as Jean Baudrillard observes, in Kellner's interpretation, "the consumer . . . cannot avoid the obligation to consume, because it is consumption that is the primary mode of social integration and the primary ethic and activity within the consumer society."[17] As noted previously, Baudrillard's analysis of consumption as the primary mode of social integration and primary ethic and activity of our culture is precisely what defines the sacred dimension and religious dynamic in our type of consumption, which is precisely what reveals the process and our engagement with it as cosmological. The mythico-ritual process of consumption defines the foundational reality of our world and our individual existence; it is obligatory and unavoidable; it functions as the sacred *is* that specifies our collective and individual *ought;* it articulates our status, our goals, our aspirations; it is our dharma; and it inspires and enchants us all. And, as is true of all cosmological cultures, its inspiration and enchantment are strongest and most far reaching at those specially designated times when the process can be most fully experienced by the culture as a whole, times of sacred focus and intensified devotion for all people. These sacred times are our holy days, and like the *akîtu* of ancient Mesopotamia, they allow us to reaffirm continuity with the sacred order on which our culture is based. The "air" in Schor's analogy may be no more clean at these times, but on holy days we inhale more deeply; and as suggested in the next chapter, we appear to do this quite often over the course of a year.

16. Juliet B. Schor, *The Overspent American: Upscaling, Downshifting, and the New Consumer* (New York: Basic Books, 1998), 24.
17. Kellner, *Jean Baudrillard*, 16.

— E I G H T —

Identifying and Classifying
Postmodern Holy Days

Using the seven elements presented in the previous chapter as a starting point, this chapter continues the analysis of the transformation of holidays into holy days by adding two additional diagnostic features — amplification of myths and expansion of ritual activity. After outlining the way these features function to reveal holy days, the chapter offers a taxonomy of holy days and other religious observances, followed by a summary listing of the holy days and other notable occasions in their annual order of appearance. Chapter 9 continues this analysis and offers a detailed overview of the postmodern liturgical year through Halloween, the eve of the Christmas religious festival — which will be the topic of part 4 of the book.

The character and function of
three primary holy-day features

The rationale for designating particular holidays as holy days is their heightened sacred significance, indicated by intensified mythico-ritual activity occurring in conjunction with their calendrical date. On the basis of my earlier remarks, the defining criteria for holy days can be found in three distinctive features:

1. the seven characteristic elements of holy days, discussed in chapter 7;

2. an amplification and dilation of myths (advertising) often focusing on holiday themes and products; and

3. a corresponding culturewide expansion of ritual activity (retail sales).

All three features are required for a holiday to qualify as a genuine holy day. Christmas, which is the holy-day paradigm, dramatically reveals all three features, but they are also present during a number of other holidays. Since the seven elements of the first feature received extensive treatment

124

in the previous chapter, we only need to remember here that their advent and experience by vast numbers of the population is contingent on the other two features. Together these two features form what can be called the mythico-ritual foundation for postmodern holy days, and the dynamic force that leads to the manifestation of the seven elements. These features can now be considered individually.

The second feature: amplification and dilation of myths

The second feature, amplification and dilation of myths, is reflected most noticeably in the proliferation of tertiary myths in advance of certain holidays. Those holidays properly classified as holy days generate both a large volume and a wide diversity of such myths, which manifest as advertisements in newspapers and magazines and commercials on TV and radio.

The most obvious illustrations of this proliferation are Sunday newspaper advertising supplements, which in advance of holy days are double or triple their size on other Sundays. Not only are there more tabloid inserts, the inserts themselves are generally longer and feature a wider array of merchandise. All the notable local retail outlets seem to be involved, especially on major holy days. From drugstores to upscale department stores, jewelers to hardware stores, and appliance outlets to discount retailers, shrines and temples in holy-day periods amplify their tertiary myths of consumption, often featuring products keyed to the particular holiday.

In advance of Father's Day, we learn about men's apparel, tools, colognes, and sporting goods. Prior to Easter, we discover narratives about the abundance of candies, plush rabbits, and spring apparel available at various shrines. Valentine's Day brings narratives of jewelry, cosmetics, and lingerie. The Fourth of July treats us to tertiary myths of cheap meats and equally cheap beer. Ecclesiastes 3:1 is just about right in affirming that for everything there is a season; and in the cosmological culture of today, for every sacred season there is an abundance of things and a spate of mythic narratives reminding us of the sacred significance of acquiring them.

To a certain extent, the significance of a holy day can be measured by the number and size of the tabloid inserts carrying these mythic narratives as well as the number of Sundays prior to the date of the holiday when they feature themes or products related to the focus of the holiday. One could even do a fairly accurate measurement on the basis of the relative weight of the tabloid inserts for different holidays. Christmas, again, best exemplifies this pattern, generating enormous advertising supplements from the weekend before Thanksgiving through the Sunday before Christmas day; but this pattern is also evident in connection with other holidays — e.g., Easter, Valentine's Day, Memorial Day, Mother's Day, and Father's Day.[1] Besides Sunday supplements, tertiary myths with holiday foci appear in other media as well; for example, Valentine's Day, Back-to-School, and Christmas are notable for TV commercials; Memorial Day and Labor Day for radio ads, and Mother's Day and Valentine's Day for advertisements in magazines.

Like other tertiary myths, holy-day advertisements and commercials communicate the same message as the meta-myth and secondary myths. Whatever the season and whatever the holiday, they serve to illuminate the sacred realm and supply a guide to the process through which it may be ritually entered. As holy-day signals, however, the number and range of these myths bring an urgency and sense of gravity to the necessity of ritual performance. Clearly the holy days they foreshadow are extraordinary religious events and our dharmic duty to acquire and consume is far greater than at other times — and so we do. This notion of obligation brings us to the third and most definitive feature of holy days, the culturewide expansion of ritual activity.

The third feature: culturewide expansion of ritual activity

What makes the third feature so significant is that it is not only the expected consequence of the amplification of holy-day myths, but in its absence the particular holiday in question lacks a critical holy-day element. In other words, without large-scale ritual activity (shopping), and in spite of the presence of the other two features, holidays that otherwise qualify as holy days are less than fully sacralized. They may bring interesting breaks from routine vocational and domestic pursuits, evince some or all of the seven holy-day elements, and generate amplifications of mythic narratives and even increased shopping in some areas. But unless a culturewide increase in consumer spending occurs, the holiday is at best a secondary or minor holy day, and perhaps not a holy day at all — at least in the cosmological sense of the term as used here. For this reason, the third feature is especially helpful in designating holy days. Most impor-

---

1. My analysis of Sunday supplements here and elsewhere is based on a two-year study of supplements in three Florida newspapers: the *St. Petersburg Times*, The *Tampa Tribune*, and the *Orlando Sentinel*. From time to time, I also consulted newspapers from other regions of the country, including Denver, Chicago, and San Francisco.

tantly, of the three features, the third can also be clearly quantified, since large-scale (culturewide) increases in shopping and consumer spending are directly correlated. This fact will be returned to at the end of this section. For now, let us consider the structure of holy-day rituals.

Like the other two features, rituals are an essential part of postmodern cosmological religion that undergo dramatic modifications (in intensity of performance, cultural extent, and religious meaning) during holy days. They are focused on acquisition, just as at other times of the year; as expressions of our dharma, they are expected duties that harmonize us with the cosmos and our immediate social world. In this regard, holy-day shopping is predicated on the same psychospiritual premise as shopping at any other time: reestablishment of the primordial relationship of individuals with the sacred power of the economy. What makes holy days different is that more of us will engage in the ritual of shopping, do so more often, and on the whole acquire more things than at other times.

Also unlike the sort of shopping that occurs routinely throughout the year, shopping in conjunction with holy days is more likely to result in an experience of sacred reality — for individuals and society as a whole. When fully experienced, as during holy days, the religious dimension of shopping becomes manifest. Shoppers may have a sense of satisfaction, upliftment, achievement, and validation. They may feel pride in the products they acquire, elation in their own religious well-being as confirmed by their ritual performance, and personal ennoblement in fulfilling their dharmic duty as essential participants in the sacred order and process of the economy.

The holy-day transformation of shopping is predicated on the general sacralization of times and places where we can maximize the experience of acquisition-consumption-disposition. As addressed in chapter 6, these temporal and physical locales are removed from the mundane sphere of work and production. In these leisure realms, mythic vistas spread out before us and the clocks without hands of sacred time replace palm pilots, date books, and time clocks. Because holidays allow a larger percentage of the population to be liberated from the profane realm of labor, one would expect a corresponding increase in consumer spending at these times. Although this increase does not occur on all holidays, those that will be designated holy days reveal this feature with striking regularity.

Myths and rituals into holy-day mythico-rituals

The religious potential of holidays is delightfully mythologized in a turn-of-the-century Corona beer commercial. In the commercial, a person is depicted lounging on a tropical beach, skipping shells into the ocean. Suddenly, the person's electronic pager begins beeping. Without missing a beat, the person chooses to skip the beeping pager into the tropical waters. Only the person's hand is seen, while a bottle of beer remains at the center of the scene throughout the narrative. As with other advertisements of this genre, the good life may involve leisure activities, but such activities require the acquisition and consumption of specific products. Weekends were made for beer; but they were also made for *buying* beer and an endless array of other products associated with overcoming difficulty, living the good life, having fun, emulating heroes, or the ritual act of acquisition itself. As with weekends, so too with days off, holidays, and especially holiday weekends.

At these sacred times, life becomes enchanted again and the burden of measured days and hours gives way to the timeless world of Being. Free of the profane shackles of beepers, cell phones, and other tools of productive labor, mythic narratives sing siren songs of sacral worlds and beckon us to acquire the requisite provisions. Nowhere is the relationship between myth and ritual more keenly witnessed than in holy-day myths and their attendant rituals of consumption.

As noted above, advertisements proliferate in advance of holy days. Their mythic narratives focus acutely on sacred objects suitable for ritual acquisition during the specific holy-day cycle: TVs and entertainment centers (along with beer and chips) for the Super Bowl, jewelry for Valentine's Day, domestic products and apparel for Easter, patio and outdoor recreation items for Memorial Day, sporting goods and power tools for Father's Day, foods and beverages for the Fourth, you-name-it at Christmas, and so on. Our response is resolute and devout. We embark on holy-day pilgrimages to the malls and shopping centers designated in the ads, intent on acquiring the sacred articles appropriate for the holy day.

Once inside the store, we seek out the advertised items, gathering them in our arms or placing them in wheeled carrying carts. We may select other products besides those featured in the ads, impulsively buying things we did not know we needed — until enchanted by the spell of the mall. The thrall of the holy-day shopping experience is created by a uniquely charged conjunction of sacred time and space; not only are we beyond the confines of profane time, we are at the epicenter of an eruption of the economy's munificence.

The sacred ambiance may prompt remembrance of other myths in addition to those that inspired our pilgrimage. Perhaps we remember them because of the alluring presence of an object they celebrate or a smiling display-sign icon of a cultural deity who embodies them. Remembering these sacred narratives, the reality of the myth expands further into our immediate world. We respond with repeated rituals. We make multiple acquisitions, just as we should on a holy day. It seems we can hardly stop. We use credit cards, if necessary, to dispel the evil of lack and limitation; listen with rapt attention to the shamans' incantations; and give money to our children so they too can share in the mythico-ritual experience, initiating them into a community that sacralizes affluence.

Songs from the myths play in our heads, their objects now conjured to existence in multiple forms in the sumptuous aisles of the shrine. We acquire, and we acquire again. On Father's Day, we try to remember the brand of cologne Dad really likes, but we remember a tertiary myth about a bold, seafaring young man and acquire his cologne instead. We acquire the related aftershave and soap as well. We acquire the deodorant for ourselves. Everybody's happy — as they should be on a holy day in a culture whose sacred truth is articulated by myths of material success and realized in rituals of acquisition.

These sorts of experiences are richest and most frequent in the month between Thanksgiving and Christmas, but they are hardly confined to those weeks and weekends. They happen at Halloween with costumes, candy, and holiday accouterments; Columbus Day with appliances and home accessories; Memorial Day with inflatable pools, garden tractors, bicycles, and swimming suits; and Back-to-School with lunch boxes, clothes, backpacks, and computers. Did Sally want the Charlie's Angels lunch box or the one with Winnie the Pooh? We buy the Pooh because we remember the Disney movie; besides, we can always take it back. The smiling priests will be happy to see us again at the shrine. Was it the Reebok logo or the Nike swoosh on Jimmy's best friend's shoes, shorts, shirt, or cap? Who knows? We remember the Tiger Woods ad and buy the Nike shoes for Jimmy. In the process, we acquire a pair of Nikes for ourselves (remembering Michael Jordan, not Woods this time), a new briefcase, and some paraphernalia for our office.

Given the relationship between myths and rituals described previously, experiences such as these are to be expected. They simply reveal how the nexus of myth and ritual is reflected in personal religious behavior during holidays. From a religious perspective, as outlined in this book, it is no surprise that Sunday papers swell with advertising supplements, stores and malls are busiest on weekends, and mythico-ritual activities expand and intensify during holidays — and most of all, on holy days. In summary, then, the formal structure of the holy-day process can be expressed as follows:

Ritual activity is influenced by mythic narratives and both tend to increase in periods of sacred time; and since holy days and holy-day cycles expand periods of sacred time for large segments of the population, there are large-scale (culturewide) increases in ritual activity at these times.

Taxonomy of postmodern holy days

The religious context of the mythico-ritual process has thus far been the primary focus of this book; as we now consider the designation and analysis of specific holy days, the process can be considered in a more conventional context. The third holy-day feature (large-scale increases in ritual activity) becomes especially helpful here since, to a certain extent, it correlates with a traditional measurement of economic (sacred) activity — consumer spending.

The importance of this correlation can be shown by first noting more conventional expressions for certain key words and terms used in my analysis. For example, my "ritual activity" might be called "retail commerce" and my "holy days" generally rendered "holidays." Thus, my concept, "large-scale increases in ritual activity during holy days," might be phrased, "retail commerce markedly increases during holidays." Other more commonly used replacement terms include: "advertising" for my "mythic narratives," "leisure time" for my "sacred time," and "holiday cycles" for "holy-day cycles." Substituting these more conventional expressions yields this rephrasing of the holy-day process summarized above:

> Retail commerce is influenced by advertising, and both tend to increase in periods of leisure. Because holidays and holiday cycles offer prolonged periods of leisure for large segments of the population, the overall volume of retail commerce increases at these times.

If I were an economist, I might offer such a summary; at least, such a summary is, on the whole, consistent with my thesis. The key feature in the translation of my religious analysis into a more conventional analysis is the direct correlation between the third feature of postmodern holy days (large-scale increases in ritual activity) and increases in what is more commonly referred to as retail commerce. In this context, increases in retail commerce are indicative of increases in ritual activity and declines are indicative of reductions in ritual activity.

The bearing of this correlation on the designation and evaluation of holy days is threefold. First, retail commerce generates quantifiable data, which is routinely recorded in documents reporting on nationwide consumer spending. Two specific documents are used here for holy-day designation and evaluation: the United States Census Bureau Monthly Retail Trade Survey (MRTS) and the Bank of Tokyo-Mitsubishi and Schroder Wertheim Weekly Chain Store Sales Index (BTM/SW). The key consumer spending category for analysis of ritual activity is designated GAF (General Merchandise, Apparel, and Furniture) by MRTS, and there is reasonably close agreement between its monthly figures in this category and the BTM/SW weekly figures.[2] What makes the GAF category relevant to this study is that it "represents those retail formats where the bulk of consumer goods shopping occurs";[3] and in the context of the analysis used here, "consumer goods shopping" is precisely what has been specified as "ritual acquisition." Note, however, that ritual acquisition exceeds this measure since it also occurs in venues not covered by the GAF category — e.g., jewelry stores and automotive dealers. These and other non-GAF spending sites are included in the Census Bureau monthly statistics but not in the Bank of Tokyo weekly index. With some qualifications, then, these documents allow for quantifiable measures of ritual activity.[4]

Further, because MRTS and BTM/SW record nationwide increases and declines in shopping and consumer spending, they also reflect increases and declines in culturewide ritual activity. Thus, "large scale (culturewide) in-

2. See Appendices for further information on these documents: Appendix A describes the two documents. Appendix B outlines the methodology used in analyzing their data relative to holy-day rituals over the ten-year period of my survey (1990–99). Appendix C offers summaries and charts of BTM/SW and MRTS data for selected holidays and holy days. The primary source used here is the Bank of Tokyo-Mitsubishi and Schroder Wertheim Weekly Chain Store Sales Index (BTM/SW). The secondary source, used for more general analyses, is the U.S. Census Bureau's Monthly Retail Trade Survey (MRTS). For slight discrepancies between the Bank of Tokyo index and the Census Bureau Monthly Retail Trade Survey, see "Chain Store Sales Snapshot" (New York: Bank of Tokyo-Mitsubishi, Ltd., 1996), 3–4. BTM/SW data is now included in BTM/UBS Warburg index. See Appendix A for more detail.

3. See National Retail Federation, "Holiday Data," Web site (accessed 12/13/99 at *www.nrf.com/hot/holiday/dec99/default.htm*).

4. As noted in more detail in Appendix B, the primary document used to measure weekly fluctuations in retail sales (BTM/SW) does not have an exact correlation with overall retail commerce, although it "mirrors the trends of GAF store sales and non-auto sales." The primary explanation for the difference in this regard is its underreporting of retail sales increases due to its exclusion of retail sales from stores opened for less than one year. It includes only "same store" (stores opened for more than one year) sales, whose sales "generally grow more slowly than new stores." See "Chain Store Sales Snapshot," 3–4. See also Appendix B for my compensation for underreported total sales in BTM/SW. Additionally, neither BTM/SW nor MRTS's GAF category include four major holiday consumer spending venues: automotive dealers, jewelry stores, restaurants, and grocery stores. MRTS does, however, include sales in these areas, and a host of others, in separate categories.

creases in ritual activity," which is characteristic of holy days, can be linked to increases in nationwide indices of consumer spending, specifically, the closely monitored GAF category of consumer spending.

Finally, because the documents report monthly as well as weekly fluctuations in retail spending, the relationship of "large-scale (culturewide) increases in ritual activity" to the calendrical dates of holidays can be specified with precision and traced over a period of years to reveal regularity. Together, these features of MRTS and BTM/SW serve as fairly reliable guides for classification and analysis of holy days, because they can be used to identify those holidays that produce large-scale increases in ritual activity annually or with a high degree of regularity.

To generate data indicative of a "regular basis" I used MRTS and BTM/SW reports from a ten-year period (1990–99). Further details on the method through which their data was analyzed is found in the appendices. In brief, and as outlined above, the documents supply quantitative measures of annual large-scale (culturewide) ritual increases in conjunction with certain holidays as reflected in increases in nationwide consumer spending across a ten-year period. Together with empirical indications of the first two holy-day features — the seven holy-day elements (chapter 7) and the amplification of myths (see p. 124) — the quantitative data related to the third feature (increased ritual activity) can be used to measure and compare the relative religious significance of various holidays and designate those that qualify as holy days.

Empirical data related to the other two holy-day features noted above is readily apparent during many holidays. These include holy-day indicators such as increased advertisements in various media and their focus on holy-day themes and products, interruptions in profane time, increases in vehicular traffic around malls and larger numbers of shoppers inside them, holy-day products on prominent display in stores, longer lines at checkout counters, more clerks and salespersons in the stores, more children buying or trying to buy things, and general increases in ritual chaos.

Phenomena of this sort and other aspects of the first two features supply the minimal criteria of a holy day; however, they do not always translate into large-scale increases in ritual activity. In the absence of such activity, the dynamic nexus of myth and ritual is shallow or unrealized and so the mythico-ritual experience is reduced in terms of culture as a whole. When this occurs, the celebration loses something of the religious grandeur and cosmological vitality that is typical of a holy day. In short, even with the other features, without large-scale expansions in rituals of acquisition, a holiday falls short of the holy-day ideal. While this result sometimes happens, even with holy days, should it occur routinely, the holiday is not a holy day — at least not in the cosmological sense of the term used here.

Using these three features, as outlined above, nine holidays can be designated as holy days or religious festivals. Their religious significance, taken as a whole, is witnessed most emphatically in their collective impact on increases in ritual activity, measured as a function of increases in retail spending. Using this measure, these holy days and religious festivals truly are the most sacred times of the year, given that they alone account for the entire increase in retail sales in the ten-year period used in this study. In other words, without increases attributable to these sacred periods, there would have been a net decline in retail spending over the ten years, and for most of the individual years as well.[5]

All holy days are not equal, however; some are clearly more religiously significant than others. For some indication of the relative religious importance of each holy day, data related to the third feature can be deployed for comparative evaluation and ranking. In this manner, holy days can be further classified into three categories: major, secondary, and minor. All reveal the first two features and increases in large-scale ritual activity on a fairly regular basis — in at least seven of the ten years surveyed in this book. To classify major and secondary holy days, I selected those that generated increases most frequently (at least nine of ten years for *major* holy days and eight of ten for *secondary* holy days) and also produced overall average increases in consumer spending that were at least double (100 percent greater than) the average weekly increase in the ten-year period.[6]

Using these criteria, three holidays qualify as major holy days (Valentine's Day, Easter, and Christmas) and two as secondary holy days (Super Bowl Sunday and Presidents' Day). Besides these definitive holy days, the Back-to-School cycle functions like a month-long holy day in terms of the year as a whole. For reasons discussed in chapter 9, Back-to-School cannot be properly classified as a holy day, but because its mythico-ritual dynamic is characteristic of holy days it can be accorded an analogous designation. As such, Back-to-School is here classified as a religious festival, with the Labor Day holy day marking its conclusion. Christmas, it may be noted, is a major holy day, and its High Holy Days cycle is also properly classified as a religious festival.

---

5. See Appendix B and supporting data in Appendix C.

6. For holy days whose cycles covered more than one week, the average weekly increase for the cycle was used for comparison. Weeks with neither increase nor decrease (zero change) were counted as increase weeks for purposes of analysis and classification. See Appendix B, esp. n. 2.

Minor holy days satisfy the minimum criteria of posting increases 70 percent of the time and may fall short of the average weekly increase for the period. Although the least significant of holy days and arguably not properly classified in this category, they make fair claim to holy-day status on the basis of their generation of fairly regular increases in consumer spending while also evincing elements of the holy-day dynamic in particularly notable ways. There are four holy days in this category: Memorial Day, Father's Day, the Fourth of July, and Labor Day.

In addition to these holy days, seven holidays that do not qualify as holy days are also worthy of consideration because of their individual mythico-ritual qualities or their distinctive role in the annual cycle of postmodern holy days. As will be discussed later, and in a way somewhat analogous to the Catholic Church's ranking of holy days, six of these holidays are aptly classified as feast days and the other as a memorial.

At this point, and on the basis of the foregoing criteria, the holy days and other yearly religious events can be designated, and their annual cycle presented as the postmodern liturgical year. They are listed here in their annual calendrical sequence and with designations and classifications introduced above. The next chapter offers an overview and analysis of the liturgical year as a whole, and discusses the relationship of holy days and other religious events to the months and seasons of the liturgical year. For now, the annual cycle of these observances can be introduced as the sacred calendar of the postmodern liturgical year, as shown on the following page.

THE POSTMODERN LITURGICAL YEAR

New Year's Eve and New Year's Day (December 31–January 1): Feast Day

Martin Luther King Jr. Holiday (third Monday in January): Memorial Day

Super Bowl Sunday (last Sunday in January): Secondary Holy Day

Valentine's Day (February 14): Major Holy Day

Presidents' Day (third Monday in February): Secondary Holy Day

St. Patrick's Day (March 17): Feast Day

Easter (from late March to late April): Major Holy Day[7]

Mother's Day (second Sunday in May): Feast Day

Memorial Day (last Monday in May): Minor Holy Day

Father's Day (third Sunday in June): Minor Holy Day

The Fourth of July (Independence Day) (July 4): Minor Holy Day

Back-to-School (August): Religious Festival

Labor Day (first Monday in September): Minor Holy Day[8]

Columbus Day (second Monday in October): Feast Day

Halloween (October 31): Feast Day

Thanksgiving (fourth Thursday in November): Feast Day

Christmas (Day After Thanksgiving through post-Christmas weekend): Major Holy Day and High Holy Days Religious Festival[9]

---

7. The date of Easter is determined by the first full moon after the vernal equinox. It is always celebrated on the first Sunday after this celestial event and can never be earlier than March 21 or later than April 25.

8. The Labor Day holy-day cycle marks the end of the Back-to-School religious festival, which occurs during the month of August.

9. Christmas includes in its cycle a number of important sacred occasions. The one noted here as the Day After Thanksgiving (fourth or fifth Friday in November) can also be called Pilgrimage Friday. This event along with Harbinger Weekend and Gift Return Day are discussed in part 4.

The Postmodern Liturgical Year

Together, the holy days, religious festivals, and other observances listed in chapter 8 comprise a liturgical year marked by feasts, fasts, and grand celebrations of consumption. This chapter presents an analysis of the liturgical year through Halloween, the last event in the liturgical year before the Christmas religious festival. The next chapter continues the study begun here, focusing exclusively on Christmas. Before considering the texture and contours of the liturgical year as a whole, some attention needs to be given to three related topics: (1) the relationship of traditional holidays to corresponding postmodern religious observances, (2) holy-day cycles and the relative sacredness of various religious events in the liturgical year, and (3) the function of ritual fasts during the liturgical year.

Traditional holidays and postmodern religious observances

Some postmodern observances are traditional holidays of American culture (Labor Day and the Fourth of July), and others have significance only in the context of postmodern religiosity — Super Bowl Sunday and Back-to-School. One holy day, Presidents' Day, is a recently established civil holiday as is the memorial day for Dr. Martin Luther King Jr. Notably, the two holy days that are the most sacred in postmodern cosmological culture coincide with the two greatest holy days in Christianity, although in postmodern culture their relative religious significance reverses their Christian religious significance — with Christmas being by far the more sacred of the two.

Obviously, several long-established holidays and others of more recent origin are not included in this liturgical year. Some of the better known ones excluded here are Ash Wednesday, Veterans Day, Armed Forces' Day, Grandparents' Day, Whitsunday, Flag Day, Secretaries' Day, United Nations Day, Mardi Gras, Lincoln's Birthday, and Washington's Birthday. The absence of the latter two is a result in part of their religiously significant combination in the new Presidents' Day holiday. These assorted non-holy-day holidays, important as they may be in their distinct religious or secular contexts, simply do not possess the sort of mythico-ritual intensity necessary to qualify as holy days — at least none I have been able to discover. There appears to be no noticeable amplification of mythic narratives and no culturewide expansion of general ritual activity in connection with these celebrations and observances. In addition, they do not appear to play any distinctive role in the annual ritual cycle, except perhaps the two president's birthdays insofar as they occur in conjunction with and have been subsumed in the generic Presidents' Day, which is a secondary holy day.

Holy-day cycles and the relative sacredness of religious observances

The sacred cycles of holy days and other observances in the liturgical year fall into four main categories: sacred Sundays, mythic Mondays, movable feasts, and religious festivals. With the exception of religious festivals, which are month-long religious events, these categories are based on the day of the week when holidays associated with postmodern religious events occur. They also serve to indicate something of the scope and duration of the event, with fixed-day (of the week) events generally being more religiously charged than fixed-date (of the month) events — with Christmas Day and Valentine's Day being notable exceptions. ·

Sacred Sundays designate those holy days that always occur on Sundays. There are three such Sundays in the liturgical year: Super Bowl Sunday, Easter, and Father's Day. Mother's Day is also a Sunday holiday and possesses certain characteristics of a holy day, but in terms of the criteria used here it falls slightly short of holy day status. Mythic Mondays are Monday celebrations. Aside from Martin Luther King Day and Columbus Day, all holidays in this category are holy days: Presidents' Day, Memorial Day, and Labor Day. As is discussed more fully later, both King Day and Columbus Day appear to be undergoing transformations, with King Day becoming more like a genuine holy day, and Columbus Day less like one.

As is already obvious to people familiar with traditional Christian terminology, movable feasts in the postmodern liturgical year differ from those classified as such in the Christian calendar. Rather than designating holidays that may be celebrated on different dates from year to year, postmodern movable feasts have a fixed date but may fall on different days of the week from year to year. Aside from Christmas Day, which is subsumed within the High Holy Days of the Christmas religious festival, and the holy days of Valentine's and the Fourth of July, the holidays in this category are feast days: New Year's Eve/Day, St. Patrick's Day, and Halloween. Only one holiday cannot be classified using this method: Thanksgiving, which falls on the fourth Thursday of November. Perhaps it is best called an immovable feast.

As suggested by these classifications, the holy-day cycles vary depending on when they fall in a given week. In some cases, the actual day of the traditional holiday marks the end of a holy-day cycle, with large-scale ritual activity ceasing on the day prior to the holiday itself (e.g., sacred Sundays, especially Easter and Super Bowl Sunday). In others, the activity continues on into the following week (e.g., mythic Mondays). In the case of Christmas, since the religious festival extends through the weekend following Christmas Day, in some years the festival is a full week longer. Following that week, however, ritual activity declines precipitously as the January ritual (shopping) fast begins. With the exception of Christmas and Valentine's Day, movable feasts are notable for their relatively low levels of annually recurring large-scale ritual activity. Sacred Sundays and mythic Mondays, on the other hand, tend to be widely observed.

While all holy days manifest the three definitive holy-day features noted previously (see p. 124), only four do so on a regular annual basis: Christmas, Valentine's Day, Easter, and Back-to-School. Christmas and Back-to-School are essentially extended holy days, and are, thus, properly classified as religious festivals. The presence of holy-day features in conjunction with Christmas is hardly surprising. It is, after all, the paradigmatic holy day of contemporary cosmological religion, with its month-long religious festival serving as the High Holy Days of postmodern culture. The Back-to-School festival is discussed in more detail later, but its manifestation of holy-day features seems likewise fairly self-evident.

That Valentine's Day and Easter also qualify as major holy days is perhaps somewhat surprising, although probably not to persons closely associated with the retail trade. Valentine's Day may appear too narrowly focused on love and romance to generate large-scale rituals, and Easter may seem too profoundly Christian to function as a postmodern cosmological holy day. In short, the former may seem too centered on passion, the latter too centered on The Passion.

In terms of the three determining holy-day features, however, especially increases in culturewide ritual activity, these two holidays closely resemble the Christmas cycle — only on smaller scales and for shorter periods. On this basis, Valentine's Day and Easter can be added to the Back-to-School religious festival and the High Holy Days of Christmas as the most sacred periods in postmodern culture, with each manifesting all three features and doing so every year. Together, these primary holy days and festival cycles anchor the four seasons of the liturgical year, with each one serving as the distinctive mythico-ritual event of a specific season. Valentine's Day is the great midwinter celebration of acquisition and is analogous to archaic planting festivals because it affirms faith in the fertility of the economy and the coming year's abundance. Easter, which is larger in scope and culturewide impact than Valentine's Day, dominates the early spring and is analogous to archaic vernal equinox festivals. For the ancients, spring signaled the beginning of the growing season; for us it signals the beginning of the spending season. Back-to-School marks the end of summer and reveals similarities to archaic harvest celebrations. Of course, at the end of the calendar year comes the greatest harvest celebration of all, the High Holy Days of Christmas, with its month-long festival of acquisition being at once a harvest festival, bacchanal, and New Year's celebration all rolled into one.

In addition to the major holy days, the postmodern liturgical year has two secondary holy days, both of which occur in the winter and border Valentine's Day: Super Bowl Sunday and Presidents' Day. Filling out the annual religious cycle are four minor holy days: Memorial Day in May, Father's Day in late spring, the Fourth of July in midsummer, and Labor Day on the cusp of summer and fall.

As noted previously, besides these genuine holy days, seven holidays do not satisfy all holy-day criteria but are, nonetheless, rightfully included in the calendar of the liturgical year. In annual sequence these are: New Year's Eve/Day; Dr. Martin Luther King Jr. Day; St. Patrick's Day; Mother's Day; Columbus Day; Halloween; and Thanksgiving.[1] Six of these are properly classified as feast days, with King Day functioning as a memorial day. Although they are not holy days, their inclusion in the liturgical year is warranted — the feast days because of their unique manifestation of the mythico-ritual process or their relationship with the liturgical year as a whole, and King Day because of a significant transformation it appears to be undergoing. The relationship of these observances to the liturgical year as a whole can now be further delineated by relating them to the four ritual (shopping) fasts that occur annually on a seasonal basis.

---

1. As a point of note, relative to the actual holy days previously designated, St. Patrick's Day, Mother's Day, and Thanksgiving have large-scale increases 60 percent of the time; New Year's 55 percent; King Day, Columbus Day, and Halloween 50 percent of the time. Since the survey began with the first week of January, 1990, the New Year's percentage is based on nine years, not ten.

Sacred seasons and ritual fasts

For purposes of general analysis, the liturgical year can be divided into four ritual seasons, roughly approximating the four seasons of the year. Each season has a duration of approximately two and a half to four months. The first two seasons are the briefest, each being a bit shorter than a natural (solar) season. Winter, the first season, begins with an extended fasting period (lasting until the week before Super Bowl Sunday when retail sales increase dramatically) and ends in mid-March, prior to St. Patrick's Day.

Like winter, spring also lasts a little more than two months. Its abbreviated length is a result of the "beginning of summer" on the sacred calendar. This event, marked ritually by Memorial Day, occurs nearly a full month before the summer solstice, thus moving the liturgical year into a new season well in advance of the equivalent solar season. As the coming of spring reduces the duration of winter, so the coming of summer reduces the duration of spring. The net result is that the first two seasons of the liturgical year last a total of only five months, of which nearly a full month (January) is given over to a ritual (shopping) fast.

The postmodern summer extends from Memorial Day to Labor Day; and just like a season of nature, it lasts for three months. At this point, however, the liturgical year is almost a month ahead of the solar year, so summer ends a full month before the date of its natural conclusion — the autumnal equinox. This accounting leaves nearly four full months for fall — the last, longest, and most ritually intense season of the year. This final season comes to an end the weekend after Christmas — a date very close to the winter solstice and the end of the calendar year.

As the liturgical year progresses, the power of the economy grows ever stronger, and through its mysterious alchemy the seasons themselves lengthen, and ritual activity (as measured by consumer spending) increases.[2] Each season, although not each month, brings increases in ritual activity over the previous season so that spring has higher levels of retail spending than winter, summer more than spring, and, of course, fall has the highest levels of all. This is, in part, a function of the lengthening of the seasons, but is also a consequence of progressive increases in shopping associated with holy days and religious festivals.

---

2. Annual, seasonal, and monthly ritual activity measured using the GAF (General Merchandise, Apparel, Furniture) category of the United States Census Bureau Monthly Retail Trade Survey. The GAF "represents those retail formats where the bulk of consumer goods shopping occurs" (National Retail Federation, Web site: *www.nrf.com/hot/holiday/dec99/default.htm*, accessed 12/13/99). For more information, see Appendices A and B.

Each season has a period of ritual contraction (or fasting), which follows a period of intense ritual activity. In strictly economic terms, prior to a holiday significant increases in consumer spending are followed by significant spending decreases in the week following. The postmodern practice of fasting *after* holy days reverses the typical relationship, in which fasting occurs prior to a holy day — e.g., Lent prior to Easter or Ramadan prior to Id al-Fitr. As with other general aspects of holy days, Christmas is again the best example of this phenomenon, with the January fast that begins the Monday after the post-Christmas weekend being the longest and most widely observed of all the seasonal fasts. The three other fasting periods follow Easter, Memorial Day, and Back-to-School. Of these three, the fast following Back-to-School is a major fast and easily quantified through use of the GAF sales index, which always registers a steep decline from August figures to those for September.

The other two fasts are classified as minor fasts because they are less widely observed. They are also a bit more challenging to quantify because of unique characteristics of the holy days they follow and periods of measurement that the spending reports use. The challenge with quantifying the post-Easter fast can be traced to the fact that Easter falls on different days each year and can influence GAF figures in March and April, depending on when it falls.

The challenge is even more complex with the post–Memorial Day fast, for two major reasons. First, and as is discussed later, both the Memorial Day holy day and the Mother's Day feast day reveal notable expansions in advertising and correspondingly large increases in consumer spending in several areas not covered by GAF categories. Increases in spending in these areas may account for lower GAF figures for both Mother's Day and Memorial Day, and more importantly here, mask the extent of the post–Memorial Day fast. Second, even though Memorial Day is a May holy day, its ritual activities may impact GAF sales in June, especially if the Monday on which it falls is one of the last days of May. Memorial Day advertisements promote ritual consumption through the weekend following Memorial Day, which could result in higher overall June sales, again masking the extent of the post–Memorial Day fast.

In spite of these difficulties, GAF statistics can be used to a certain extent to suggest the extent of ritual contraction following these holy days. In the case of Easter, monthly GAF sales figures help to reflect the post-Easter fast by generally showing increases in March and declines in April in those years when Easter occurs in late March or early April. The March increases in these years would be consistent with all or most Easter ritual activity occurring in that month and the April declines would be reflective of all or most post-Easter fasting occurring in April.

The BTM/SW weekly index is even more conclusive, indicating declines or slower increases in sales in the week after Easter in nine of the ten years in the survey, with actual declines occurring in seven of the ten years — regardless of the month. The one year in which there was an increase greater than the Easter increase, it was followed the next week by a steep decline in retail sales.

For quantifiable measurement of the fast following the May holy days, GAF June sales are perhaps the only reliable guide, and these reflect a decline in eight of the ten years in the survey. On the other hand, and perhaps due to complexities noted above, the Tokyo figures do not reveal an annual drop-off in ritual activity in the week immediately after Memorial Day.

This analysis is not meant to suggest that the two minor fasts in the liturgical year are anything more than that. Neither rivals the major fasts in January and September, which are sizable contractions. Nonetheless, both may be more extensive than available quantitative tools can accurately measure.

On the basis of the foregoing data, the liturgical year can now be further delineated as an annual cycle of four seasons, each with a major holy day or religious festival, other less-significant holy days and sacred observances, and a ritual fast. As a sacred calendar, the annual cycle is as follows:

WINTER
  New Year's Eve/Day (Feast Day)
  January Fast (Major Fast)
  Martin Luther King Jr. Day (Memorial Day)
  Super Bowl Sunday (Secondary Holy Day)
  Valentine's Day (Major Holy Day)
  Presidents' Day (Secondary Holy Day)

SPRING
  St. Patrick's Day (Feast Day)
  Easter (Major Holy Day)
  Post-Easter Fast (Minor Fast)
  Mother's Day (Feast Day)

SUMMER
  Memorial Day (Minor Holy Day)
  June Fast (Minor Fast)

Father's Day (Minor Holy Day)
The Fourth of July (Minor Holy Day)
Back-to-School (Religious Festival)
FALL
Labor Day (Minor Holy Day)
September Fast (Major Fast)
Columbus Day (Feast Day)
Halloween (Feast Day)
Thanksgiving (Feast Day)
Christmas (Major Holy Day and High Holy Days Religious Festival)

Holy days and the seasons of the liturgical year

As explained previously, the progressive nature of ritual activity from season to season over the course of the year and the significance of holy days can be measured using monthly fluctuations in consumer (GAF) spending. Using this data as a base for analysis and factoring in the ritual fasts discussed in the previous section, the postmodern liturgical year can now be presented as an organic whole, a living organism comprised of four interrelated seasons, each with periods of fasting, feasting, and sanctified periods of ritual acquisition.

Each of these various religious observances serves as both cosmic monitor and cultural mediator of the economy's sacred respiration as it travels on its own annual pilgrimage from the depths of darkness and near death in January to the heights of shimmering light and puissance in the High Holy Days of December. As the economy moves forward through the seasons, we follow in step with its progress and pauses, alert to its expansions and contractions — and ritually breathing in perfect synch with its sacred respiration.

Winter

Winter is the nadir of religious activity in postmodern culture, with January and February invariably being the least active months of the entire year. Not only is the natural world cold and listless across much of the United States in these months, so too is the economy. The ritual fasting period from the weekend after Christmas to the week before Super Bowl Sunday serves as the transition from one liturgical year to the next. It is both a period of collective rest and recuperation from the High Holy Days as well as a time of preparation for the coming year. The January fast can also be understood as a piacular ritual, with culture as a whole mourning the symbolic death of the economy.

In these early weeks of the year, the economy is in repose and its sacred realm difficult to enter. The reality of the meta-myth seems distant, and the nexus of myth and ritual tenuous. Tertiary myths become whispered echoes of those that filled the High Holy Days just past. Ritual sites are depopulated, and holy-day priests return to more mundane callings. The world of religious experience seems as barren as the natural world, as though the Great Mother is asleep and no one dares awaken her. In strict economic terms, however, this extended ritual (shopping) fast accounts for sharp declines in January spending, usually making it the lowest of all months in GAF sales.

The January fast may in part explain the absence of significant mythico-ritual activity in connection with the King Day holiday, which functions as a genuine memorial day in the postmodern liturgical year, just as it does in the liturgical year of civil religion. On the other hand, the solemnity of the day may contribute to the already extensive ritual fasting during the month. In either case, the mid-January date for the King Day memorial is especially apt, since it occurs during a time of negligible consumer spending. This fasting may result in more attention given to the famous man and his work than would be the case if the holiday were transformed into a typical postmodern holy day. Nonetheless, and in spite of the fact that there is virtually no advertising support, this very sort of transformation may be occurring as retail commerce appears to be increasing in conjunction with the King Day holiday.[3]

Although still largely dormant through most of January, the first signs of the economy's return to life appear in the week prior to Super Bowl Sunday, the first holy day of the year. Indications of its resurrection become even more noticeable in February, which brings the first major holy day, Valentine's Day, and shortly thereafter, Presidents' Day, one of only two secondary holy days in the entire year. The conjunction of these two holy days and their high levels of ritual activity may explain why February usually has higher overall GAF sales than January — in spite of the fact that it marks the "dead of winter" and is two or sometimes three days shorter in length.

---

3. The King Day holiday may be undergoing a transition, with holy-day phenomena replacing its memorial-day aspects — e.g.: in the last three years of the ten-year period used here, the Bank of Tokyo Index indicates large increases in consumer spending during the King Day holiday period. The King Day holiday may yet emerge as a genuine holy day. Curiously, these increases have occurred without significant increases in tertiary myths.

In addition, February routinely brings considerable increases in two areas of retail spending not included in the GAF category or measured in the Bank of Tokyo weekly sales index. Both of these areas, jewelry sales and vehicle sales, are directly impacted by mythico-rituals of the two holy days. Jewelry acquisition rituals are a major part of the Valentine's Day cycle, and vehicle acquisition rituals are an important feature in the cycle of Presidents' Day. While sales in these two areas are not covered in the GAF index or accounted for in the BTM/SW weekly index, they must be considered indications of mythico-ritual activity, especially when considered in the context of the proliferation of advertising focusing on jewelry in the Valentine's Day cycle and vehicles in the Presidents' Day cycle. If sales in these areas were added to GAF, February would always exceed January, and if they were included in the BTM/SW index, the two holy days would doubtless reveal an even larger increase in ritual activity than they do already.

March continues the economy's regeneration process, always exceeding the GAF sums of the two previous months. In the middle of the month is St. Patrick's Day, a feast day for culture as a whole, and in some parts of America, a genuine holy day. In fact, were it not for the absence of distinct amplifications in mythic narratives and slightly higher regularity of annual spending increases, St. Patrick's Day would qualify as a holy day. Falling on March 17, this movable feast with holy-day characteristics signals the end of the winter season and the transition into spring. It also prefaces the second greatest holy-day cycle of the entire year — Easter.

Spring

As a mythico-ritual cycle, Easter is remarkably similar to Christmas, only on a smaller scale. Advertisements featuring Easter and spring themes and products begin appearing four to five weeks in advance of the holy day, and ritual consumption shows a pronounced increase during this period, especially in the week just before Easter Sunday. So dramatic is the expansion in ritual acquisition that increases in retail spending for the two-week period are, on average, seven times (600 percent) higher than other weeks during the year. By comparison, the first major holy day of the year, Valentine's Day, averages an increase of about eight times higher than other weeks, but its cycle lasts only one week. Easter also serves to inspire the entire spring season, establishing a high level of ritual activity that is then continued through the month of May.[4]

---

4. Spring weather is also a factor, but is beyond the scope of this book to quantify.

In addition to increased sales during the Easter cycle, its ritual significance is also reflected in GAF spending during March and April. As previously discussed in the context of the post-Easter fast, in years when most of the Easter cycle occurs in March, that month posts higher GAF sales than April; in years when the bulk of the cycle is in April, April surpasses March in GAF sales. Also like Christmas, and unlike Valentine's Day, a week of ritual fasting occurs immediately after the holy day. This week of fasting bears a striking resemblance to the January fast after Christmas and doubtless functions in the same manner, serving as a time of rest and recuperation from a major holy day as well as a period of preparation for subsequent ritual events.

Following Easter are two less significant celebrations: Mother's Day and Memorial Day. Both are insignificant compared to the major holy days, yet when combined with graduation acquisition rituals, they likely account for May annually posting higher GAF sales than any previous month. Although their annual ritual increases are modest in terms of the ritual-to-sales comparison being used here,[5] two important considerations must be taken into account when evaluating their sacred significance. First, they occur in a month that posts remarkably high overall increases in GAF spending, so their modest increases occur in conjunction with a general expansion in spending. In spite of this general increase during the month, Mother's Day still posts increases 60 percent of the time and Memorial Day 70 percent.

In addition, both days feature distinct mythico-ritual activities in several non-GAF categories that post marked increases in spending in May.[6] For example, Memorial Day rituals may be the chief cause of conspicuous increases during May in grocery store sales and vehicle sales. Memorial Day picnics and cookouts may account for May annually being higher than all previous months in grocery store sales; and vehicular acquisition rituals occurring in the Memorial Day cycle may account for May usually (nine of ten years) being higher than all previous months in vehicular sales. In addition to these two areas, a third area of Memorial Day consumer spending is also not included in the GAF category—movie theater ticket sales.

For its part, Mother's Day also features mythico-rituals linked to two

---

5. See additional comments in the text; note 6, below; note 4 in chapter 8; and Appendices.

6. These categories are grocery stores, automotive dealers, jewelry stores, restaurants, and movie theaters. Although not included in the Commerce Department's GAF category or the BTM/SW weekly index of consumer spending, with the exception of movie theaters, all areas are included as spending categories in the Commerce Department's monthly trade survey.

areas not included in the GAF category or the Tokyo weekly sales index—
jewelry store and restaurant sales. The mythico-ritual linkage of jewelry
and restaurants with Mother's Day may account for May annually being
higher than all previous months in sales in these two areas. May even
exceeds February (Valentine's month) in jewelry sales, which may also be
a result of advance purchase of jewelry for June weddings and graduations.
As with Valentine's Day and Presidents' Day in February, if these non-GAF
categories were included in the GAF, the month's increase would be even
larger, and if factored into the BTM/SW index, the religious significance
of Mother's Day and Memorial Day would be even more pronounced.

Summer

The spring cycle comes to a close with Memorial Day, which is followed
by the June fast. Following the religiously charged month of May, June is
a month of ritual contraction, usually (eight of ten years) posting lower
GAF figures than May. The lower levels of ritual activity during Father's
Day are indicative of this contraction. In addition, unlike Mother's Day
and Memorial Day, there are no significant ritual increases in non-GAF
areas of consumer sales during the Father's Day cycle. The one non-GAF
category where there are regular June increases, which are likely traced
to the Father's Day rituals, is sporting goods stores. While sales increases
here are routine in June, they are generally only slightly higher than May.
Curiously, in June there is a high level of vehicular sales,[7] but these cannot
be accounted for in the context of the holy day since there is no indication
of increased advertising relating vehicle acquisition rituals to Father's Day
per se. While many fathers in America would doubtless prefer it to be
otherwise, Father's Day is thus best classified as the least sacred of all holy
days. It is a minor holy day in a month of ritual contraction.

Summer's midpoint is signaled by the Fourth of July, a minor holy day.
The month as a whole usually has slightly less ritual activity than June and
always less than May. The one area where there is often a marked July
increase is in the non-GAF category of grocery store spending. In fact, in
many years July is the second highest month (behind December) in expenditures made at grocery stores. As with Memorial Day, this increase is
most likely a consequence of Fourth of July being celebrated with picnics,
cookouts, beer, and soda.

Aside from these increases, which can be fairly traced to feast-day cele-

---

7. Vehicle sales in June are higher than May in six of the ten years in the survey and the
highest for the entire year in five of ten.

brations, the Fourth of July remains only a minor holy day because it generates increases in retail sales only 70 percent of the time. This is notable since advertisements with Fourth of July themes are extensive. In spite of this amplification and dilation of mythic narratives, there appears to be no corresponding expansion in ritual activity, even in vehicle sales, which are one of the major foci of the Fourth's mythic narratives. Over the ten-year period surveyed here, average retail sales in the Fourth of July cycle were only a little more than half the overall weekly average. In years when increases did occur, they were usually small, and more than offset by years with actual declines in sales.

The relative lull of late spring and early summer lasts until August and the annual Back-to-School religious festival. Like the High Holy Days of Christmas, the Back-to-School festival covers an entire month, essentially turning August into a single prolonged holy day. Back-to-School does indeed have a Christmas-like quality. All three features of the holy day tableaux are manifest: the seven holy-day elements are certainly evident, there is an increase in tertiary myths with a holy-day focus, and a corresponding expansion in ritual activity occurs.

Curiously, in spite of these features, August has no distinct holy days, and the Back-to-School festival itself lacks a discernible beginning and distinct conclusion. There is not a "Back-to-School Day" as there is a Christmas Day, Easter, or Valentine's Day. Moreover, unlike May, with which August also has religious affinities, no annual holidays occur during the month, which might be used to help capture ritual activities in a measurable form. Finally, the beginning of the school year varies throughout the country, and even between adjacent counties and school districts. Schools of different grade and age levels begin on different dates. Similar differences can be found between private and public schools and among institutions of higher learning. Developing quantifiable data using the weekly measure of consumer sales increases for the Back-to-School mythico-ritual period is thus impossible. Still, the festival is without question one of the most important religious cycles in the liturgical year and cannot be dismissed or overlooked.

To gauge the extent of ritual activity for the Back-to-School festival, I considered consumer spending for the entire month of August, with Labor Day marking its conclusion. This allowed me to use GAF data exclusively for purposes of analysis, rather than the BTM/SW index. Using this criterion, Back-to-School stands out as the dominant mythico-ritual event of every year until the fall season. In short, August always has GAF spending totals higher than any previous month, and it is the highest month of the year until November, except for rare occasions (two of ten years surveyed) when October is slightly higher. The Back-to-School cycle comes to an end with Labor Day, a minor holy day, which marks the end of summer and the beginning of fall.

Fall

Labor Day's classification as a minor holy day results at least in part from following so closely the Back-to-School festival. Its role in the liturgical year is thus somewhat like that of Presidents' Day, which also closely follows a major holy day, Valentine's Day. A distinct holy day in its own right, Labor Day, like Presidents' Day, may benefit from the high level of ritual activity engendered by its more sacred antecedent, but to show increases at all it must overcome the ritual contraction that follows major religious events. That Labor Day does so, and especially in light of following the enormous, month-long Back-to-School festival, makes it somewhat more significant than other minor holy days. By contrast, New Year's Eve and Day, whose relationship with the Christmas festival is analogous to Labor Day's relationship with Back-to-School, routinely reveals reductions and often sharp declines in ritual activity.

Following Labor Day, the rest of September is given over to ritual fasting, as is common in months after major religious cycles. The fast is clearly reflected in September's GAF sales figures, which are always lower than August's, and often lower than months earlier in the year, especially May. The fall season thus begins with a major fast, just like the liturgical year, with September serving as a time of recuperation and preparation similar to January.

This major postmodern fast usually overlaps the High Holy Days of Judaism, which are commemorated with ancient rituals of fasting and repentance predicated on belief in a transcendental God. Like Judaism's "Days of Awe," the September fast marks a major turning point in the postmodern liturgical year. In the case of Judaism, this period serves as the bridge from one year to the next, while in contemporary cosmological culture it marks the approach of the fall season — the most sacred season of the year. As with the King Day holiday in January, the coincidence of a postmodern fasting month with a period of functionally similar ritual practices in a very different religious system may enrich and amplify the sacred meaning of the period in both systems.

Columbus Day falls on the second Monday in October. Historically, this holiday has been widely celebrated throughout America, and indeed throughout the Americas. Since the early 1990s, however, the holiday has been marked by controversy and protests centering on the lingering effects of European colonialism and affirming the rights of indigenous peoples. As a result, the postmodern religious significance of the holiday appears to be in decline, with mythic narratives tied to the holiday contracting and ritual activities subsiding.[8] Columbus Day is thus a holiday in transition, and if current trends remain in place, it may well disappear from the liturgical calendar entirely.

Even should this occur, there will not likely be any reduction in the overall increase in ritual activity for the month of October. Not only does October always reveal higher levels of ritual activity (measured in GAF sales) than September, it initiates a three-month cycle of ritual expansion that continues through the High Holy Days of Christmas. Although the contribution of Halloween to October's general ritual expansion appears to be negligible, the holiday has become one of the great feast days of our culture — ranking second only to New Year's Eve in the number of parties it spawns.[9]

The designation of Halloween as a feast day rather than a holy day may seem somewhat surprising, especially in light of its growing popularity as a holiday and reports of large increases in sales of holiday-related paraphernalia. Recent business and commerce reports indicate that the Halloween shopping season is today second only to Christmas.[10] Halloween sales have definitely been increasing in recent years, summing to an estimated $6.8 billion in 2000, compared with $2.5 billion as recently as 1996.[11] Candy sales were projected to reach $2 billion in 2000, costumes $1.5 billion, and other holiday items (like pumpkins and party supplies)

---

8. For example, in the last three years of the survey, the Columbus Day cycle has posted increasingly steep declines in ritual activity as measured by the Bank of Tokyo index.

9. Jennifer Roberts, spokesperson, International Mass Retail Association, in interview with Kathleen Schalch, National Public Radio, "Morning Edition," October 29, 1998. Roberts reports that it has just recently passed Super Bowl Sunday to move into second place behind New Year's Eve. For more details see, "The Halloween Industry," The Halloween Association: *www.halloweenassn.org/industry.html* (accessed 10/27/00). This site ranks it third, behind the Super Bowl and New Year's.

10. See, for example, Lori Johnson, "Halloween Sales Treat for Retailers," *Business Journal* (Charlotte, N.C.), October 25, 1999; accessed online at *www.bizjournals.com/charlotte/stories/1999/10/25/story3.html* (accessed 10/27/00). See also reports of Halloween being second only to Christmas from spokespersons for Walgreen's and K-Mart in Felicia Levine, "Halloween Sales Heading from 'Boo' to Boom," *South Florida Business Journal — Broward Edition,* October 28, 1996), accessed online at *www.bizjournals.com/southflorida/stories/1996/10/28/story2.html* (accessed 10/27/00).

11. For 2000 estimate, see Pam Rucker, "press release," National Retail Federation (October 4, 2000). For 1996 estimate, see Felicia Levine, "Halloween Sales Heading from 'Boo' to Boom."

$2.7 billion.[12] As suggested by these high and increasing sales figures for holiday-related merchandise, advertisements for Halloween products have also been expanding. Halloween thus reveals certain characteristics associated with holy days and, arguably, the first two features in the holy-day criteria being used here. What it lacks, however, is the critical third feature — a culturewide expansion in ritual activity. Such expansion is simply not apparent in conjunction with the holiday, at least insofar as it can be measured by the consumer sales data used here, for three major reasons.

First, although Halloween does generate a considerable volume of holiday-specific ritual acquisitions (second only to Christmas), it does not appear to engender a mythico-ritual cycle that would contribute to increases in other areas of ritual activity. The large sales figures related to the holiday represent only three areas of ritual acquisition, all of which are directly tied to the actual celebration of the holiday — candy, costumes, and holiday accessories. Sales in these areas are indeed enormous and certainly reflect a distinct mythico-ritual cycle in their own right. In this regard, precisely because Halloween sales are so specialized, the holiday cannot be used to account for the culturewide expansion in ritual activity that occurs in October. In fact, because of their highly specialized focus, rituals related to these three areas may actually draw worshipers away from other ritual acquisitions.

Second, while Halloween rituals do contribute to the general increase during the month because of the wide observance of its mythico-ritual cycle, little if any direct correlation appears to exist between the holiday and increases in ritual activity outside the three areas noted above. No significant amplification of advertisements takes place featuring items without a direct connection to the holiday. One seldom finds Halloween ads about general merchandise: shoes, ties, televisions, skirts, bicycles, cosmetics, luggage, etc. Costumes, yes; candy of all varieties, yes; plastic and organic pumpkins, flashlights with ghost-heads, and rubberized skulls that make spooky sounds when vibration activated are all prominent. We do acquire all these things and many others in the Halloween cycle, and we do so because of the feast-day myths. But we probably are not acquiring parkas, halogen torch lamps, rakes, and DVD players because it is Halloween. In other words, aside from sales of specific Halloween products, October sales increases appear to be unrelated to the holiday.

Third, and most importantly, using the BTM/SW weekly index as a measure, over the ten-year period of this study, during the Halloween cycle

---

12. Rucker, "press release."

ritual activity, on the average, declined. The decline became particularly noticeable in the last few years of the study, which were precisely the years when retail trade studies were reporting significant increases in Halloween spending. While several explanations may account for these increases,[13] the simple fact remains that Halloween does not inspire culturewide rituals of acquisition that are definitive of postmodern holy days.

Halloween does indeed rightly stand next to New Year's Eve/Day as our second greatest feast day, and as such, a fitting preface to the two most sacred months of the year. Today, just as in medieval Europe, October 31 is the eve of an especially hallowed event, in fact, the most hallowed event in the postmodern liturgical year. Rather than All Saints' Day, in postmodern culture the day after Halloween is more notable as marking the beginning of the Christmas season. The next section explores the religious dynamic of the postmodern Christmas festival and considers its meaning and function in contemporary cosmological culture.

---

13. Most importantly, perhaps, increases in grocery and drugstore Halloween sales, which would not be covered in the BTM/SW index of department stores. Even factoring in increases in these areas, however, does not fully account for the steep drops for the last five years of the study (1995–99). Another possible explanation is the recent emergence of Halloween-specific retailers.

Part IV

RELIGIOUS DIMENSIONS OF CHRISTMAS IN POSTMODERN CULTURE

Christmas by the Numbers

November continues the accelerated rate of ritual activity begun in October. As one would expect, ritual increases in November are striking, with GAF sales figures being from 10 to 15 percent higher than the highest previous month (usually August) in any given year. In fact, were it not for December, November would be the sacred apex of the liturgical year. Then again, without the Christmas cycle, which commences in November, the month might otherwise be rather insignificant. In point of fact, however, as the month that marks the beginning of the High Holy Days of postmodern culture, November stands apart from all other months — except the even greater month that immediately follows.

November and the advent of the High Holy Days

The signs of the High Holy Days' approach appear in late October when the November issues of magazines begin arriving at newsstands and grocery-store checkout racks. Many magazines have covers with Christmas-related images or scenes. More importantly, however, they invariably contain within their pages a wide assortment of tertiary myths (advertisements) featuring Christmas themes and objects for ritual acquisition during the festival season. Shortly thereafter, Christmas myths begin to be noticeable in other media. A gradual increase in these myths occurs until the weekend before Thanksgiving, at which time their volume expands enormously. This weekend before Thanksgiving, rather than the Friday after Thanksgiving, is the first great harbinger of the Christmas season.

Prior to this time, several traditional observances occur in November. All Saints' Day (November 1), the original hallowed day for which October 31 is the eve, passes virtually without notice in the postmodern liturgical year — save for one notable event. On November 1, malls begin decorating for Christmas.[1]

The Tuesday after the first Monday in November is marked by the voting ritual of civil religion, which in presidential election years results in considerable public activity, but apparently no religious celebrations. Another civil religious observance, Veterans Day on November 11, generates a smattering of tertiary myths but is otherwise uneventful religiously — aside from the presence of Christmas items in some of the myths.

Soon after Veterans Day, Santa Claus arrives at most malls.[2] His appearance sanctifies the mall as a holy site and signals the beginning of "Harbinger Weekend," the pre-Thanksgiving weekend when avoiding exposure to High Holy Day myths is virtually impossible. Sunday newspaper supplements are larger and more numerous than usual, with gift items and Christmas decorations prominently featured. Television commercials for malls and department stores proliferate, and all manner of products are presented with a Holy Day glamour. If by chance the myths should be missed, other portents of the season begin to appear in public and private spaces during the shortened week before Thanksgiving. Christmas banners are hung from street lamps in urban centers and holiday decorations become even more prominent in retail shopping venues. Wreaths are hung on doors or in windows, and multicolored lights begin to multiply in residential areas. Grocery stores begin packing purchases in bags with symbols of the season, and we pass by images of Santa as we trundle toward checkouts with frozen turkeys and canned cranberry sauce.

Harbinger Weekend has little to do with Thanksgiving, aside from the fact that it occurs the weekend before the holiday and ads featuring ritual items associated with Thanksgiving are inevitably mixed in with Christmas advertisements. The primary function of Harbinger Weekend is to herald the advent of the Christmas season that begins bright and early on the Friday after Thanksgiving, a day that witnesses what is arguably the greatest mythico-ritual event in the liturgical year. Not only is the day after Thanksgiving presaged by Harbinger Weekend, it is again dramatically prefigured on Thanksgiving itself with yet another even more massive eruption of advertising tabloids in newspapers, corresponding commercials on television, and parades in the public sector, of which Macy's Thanksgiving Day Parade in New York City is the most famous.

---

1. See "ICSC Holiday Fun Facts 2000," International Council of Shopping Centers (2000), accessed online at *http://holiday.icsc.org/funfacts00.html* (accessed 3/15/01).
2. On November 18, in 2000. See ibid.

The Thanksgiving feast day

As a formal annual observance, Thanksgiving functions as a major feast day in the liturgical year. Like Halloween and other feast days, Thanksgiving has its own distinctive mythico-ritual cycle that doubtless contributes to the increase in retail sales during the month. Grocery stores are, of course, the primary locus of feast-day religious phenomena; feast-day myths generated by these most utilitarian of all shrines herald the coming holiday with grand and vivid narratives featuring foods, beverages, and holiday accessories. Thanksgiving is especially representative of feast-day cycles. Of all the feast days, it requires the largest quantity and widest array of edible products. Turkeys are, naturally, the central theme of Thanksgiving myths, but a host of related edible products also appear: jellied cranberry sauce, potatoes (sweet and otherwise), corn (especially fresh ears), canned gravy, seasoned breading for stuffing, pickles and garnishes, assorted canned and frozen vegetables, frozen pies (especially pumpkin), synthetic cream topping, marshmallows, and so on. As with other mythico-ritual cycles, feast-day myths are the first of a two-part process, and the Thanksgiving rituals of acquisition that follow them are just as dynamic as any that occur on holy days. In spite of the fact that they are almost entirely restricted to grocery shrines, the extent and intensity of their performance is striking.

Like holy-day cycles, shopping increases as Thanksgiving nears, with the day before being a particularly exciting time. On Thanksgiving eve, parking lots at grocery stores are filled with vehicles, and the stores themselves teem with an energy that resembles the ritual frenzy seen otherwise only during the Christmas festival at malls and department stores. The day before Thanksgiving is, thus, properly designated the Christmas Eve of grocery shrines. It is also the "eve of the eve" of the High Holy Days, which begin on the Friday after Thanksgiving. Framed, as it is, by Harbinger Weekend before and the beginning of the Christmas festival on the Friday after, the Thanksgiving feast-day cycle can be easily overlooked as a distinct event in the liturgical year. And while Thanksgiving itself is not a holy day, its miniature mythico-ritual cycle functions as a sacred bridge between two of the most religiously charged weekends of the year.

Following the conclusion of Thanksgiving's mythico-ritual cycle, the holiday is given over to communal activities and the consumption of items on the Thanksgiving ritual menu. Although specific Thanksgiving activities and menus vary, and traditional holiday practices appear to be waning, the feast day's classical ritual process is still widely observed.

The focal point of the Thanksgiving ritual is a lavish meal shared with family members. The preparation of the meal is a complex, multipart enterprise. Many hands and many skills are needed. Traditionally, the undertaking is presided over by the senior matriarch, assisted by other female members of the clan. The presence of ancestors may be keenly sensed during this part of the ritual, as recipes and cooking techniques of deceased matriarchs are resurrected and discussed. The authority of the living matriarch may even be challenged with the invocation of recipes used by ancestral matriarchs.

Males in the household are usually excused from meal preparation rituals, unless they have a particular talent and have been formally welcomed into the holiday kitchen. For their part, males spend meal preparation time in a room separated from the kitchen, usually a television viewing room (often called a den); there they will watch one of several NFL games broadcast on Thanksgiving Day. One of the games will always involve the Detroit Lions, and in this regard, the Lions are as much a part of the postmodern Thanksgiving observance as are turkeys.[3] If communal activities begin early enough, Macy's Thanksgiving Day Parade may be included in the viewing fare for the day, in which case the entire clan may watch the parade together.

All the foods acquired at the grocery shrine in the days immediately preceding the feast day are carefully prepared according to family traditions. As mealtime approaches, each food is brought to the communal dining table and arranged in a systematic manner. The best tableware and eating utensils are reserved for the occasion. Salt and pepper shakers shaped like turkeys, seventeenth-century Puritans, or Native Americans also may be part of the arrangement. The center of the table is always left vacant until the very last moment before the meal is to begin. Only when everything is in proper order can the consumption phase of this classic feast-day ritual commence. It all depends on the turkey. When it is "done," as the saying goes, the men are summoned from their den, the women from their kitchen labors, and the turkey from the oven. The turkey is carried ceremoniously to the table and placed in the vacant place reserved for its presence.

At this point, supervision of the ritual shifts from matriarchal to patriarchal authority. If the family is religious (in a traditional sense), a prayer is offered, usually by the senior patriarch or someone he has designated, such as a clergy person in the family or someone deemed to be particularly

---

3. In recent years the Dallas Cowboys have also regularly played a game on Thanksgiving. The Lions, however, remain the classic Thanksgiving team.

religious. Patriarchal authority is then further reinforced when the fowl is cut up and its flesh distributed to members of the clan. Here again the senior patriarch presides, usually receiving empty plates in sequence from each member of the clan, asking each whether she or he desires "white" or "dark" meat, and then fulfilling their desires. Everyone in attendance joins in as plates are passed around the table, each supplying a different food product; one adding potatoes and gravy, another green beans topped with almonds or those little fried onion strips, another the jellied cranberry sauce (which seldom is eaten). In the end, all at the table have full plates of holiday food, and eating begins in earnest. While not all foods are consumed, especially the jellied cranberry sauce, a primary requirement is that everyone consume some portion of the turkey. As some of my friends and I, who are vegetarians, have discovered, in families that observe the classic Thanksgiving ritual, to forego the consumption of turkey is virtual sacrilege. One source reports that 91 percent of Americans eat turkey on Thanksgiving, consuming 45 million birds on that day or (in sandwiches) during the subsequent week.[4]

Following the meal and after praise is extended to the cooks, the men again retire to their den and the women again to the kitchen; the men to resume game viewing and perhaps to doze, the women to clean up. If not served immediately after the meal, dessert is served after the clean-up is completed. Traditional desserts are pies topped with thawed or partially thawed frozen whipped cream — which is often synthetic. Pumpkin is the classic holiday pie, but others, such as cherry, mincemeat, and apple, are also frequently served. Postmeal conversations are rarely about the president's official proclamation of the national day of thanksgiving or the mythic origins of the holiday among seventeenth-century Puritans in Plymouth Colony. They may, however, concern the High Holy Days and its first sacred pilgrimages, which for many will begin early in the morning the very next day.

The mythico-ritual cycle: from Pilgrimage Friday to Gift Return Day

In terms of postmodern religiosity, Thanksgiving is, of course, eclipsed by the Day After Thanksgiving, the annual religious event that defines the central importance of November in the liturgical year. Although the

---

4. See "Thanksgiving Facts," at *www.arose4ever.com/karen/thanksgiv/factsthanksgiving .htm* (accessed 3/10/01).

highest levels of retail spending occur closer to Christmas,[5] the Day After Thanksgiving is the sacred epicenter of the annual religious cycle. On this Friday the entire culture is rocked by a massive mythico-ritual paroxysm as countless millions leave their homes and flock to sacred sites of all varieties. This first day in the most sacred cycle of the year is as much a time of pilgrimage as ritual performance. Because of its dedication to large-scale ritual pilgrimages, the Day After Thanksgiving is also aptly titled Pilgrimage Friday.

The pilgrimage festival begins at dawn, and even earlier in some locales. The myths of Harbinger Weekend and Thanksgiving trumpet the start of the celebration with various well-known mantras: "Early Bird Sale," "Doors Open at 6 A.M.," "Shop Early!" "Great Values 7 A.M. to 10 A.M. Only." And the pilgrims hearken. From dawn until late at night (11 P.M., midnight, or later), legions of dedicated votaries devotionally respond to these dharmic goads. This day is the grand commencement of "the most wonderful time of the year." Department stores and malls are visited by vast multitudes, their sacred avenues toured by throngs of festival participants, and the first ritual acquisitions of the High Holy Days occur. Pilgrimage Friday is, however, only the beginning of the High Holy Days, and for most persons these Friday travels are only the first of many journeys that will be made during the Christmas festival.

The festival itself lasts from Pilgrimage Friday through Gift Return Day, a ritual event whose precise date varies from individual to individual but usually occurs no later than the Sunday after Christmas.[6] During this period of slightly more than a month, every day is a functional holy day for countless millions, with weekends being the holiest days of all. Christmas-inspired advertisements and promotions are inescapable as these tertiary myths of the season stream ceaselessly from all the media pores of culture. Wherever we look (if we look very long at all), Christmas appears everywhere from Pilgrimage Friday through the month of holy days that follow.

Throughout this month of holy days, shopping venues are as crowded

---

5. It is not uncommon for the Day After Thanksgiving to be among the top-ten holiday shopping days of the year, but usually not among the top five and never higher than fifth. Occasionally, the following Saturday is also among the top-ten. Otherwise, the top-ten shopping days are all in December. Data from a six-year period (1994–99). See "Top Ten Holiday Shopping Days Yearly Daily Sales Comparison," International Council of Shopping Centers (2000), accessed online at *http://holiday.icsc.org/10days00.html* (accessed 3/10/01).

6. The one exception to this cycle occurs in years when Christmas falls on a Sunday, which means New Year's Day also falls on a Sunday. In these years, most returns are made prior to the post-Christmas Sunday, but no later than the Monday after New Year's Day.

on weekdays as they are on weekends at other times of the year — as busy or busier, in fact, on midweek days as on weekends during other holy-day cycles. Many of the advertisements early in the season feature clothing, but as the festival continues an incredible array of other items appear in the ads, filling our consciousness and goading us on to journeys of sacred acquisition. If we do not begin our festival rituals on Pilgrimage Friday, we will soon enough. Inspired by the mythic power of Christmas ads, in this season more so than all others, we discover again our sacred obligation to acquire. Like animate beings, malls and department stores seem somehow alive — filled with a vitalizing power and sacred energy not unlike what one might have found in the temples and shrines of antiquity. They welcome and enchant us, hold and enfold us, and guide us on through aisle after decorated aisle, all teeming with the mythic objects of our culture's dharmic dreams.

Dream we do, but acquire we must. At Christmas it seems that we can. Every desired object stands before us, and every desire can be ritually satisfied during this month-long stretch of numinous days. Anything imaginable seems within ritual reach. The grand temples (our suburban shopping malls) are the most popular locales, but every religious outpost of culture is a potential destination. From roadside vendors selling Elvis Presley velvet paintings and area rugs with images of the Dao to tony apparel stores on Rodeo Drive and high-end jewelers in Palm Beach, every type of retail venue is alive with ritual activity. A sense of excitement fills the air and ritual chaos is commonplace.

With tabloid ads in hand and mythic images dancing like metaphorical sugarplums in their heads, Christmas pilgrims peregrinate from one sacred site to another. An electronics store has that long-pursued Dolby Pro-Logic home theater system while the department store down the way features the much desired Bissell carpet cleaner. Both were imaged sleekly in Harbinger Weekend ads produced by the stores being visited. At the discount store in another part of the mall we find the NordicTrack Ellipse and next to it a Char-broil gas grill (with free grill cover). Can we afford all this? Of course we can. It is Christmas after all.

At another sacred site we happen upon a panoply of televisions: Hitachi, Toshiba, Sony, Panasonic, RCA, Philips/Magnavox, Zenith. The more desirable ones were depicted in a Thanksgiving Day advertising supplement with scenes of Santa riding a snowboard on their screens. Later in the season come mythic advertising narratives about bicycles and watches, crystal sets and power tools, silver heart pendants and Gucci luggage, ties and microwave ovens, shoes and seventy-eight-piece flatware sets. The cornucopia of the economy's fertility is vividly depicted in the seemingly endless flow of advertisements throughout the season; at the sacred sites themselves we find the mythic narratives of the ads are accurate, or even understated. Everywhere we look we find a stunning array of the best and brightest, fastest and smoothest, hottest and coolest objects of desire. Now is the time to acquire, and we do.

Pilgrimage Friday and the weekend that follows set the tone and pace for the entire season. On those three days, between 8 and 10 percent of all Christmas spending occurs.[7] After the initial celebratory eruption on Pilgrimage Friday and the following weekend, the ritual process slows somewhat, only to gradually pick up momentum with each succeeding week of festival, until again becoming frenzied during the final week before Christmas Day.[8]

Even after the holy day itself passes, the celebration continues, as vast numbers of persons continue the ritual cycle by returning unwanted products received during the season. Tales of the "unwanted gift" are among the best known of the holiday season. Occasionally the basis of Funny Story commercials or included in sitcom plots on TV, they are more often highly personal narratives shared with friends and family members. These are the stories of the weird tie or the inappropriate calendar, the "too grown up" gift for a child, the bad-smelling cologne or perfume, cheap jewelry, clothes that do not fit, and stereo components that do not integrate. Such narratives have a remarkable motivational power, and stores spring to life again as undesired items are returned to their places of acquisition. Curiously, beginning on the day after Christmas (the traditional Gift Return Day) and for several days thereafter, more people are bringing bags or boxes into shrines than there are people leaving with similarly packaged acquisitions.

The gift-return ritual is a rather vivid example of the acquisition-consumption-disposal cycle, since the items disposed of on Gift Return Day are so new they are, in fact, unused and often unopened. Consumption thus becomes an entirely symbolic performance, a virtual act, with the object itself distilled into its purest essence: a thing to be disposed of

---

7. From 1996 to 1999, Thanksgiving weekend accounted for an average of 9.1 percent of all Christmas sales. The high was 10 percent, the low was 8.5 percent. See "Weekly Distribution of Mall Sales 1996–1999," International Council of Shopping Centers (2000), accessed online at *http://holiday.icsc.org/wdsales00.html* (accessed 3/10/01).

8. For the Christmas spending cycle and increases during the period just before the holiday, see ibid. For last minute spending, see Lydia Saad, "More Than Half of Americans Delayed Gift Shopping until Final Pre-Christmas Days," The Gallup Organization (November 23, 1999), accessed online at *www.gallup.com/poll/releases/pr991223.asp* (accessed 4/20/01).

so that the sacred process can begin again. Moreover, since most persons either desire something quite like what they have returned or receive ritual "credit" for the returned item, they are able to immediately begin the religious process again — seeking out new objects to acquire. Traditionally, Gift Return Day is observed on the day after Christmas, which is one of the busiest days at malls and other shopping sites; however, return rituals can be performed anytime during the following week, but usually no later than the day before New Year's Eve.

Although the conclusion of Christmas activities may vary somewhat, depending on whether and when Gift Return Day is observed by individuals, the celebration is certainly over by the first week of the new year, at which time the January fast begins. The symbolic end of the festival occurs slightly earlier, however, on a date fixed with exacting precision. The date is Christmas Eve and the event that marks the passing of the season occurs with little or no notice at all: Santa Claus disappears. He will not be seen again until Harbinger Weekend, the following year. What Santa means to Christmas will be taken up in chapter 12, but for now, some indication of the religious significance of the festival can be considered.

Christmas by the numbers

At this point, stating that the Christmas festival is the central religious event in postmodern culture would be quite redundant. As previously noted, it is at once the greatest celebration of the sacred truth of our culture and the paradigm for all other holy-day cycles. In this regard, the Christmas season has structural affinities with the mythico-ritual cycles of other holy days in the postmodern liturgical year. Where Christmas differs from all the others, of course, is in its enormous size, and when it comes to cosmological religious celebrations, size does matter: the bigger the better, the biggest the best. Christmas is by far the best, by this and any other measure one can use.

To put the Christmas celebration into its proper religious context, let me briefly revisit the criteria used earlier to classify holy days. First, in chapter 7, I proposed that postmodern holy days manifest contemporary versions of seven mythico-ritual elements that are characteristic of ancient cosmological religious celebrations — most typically, those of archaic New Year's celebrations. To these, in chapter 8, I added various commercial and economic indicators, using the rationale that increases in advertising indicated an amplification of myths and increases in retail commerce paralleled increases in ritual activity. This method of analysis resulted in the designation of a number of holidays as holy days and a further classification of these holy days in terms of their sacred significance.

This approach reveals Christmas as the holiest of all holy days and the month-long Christmas season as the greatest religious festival of postmodern culture — our High Holy Days. Others are similar — Valentine's Day, Easter, Back-to-School — but none come even close to being Christmas's equal. Only by scanning the sacred landscapes and calendars of other cosmological civilizations can possible analogies be found. Such a search suggests parallels between our Christmas spectacle and archaic agricultural festivals and New Year's celebrations; e.g., the Saturnalia of ancient Rome and the *akîtu* of Babylon. Christmas also has affinities with Hinduism's Kumbha Mela, which is still celebrated in India today. But Christmas surpasses them all, if not in sheer religious intensity, certainly in terms of its culturewide impact.

Perhaps the most fitting place to begin to gauge the religious significance of Christmas is with the U.S. Census Bureau's Trade Survey, comparing December's GAF sales figures with other months of the year. As noted at the beginning of this chapter, November's GAF sales are always the highest of the year until that time, usually ranging from 10 to 15 percent higher than the next highest month. Since the Christmas cycle begins in late November, Christmas spending accounts for some portion of this increase, and so the High Holy Days' impact is, to some extent, already being registered in those high November figures. The full impact becomes evident, however, when December's GAF figures are compared against November's.

As dramatic as November's sales are when compared to other months of the year, they pale beside those of December. In this, the Christmas month, GAF sales are routinely 40 to 50 percent higher than November, which itself is 10 to 15 percent higher than any previous month of the year; for example, in 1999 November GAF sales totaled nearly $74 billion (compared with about $64.5 billion for the next highest month [August]). By comparison, December GAF sales summed to $112 billion — a bit more than 14 percent of the total sales for the year.

Extending the comparison to other categories reveals equally dramatic increases in December. For example: December sales of all nondurable goods categories summed to $192 billion compared to November's (next highest) $153 billion, and December's total retail sales summed to $312 billion compared to November's $257 billion.[9] These sorts of dramatic dis-

---

9. See "Monthly Retail Trade Survey (1999 Sales)," U.S. Census Bureau, accessed online at *www.census.gov/mrts/www/data/html/sal99.html* (accessed 1/10/01).

parities occur annually, thus suggesting the enormous impact of Christmas on retail spending. Insofar as this spending is a measure of mythico-ritual activity, as argued in this text, the statistics offer a rather striking indication of the staggering religious significance of Christmas.

A further indication of the sacred magnitude of Christmas is found in the Bank of Tokyo weekly sales index. Using this index as a measure of ritual activity (as described in chapter 8) reveals increases during the Christmas season every year. This result is to be expected given that Christmas is a major religious event. The same sort of annual increase is seen in conjunction with Valentine's Day, Easter, and Back-to-School. For this reason, Valentine's Day and Easter are major holy days and Back-to-School is a religious festival. All are extremely sacred times, but where the heightened sacred significance of Christmas comes to light is in the comparison of its increases to those of the other major religious events in the liturgical year. In this context, then, we may remember that of the other three mythico-ritual cycles, Valentines and Easter are the most sacred, with ritual acquisition increases that are on average more than seven times (600 percent) higher than average weeks. By comparison, Christmas ritual (spending) increases are on average over four times (300 percent) higher than the average week, but it maintains this weekly average for five to six weeks, compared with only two weeks for Easter and one week for Valentine's — and it does this every year.[10]

While these statistics are indeed striking, they only begin to suggest the gigantic scope of the Christmas festival. Because of our culture's intense preoccupation with economic phenomena (and religious veneration of the economy, in terms of my thesis), a wealth of additional data indicates the sacred enormity of the Christmas festival. Among the other quantifiable measures of ritual activity that could be considered here, several are especially revealing: the top-ten shopping days of the year, department store sales figures during the Christmas season, Christmas sales figures in other venues, and Christmas greeting-card sales.

In addition to the GAF and Bank of Tokyo sales figures, the sacred significance of Christmas is reflected in another measure of ritual activity — the top-ten shopping days of the year. Annually, these ten days all occur during the Christmas festival. As previously noted, Pilgrimage Friday is always among this decalogue of dates, usually in the second half. Aside from Pilgrimage Friday, in the six years covered in a recent trade survey,[11]

---

10. See Appendices B and C.
11. See "Top Ten Holiday Shopping Days Yearly Daily Sales Comparison," International

in only one year did any other November date have a sales volume included among the top-ten dates, and that was a Saturday after Pilgrimage Friday. All other dates are days in December; the highest ranking dates in any year generally fall on days within a week of Christmas Day, with the Saturday immediately before the holiday usually being the highest of all. Curiously, and in contradiction to what appears to be a traditional holiday legend, Christmas Eve is not one of the "biggest shopping days" of the season. It is never in the top five, and in some years, it is not even among the top ten.

Since the mythico-ritual status of the Christmas cycle is consummated in rituals of acquisition, tremendous increases in consumer spending occur during the High Holy Days. These increases have already been cited, in a general sense, in the analysis of GAF figures for November and December. They can be further specified by considering retail sales at one of the primary religious centers of postmodern culture — department stores. As is to be expected, the percentage of increase in department store sales closely parallels GAF sales from November to December, usually in the range of 40 percent. The year 1998 offers a representative example. In that year, department store sales for December increased 45 percent over those of November, summing to $40.9 billion.[12] In its annual reports on the Christmas season, the Census Bureau routinely notes December's increases over November in various spending categories, often noting: "No other month-to-month increase came anywhere near that."[13] No other month compares with the Christmas month, which annually accounts for one-seventh of the yearly sales at department stores.

Department stores are, of course, not the only sites that experience enormous surges in consumer spending during the holy day festival. Nearly every other major retail venue reflects similar dilations. The one exception is the automotive sector, where December is typically one of the slowest months of the year. As the president of one advertising agency observed, when it comes to selling cars, "You can't compete with Santa Claus."[14]

Council of Shopping Centers (2000). Full citation in n. 5. Data in this paragraph from this source.

12. See "The Holiday Season," U.S. Census Bureau, Press Release (December 2, 1999), accessed online at *www.census.gov/Press-Release/www/1999/cb99ff16.html* (accessed 12/23/99). Data in this paragraph from this source and related "Holiday Season" press releases for other years.

13. For example, see ibid. and the same statement in the "Holiday Season" press release of December 17, 1998, accessed online at *www.census.gov/Press-Release/cb98ff15.html* (accessed 12/23/99).

14. Eric Gerard, president, BigGross.com, Largo, Florida. Interview with the author, July 7, 2001.

Since the competition begins in November, the Christmas contraction in automotive sales begins in that month, which in many years posts even lower sales figures than December.[15]

Aside from automotive shrines, most other religious locales record their highest ritual (sales) volume during the Christmas festival, evincing stunning increases over already high November figures. Some of the most dramatic increases occur at sites specializing in products imbued with considerable sacred potency. These include apparel and accessory stores, jewelry stores, and electronics stores. Equally large increases are found at variety stores, bookstores, and sporting goods stores/bicycle shops. A sense of the importance of these sites to holy-day pilgrims is indicated in the jump in sales they experience between November and December, as shown in the following table:

Store Type	1996 increase	1997 increase	1998 increase
Apparel and accessory	40%	44%	45%
Jewelry stores	144%	159%	172%
Electronics stores	44%	48%	49%
Variety stores	57%	41%	47%
Bookstores	76%	78%	87%
Sporting goods/bicycle shops	66%	72%	69%[16]

What makes these sizable increases all the more meaningful is that they are expansions above the already high sales figures for these stores in November. Moreover, as reported by the Census Bureau (in its 1996 holiday report): "The only other month-to-month rise for any of these retailers that came even close [in 1996 and presumably other years] was a 73 percent increase in book store sales from July to August."[17]

Taken together with department stores, these six venues appear to be the most important centers for holy-day worship. They are, however, not the only destinations for Christmas pilgrims. As noted by Leigh Eric Schmidt in his fine study of the commercialization of the holidays, *Consumer Rites,*

> Indeed, many department stores as well as smaller retailers count on Christmas for a quarter of their annual sales and, because of

---

15. For declines in auto sales during November and December, see any Census Bureau "Monthly Retail Trade Survey"; e.g., 1995, at *www.census.gov/mrts/www/data/html/sal95.html* (accessed 1/4/00). Over the ten years surveyed in this study, November had higher sales than December five of the ten years.

16. See "The Holiday Season," U.S. Census Bureau Press Releases for 1999, 1998, 1997. All accessed online using references given earlier.

17. "The Holiday Season," U.S. Census Bureau, Press Release (December 2, 1999), accessed online at *www.census.gov/Press-Release/fs97-13.html* (accessed 12/23/99).

higher margins in pricing, half of their annual profits. And some-times the percentages for Yuletide earnings run even higher — up to 70 percent of the year's profits. In all, according to one recent esti-mate, Christmas gift giving is worth some $37 billion to the nation's economy.[18]

In fact, as one scans over Census Bureau surveys from year to year, one finds December increases in nearly every major area of consumer spend-ing. As noted above, the only major exception is the automotive sector. Building supply stores, which do not typically function as sites of ritual acquisition, also have low sales during the Christmas season. Although weather may account for some shrinkage of sales in this area, it seems probable that the primary cause is Christmas spending in other areas, and like auto dealers, building supply retailers cannot compete with Santa either.

Aside from these two areas, the Christmas season brings increases in nearly every category of consumer spending.[19] Again, these are increases above November spending figures, which in most major retail categories are already higher than all other months. In the final analysis, then, Decem-ber sales in nearly every retail spending category are not just higher than those of November but the highest of the year — every year. Caught up in the sacred frenzy are such otherwise mundane locales as grocery stores and bakeries, drugstores and shoe stores, meat markets and fish sellers. In these areas, too, the Christmas season brings the highest levels of retail sales, transforming even them into sacred sites of ritual acquisition. Per-haps less surprising are the dramatic increases in liquor store, mail order, and Internet sales.[20]

---

18. Leigh Eric Schmidt, *Consumer Rites: The Buying and Selling of American Holidays* (Princeton, N.J.: Princeton University Press, 1995), 4. "For statistics on the Christmas market," Schmidt cites William Severini Kowinski, *The Malling of America* (New York: William Morrow, 1985), 78.

19. For supporting data, see any Census Bureau "Monthly Retail Trade Survey," such as those cited earlier in this chapter. December sales in categories reported in this paragraph are based on Trade Surveys from 1990 to 1999.

20. Statistics on mail order sales and liquor store sales are included in the Census Bureau trade surveys. Internet sales are not, and so holiday Internet sales are a bit more difficult to quan-tify. It appears, however, that they are considerable. According to Pamela Rucker, spokesperson for the National Retail Federation (NRF), estimates for 1999 Internet holiday sales were $3 bil-lion to $11 billion. Using NRF projections for Internet retail sales as a base, these figures suggest that holiday sales comprise a significant portion of total annual sales (projected to be $38.8 billion in 2000). In addition, 9 percent of holiday shoppers in 2000 reported that they would be "very likely" to use the Internet, up from 8 percent in 1999 and 4 percent in 1998. Notably, the 9 percent using the Internet is still less than those using conventional mail order catalogs (12 percent). See Rucker citation in Robert Goldfield, "Christmas 1999: Retailers Revel In Profit-Packed Internet Sales," *Portland Business Journal* (December 10, 1999), accessed online

Before leaving this section, some comment must be made on one of the oldest and most widely observed sacred obligations of the Christmas holy-day cycle — the ritual acquisition of holiday greeting cards. The origin of this ritual predates the postmodern period by more than three-quarters of a century, thus distinguishing it as one of the earliest precursors of the contemporary Christmas religious festival. As Penne L. Restad tells us in *Christmas in America,* a wonderful study of the history of Christmas in America, the cultural roots of the American Christmas card can be traced back to the commercial sector and the work of R. H. Pease and, later, Louis Prang.[21] Already a holiday custom in England and on the European continent, the Christmas card's Americanization came courtesy of Pease, who produced the first one in the early 1850s. In light of the subsequent emergence of postmodern culture and its paradigmatic holy day, Restad's description of Pease's first American Christmas card is illuminating:

> [U]nlike its English forerunner, the images on each of the card's four corners made no allusion to poverty, cold, or hunger. Instead, pictures of a "small, rather elf-type Santa Claus with fur-trimmed cap, sleigh and reindeer, a ball-room full of dancers, the building marked 'Temple of Fancy,' and an array of Christmas presents and Christmas dishes and drinks" suggested the bounty and joys of the season.... Where the English one wished the season's greetings, the American card added a self-promotion "Pease's Great Varety [*sic*] Store in the Temple of Fancy."[22]

What for Pease and other early card producers had been "merely ephemeral business,"[23] Prang transformed into an industry. Like the vast array of products designed for large-scale ritual acquisition that came on the scene with the Industrial Revolution in America, the key to Prang's invention of the Christmas card was mass production. Already the owner of two-thirds of all the steam presses in America, in 1875 he turned his

---

at *http://portland.bcentral.com/portland/stories/1999/12/13/story2.html* (accessed 2/5/01). For NRF projections, see "On-Line Retail Sales Projections (1999–2003)," reported in "Holiday Sales Data (1999)," accessed online at *www.nrf.com/hot/holiday/dec99/default.htm* (accessed 12/13/99). For "very likely" Internet shoppers and mail order shoppers, see Saad, "More Than Half of Americans Delayed Gift Shopping."

21. Penne L. Restad, *Christmas in America: A History* (New York: Oxford University Press, 1995), 119–20.

22. Ibid., 119. The description given by Restad is apparently from George Buday, *History of the Christmas Card* (no citation given), 277–78. She reports that a picture of what Ernest Dudley Chase "claims" is one of Pease's cards is in *Two Thousand Years of Seasons' Greetings: An Album of Holiday Cards and Their Precursors, Christmas 1951* (New York: Photogravure and Color, 1951), 13.

23. Ibid. Restad cites Buday's *History,* 37.

attention to Christmas cards. By the following year Prang's presses and workforce was geared up to produce over 5 million cards annually. In 1890 he withdrew from the market due to increasing competition from other firms that could produce the cards more cheaply.[24]

The process set in motion by Prang's presses led to the birth of the greeting-card industry in America. Today they are produced for more than twenty different holidays as well as transitional events (birthdays, anniversaries, etc.) and other occasions. As of 2000, Americans were purchasing over 7 billion cards annually, with sales summing to $7.5 billion.[25]

Half of all cards acquired are seasonal in nature, and of that number the top-selling cards are those for five holidays that have here been analyzed: Valentine's Day, Easter, Mother's Day, Father's Day, and, of course, Christmas. The ritual acquisition of greeting cards is thus rightly cited as an important part of the religious observance of these events. Far above all other holidays in card sales are Valentine's Day and Christmas, with the former accounting for 25 percent of all holiday cards sold and the latter (as in so many other categories of ritual acquisition) vastly exceeding all others, and accounting for 61 percent of total sales. Other holidays rank far behind these two, with Mother's Day at 4 percent, Easter 3 percent, and Father's Day 2.5 percent.

So, in addition to all the many other areas of retail (ritual) activity that dramatically increase during the High Holy Days, we can add one of the oldest and still most popular rituals: the acquisition of Christmas cards. Of course, most of us also send the cards, but prior to the sending they have to be acquired. The acquisition of more than 2 billion cards certainly accounts for a considerable amount of ritual activity: amounting to over $2.25 billion in retail sales.[26]

To repeat the point made earlier, during the Christmas festival every object of desire is available and every desire can be satisfied. We can now also observe that nearly every conceivable object may be transformed into an object of desire during this "most wonderful time of the year." From cards to camcorders, washers to watches, fur coats to Furbys, everything is available for ritual acquisition. In this one grand month of holy days, the entire cultural landscape seems transformed into a seamless mythic vista,

---

24. Ibid., 118, 122.

25. Greeting Card Association (GCA), "State of the Industry" (2001), accessed online at *www.greetingcard.org/gca/facts.htm* (accessed 5/15/01). Other information on card sales, from this source.

26. Figures here are estimates by the author derived from statistics in the GCA report. See ibid.

making ritual acquisitions both easy and frequent, and allowing dharmic obligations to be effortlessly fulfilled.

But the celebration of Christmas involves even more than the mythico-ritual cycle and our personal religious observances. We do not spend all our time at the shrines. There are other seasonal narratives and traditions besides those directly related to our dharmic obligations. While these elements are not explicitly religious, they serve to support and enhance the religious celebration — often quite directly. Thanksgiving, as presented earlier, is a good example of how such narratives and traditions function. Besides this notable feast day, a number of other seasonal narratives and observances deserve elucidation in the context of this study. Thus, to better understand the postmodern Christmas cycle and also to help introduce the subsequent study of Santa Claus, the next chapter examines several especially pertinent nonreligious (not directly related to the divine economy) seasonal narratives and traditions.

— E L E V E N —

Supporting Seasonal Narratives
and Traditions

Besides generating the most dynamic mythico-ritual cycle of the liturgical year, the Christmas festival also occasions the appearance of other cultural phenomena directly and indirectly related to the religious celebration. Broadly considered, these auxiliary components of the festival can be classified as seasonal narratives and seasonal traditions. Properly speaking, these are not genuine myths and rituals; yet because of the culturally engulfing quality of the celebration and its profoundly cosmological basis, separating these secondary narratives and observances from the general religious tableau is difficult. Nonetheless, they are not usually part of the formal mythico-ritual cycle, and although they may contribute to religious activity, they are best conceived of as supporting elements that complement and enhance the festival's more sacred aspects. Both begin as early as Harbinger Weekend and become increasingly evident by Pilgrimage Friday. Like the myths and rituals, they continue on throughout the High Holy Days, and then decline precipitously after Christmas.

It is not feasible to present an exhaustive analysis of these narratives and traditions or explore any in particular in detail here; other books on the traditional celebration of the season do an excellent job of that.[1] Rather, I offer a brief overview of their general character and some selected examples that appear to have a direct bearing on the more explicitly sacred aspects of the Christmas celebration.

Seasonal narratives

At precisely the same time as most people are making their first festival journeys on the Day After Thanksgiving (Pilgrimage Friday), an assort-

---

1. For example: Karal Ann Marling, *Merry Christmas! Celebrating America's Greatest Holiday* (Cambridge, Mass.: Harvard University Press, 2000); Stephen Nissenbaum, *The Battle for Christmas* (New York: Alfred A. Knopf, 1996); Penne L. Restad, *Christmas in America* (Oxford: Oxford University Press, 1995); and William B. Waits, *The Modern Christmas in America* (New York: New York University Press, 1993).

ment of holy-day narratives thunder into popular culture with a celerity that is as sudden as it is expected. As noted above, Santa is already ensconced in most shrine centers by Pilgrimage Friday, and just as he presides over the mythico-ritual spectacle that begins on this day, his appearance also signals the annual commencement of these seasonal narratives. Like the unending torrent of Christmas music playing on the radio (itself a type of seasonal narrative), these background stories continue for the duration of the festival. They can be divided into four categories: news coverage, personal communication, television specials, and films.

Among the first of these narratives are news reports about shopping on the Day After Thanksgiving. Usually described as "the official beginning of the holiday shopping season," from time to time it is mistakenly identified as "the biggest shopping day of the year." Typically, this narrative involves television reporters doing on-camera interviews with shoppers, inquiring about the purchases they have made, the availability of various products (especially highly desired "toys of the season"), prices, how much they are planning to spend, and so on. Merchants are also interviewed fairly frequently, with questions being asked about how successful their sales have been and their expectations for the rest of the Christmas season. Newspapers on the Saturday following Pilgrimage Friday contain their own versions of this distinctive narrative, featuring photographs of shopping scenes, usually including an aerial photograph of a mall parking lot filled to overflowing with cars.

News reports dealing specifically with the Christmas festival continue throughout the month of December, with print and broadcast media sources reporting regularly on various aspects of the season. These reports include retail-sales forecasts for the Christmas season offered by industry and government officials, daily reminders of how many days are left until Christmas, and special coverage related to the most desired children's toys. Almost daily, reports from the U.S. Postal Service are aired offering official decrees about the deadline for mailing Christmas cards and packages if one desires to have them arrive before Christmas. The coverage of these more sacred features of the season are complemented by stories in papers and on TV about overly decorated houses, "toys-for-tots" collection drives, and persons wrestling with tragedies during "the most wonderful time of the year."

At the individual level, Christmas spawns a host of personal narratives, generally communicated through interpersonal dialogues. As the festival approaches, persons begin talking with others about various aspects of the season. These dialogues are as varied as they are ubiquitous. Gifts are a general subject of conversations, especially within families. We talk about what the children want, what spouses and significant others desire, what we should buy for the home. We talk to friends about when we are going to the shrines and the products we are seeking. If we have already begun our pilgrimage rounds, we talk about the journey, what we discovered, which shrines were the best, which are less desirable. If we are mailing cards, we ask others if they are too, and if so, whether they have finished the task. An interesting subspecies of the card-sending narrative is the complaint narrative about people who send cards too early or too late. Another complaint narrative deals with persons who send annual chronicles of their activities over the previous year.

Families talk about seasonal obligations: when the house will be decorated and whether to buy a "real tree" or use the artificial one in the attic, who might be stopping by for a visit, and when visits to others should be made. If relatives are visiting for the festival, holy-day conversations may deal with accommodations and features of the relationship. The travel plans of the immediate family are also discussed, even if they are only driving tours to "look at the lights." In families with children, there are usually long discussions of how the celebration will be choreographed for them.

Children, of course, have narratives all their own. These usually concern products they will receive on the holy day itself, but they may also deal with family activities. These they share with their parents, friends, and especially the festival's presiding deity. One source reports that an average of 7,720 children visit Santa per mall in America.[2] The seasonal narratives of workers focus on whether or not to buy gifts for coworkers, the Christmas bonus check, whether colleagues are "going out of town for the holiday," and the employee Christmas party. If the party is part of the narrative, there are invariably reminiscences about those of previous years. The personal narrative is most grandly communicated on the TV talk show, when mythic figures talk with talk-show hosts about what they are doing and planning to do during the season.

As important as they are to the postmodern milieu, talk shows comprise only a tiny portion of televised Christmas narratives. The real core of the TV Christmas celebration is found in what is commonly referred to as

---

2. "ICSC Holiday Fun Facts 2000," International Council of Shopping Centers (2000), accessed online at *http://holiday.icsc.org/funfacts00.html* (accessed 3/15/01). Average number of visits based on a sample survey of "120 regional and superregional malls...only a small portion of the 1,300–1,500 enclosed regional and superregional malls in the U.S." — statement to the author, July 21, 2001, from Mike Rubridy, assistant librarian/writer, Albert Sussman Library (ICSC).

"holiday programming." This programming takes three general forms: the inclusion of holiday themes in sitcoms and sitdrams; Christmas movies or "made for TV movies"; and children's (cartoon) specials. As argued by Robert J. Thompson in his study of "Christmas Television Specials," this programming often elides the otherwise strict line of separation between religion and network programming.[3] The way Christian religious themes are smuggled into these programs, according to Thompson, is through the music, which typically includes Christmas religious hymns. Still, as he later notes: "Aside from hymn lyrics, practically none of the network Christmas programming is overly Christian" (48).

What is overly (and overtly) religious, however, at least as argued in this book, are the commercials broadcast during the holidays. As at any other time of the year, these tertiary myths bring us into closest proximity to the meta-myth, making it vital to our existence and revealing how we are to properly perform our dharma to consume. To a certain extent, it is incidental that they happen to do so in the context of Frasier's plans for a big Christmas party and Walker, Texas Ranger, going after bad guys who are wearing Santa attire, or movies like *Olive, the Other Reindeer* and *Santa and Pete*. Then, again, as Thompson notes:

> [C]ommercials thrive in the healthy environment that Christmas television provides. The shows are designed to appeal to many people, and the moods they set are those that will open wallets as well as hearts. The old complaint that "Christmas is too commercial" is a tired cliché, and the claim that "television is commercial" is redundant, but the identity between these two statements is significant. In contemporary American society, the style of Christmas and the style of television are both dictated by consumption. (52)

To Thompson's cogent observations, I would only add that these two styles are synergistically commingled; both, after all, are sacred styles.

Another type of holiday narrative, and one of the most popular, is the feature film. Annually, theater attendance soars during the Christmas festival, and Hollywood studios time projected blockbuster films for release during the holy-day season. In this regard, the 2000 Christmas hit *Dr. Seuss' How the Grinch Stole Christmas* is just the most recent in a long line of Christmas movies dating back to the 1942 classic *Holiday Inn*. The popularity of going to movies accounts for theater attendance

---

3. See Robert J. Thompson, "Consecrating Consumer Culture," in *Religion and Popular Culture in America* (Berkeley: University of California Press, 2000), 44–55, esp. 45–47.

being included among seasonal traditions and perhaps a component part in Christmas pilgrimages. Even so, the classic Christmas films persist in popular culture, supplying yet another of the season's narrative elements.

Like Santa himself, these films annually return, showing up on television screens around the country, and now the world. If one misses their broadcast over commercial airwaves, they can always be rented at video stores, or purchased outright from video or DVD merchants. For many, Christmas would not be quite the same if they did not see *Miracle on 34th Street,* the 1947 masterpiece. For others, it might mean watching Jimmy Stewart in the role of George Bailey in the 1946 classic *It's a Wonderful Life,* which is reportedly "America's favorite Christmas-movie-on-TV."[4] Then, again, for some, required viewing might be one of the several movie versions of Dickens's *A Christmas Carol,* including perhaps the postmodern version, *Scrooged,* starring Bill Murray. Finally, for younger persons, films like *The Nightmare before Christmas, Jack Frost,* or *Home Alone* may be the representative Christmas movie-narrative. Perhaps in future years, Jim Carrey's Grinch in the 2000 Christmas blockbuster will function like Stewart's George Bailey does today.

Seasonal traditions

Traditional Christmas activities are as wide ranging and diverse as are the seasonal narratives. While many of these traditions have their origin in the modern period (and some are actually quite ancient), most have been integrated into the tableau of the postmodern festival. Some of the more notable ones are briefly surveyed here: home decorating, nonreligious journeys, and gift exchanges.

Decorating the home

Among the most widely observed of all Christmas traditions is decorating the home. From the most modest of human habitations to the grand mansions of the cultural elite, the Christmas festival is an occasion for adorning one's residence with festive embellishments. As noted above, shrines begin decorating around November 1; personal dwellings soon follow, with decorations becoming widespread soon after Pilgrimage Friday.

As with the shrines, the centerpiece of most domestic environments during the holidays is a richly decorated evergreen tree — usually a fir or pine,

---

4. As noted by Marling, *Merry Christmas!*, 355. Marling's book and Restad's *Christmas in America* both contain good treatments of Christmas movies and their role in shaping contemporary concepts of the holiday.

five to seven feet tall. The custom of decorating trees extends at least as far back as ancient Rome and its solstice celebration, the Saturnalia festival. It has been part of the American holiday since the 1850s, when holiday trees were first sold commercially. Today the Christmas tree tradition accounts for the annual acquisition of over 30 million "live trees," and millions of artificial trees (most imported from the People's Republic of China).[5] The "live trees" have a limited life expectancy, and the artificial trees last about six years.

Trees are the largest and often the most costly of Christmas decorations, but they are only one of a vast collection of commodities acquired to decorate homes for the season. Among the most popular products are: glass and plastic ornaments, strings of small (indoor/outdoor) electrical lights, synthetic icicles, garlands, Santa mugs (some in the shape of his head), natural and artificial wreaths, electric candles and candelabra, electrically illuminated blow-mold lawn figures (e.g., Santas and snowpersons), holiday pillows and throws, "elf" caps, and artificial snow in aerosol cans. Flowers are another popular decoration — so popular, in fact, that (as in so many other areas) Christmas flower sales are the highest of any holiday season, surpassing even Mother's Day.[6] Needless to say, the acquisition of this wide array of Christmas-specific items is seamlessly integrated with the festival's other rituals of acquisition.

Of course, not everyone has to acquire this holiday paraphernalia. Many persons save and reuse their decorations year after year. This unique tradition is one of the few instances where the saving of used products is culturally condoned. It also gives rise to yet another tradition, colloquially known as "getting out the Christmas stuff." For those who observe this tradition, the event signals the annual commencement of the domestic Christmas celebration. For children (although not necessarily their parents), this is a glad and happy time, as well-known holiday decorations begin to appear, coming out of the garage, down from the attic, or in from the shed. Once all the material is acquired or resurrected from storage, the process of arranging it begins. Again, if children are involved, this is a time of merry excitement. The tree is placed in a prominent location in the house and decorating begins; strings of lights are affixed to houses or

---

5. Tree sales figures from University of Illinois Extension, "Christmas Trees and More," accessed online at *www.urbanext.uiuc.edu/treefacts.html* (3/10/01). PRC as nation of origin from U.S. Census Bureau, "Facts for Features," accessed online at *www.census.gov/Press-Release/www/1999/cb99ff16.html* (12/23/99).

6. Society of American Florists, "Holiday Statistics," accessed online at *www.aboutflowers.com/pressb3a.html* (5/20/01). Poinsettias are the most popular, accounting for 87 percent of all holiday sales.

in interior windows; blow-mold figures are implanted on lawns; wreaths are hung on doors; plastic mistletoe is hung in prominent locations; moms and dads or other pairs of significant others share Christmas hugs and kisses; refreshments are served in Santa mugs; and stockings are hung by chimneys with care.

As suggested above, the tradition of home decorating is often conjoined with the festival's sacred pilgrimages. This is certainly the case when new decorations are acquired, but it also occurs when holiday accessories need to be replaced (usually at the "last minute"), especially bulbs for all the many light fixtures that come into use at this time of the year. Besides these pilgrimages, for many persons, the High Holy Days are a traditional period of travel. These journeys can be of long or short duration and cover great or very modest distances. Of the various types of journeys made during the Christmas festival, several are of special note: "going home for the holidays," the trip to the post office, the tour of the town, and going to church.

Holiday trips

As with so many other areas of cultural activity, Christmas is also the leading holiday in terms of out-of-town travel. In the 2000 season, for example, over 60 million Americans (more than 20 percent of the population) went on trips of over one hundred miles. The next highest holiday, by comparison, was Thanksgiving, with slightly less than 40 million persons going on extended journeys.[7] For a sizable majority of Christmas travelers, the destination is the home of a relative or friend, thus giving a tangible indication of the motivating power generated by the nostalgic notion of "going home for the holidays." Not surprisingly, airports are especially busy from Thanksgiving through New Year's Eve. Highways, which are already busy enough with holy-day pilgrims, are busier still, with over 40 million persons making their long-distance Christmas journeys in personal vehicles. Judging from the number of persons finding holiday lodging with family and friends (nearly 35 million), perhaps Christmas in the post-

---

7. Data from a 2000 survey by Travel Industry Association as reported by AAA South. In terms of number of travelers, the five major holidays are: (1) Christmas-New Year's (60 million travelers); (2) Thanksgiving (38.9 million); (3) Fourth of July (36.6 million); (4) Memorial Day (34.2 million); (5) Labor Day (33.7 million). For Christmas report, see AAA Auto Club South, "Travel News and Holiday Travel Projections," 12/13/00, accessed online at *www.aaasouth.com/acsnews/10109.asp* (accessed 4/20/01). Additional information in the paragraph from this source and Dawn Landrum, Project Coordinator, AAA Auto Club South.

modern world offers something of a corrective to Thomas Wolfe's oft-cited adage that "you can't go home again."

Once at their destinations, relatives and friends join in the Christmas celebration with their hosts. They may help decorate the domicile if they arrive early enough, wrap gifts, assist with the preparation of holiday foods, watch old movies with their hosts, tell stories of past Christmases, and share in the Christmas Day gift exchange. Needless to say, they will also join their hosts on pilgrimages to sacred sites throughout the season. A particularly farcical vision of these communal holiday celebrations is offered in another of the growing number of postmodern Christmas films: *National Lampoon's Christmas Vacation.* Although the film is a ludicrous parody, the experiences of the Griswold family are simply greatly exaggerated versions of several widely practiced holiday traditions — including the visit of relatives.

With or without out-of-town visitors, people make several other traditional nonreligious journeys during the holiday season. The first of these is the trip to the post office. Typically, this trip occurs sometime after Pilgrimage Friday and before the middle of December. The purpose of this journey is the mailing of Christmas packages and cards. After all, those 2 billion cards that have been purchased need to be mailed before the deadline "to arrive before Christmas." Thus, like the various religious sites, post office branches become extremely busy during the High Holy Days; they too join in the sacred spirit of the season, offering special holiday stamps for ritual acquisition. These stamps come in two varieties, one with a distinctly Christian religious image, the other with a generic holiday image. Appropriately, the Post Office refers to the Christian stamps as "traditional" and the generic stamps as "contemporary." The first U.S. Christmas stamps were issued in 1962 and have had press runs as high as 3.3 billion (1995). Notably, for the first time since the Post Office began issuing Christmas stamps, the 2000 edition was postponed, due to high inventories of unsold 1999 stamps.[8]

Driving tours

Another time-honored journey during the season is the nighttime driving tour of holiday decorations. In many cities, municipal governments or

---

8. Information on sales and history from CBS News (December 7, 2000), "No New Christmas Stamps This Year," and Dorothy S. Gelatt, *Maine Antique Digest,* "Post Office Prints 3.3 Billion Ephemera Christmas Stamps." Sources accessed online. For CBS News, see *www.wwjtv.com/now/story/0,1597,179782-232,00.shtml* (accessed 4/20/01); for Gelatt, see *www.maineantiquedigest.com/articles/vic1095.htm* (accessed 4/20/01).

private-sector groups sponsor large-scale outdoor Christmas displays in parks or along major thoroughfares. Popular items used in these displays are cards and trees (e.g., Christmas card parks and Christmas tree boulevards). These are major community events, with businesses, civic groups, schools, and religious communities joining in the project by sponsoring individual cards or trees. Other themes for these outdoor displays may include Santa workshops, gigantic Christmas trees (like the National Tree in Washington, D.C.), and Christmas wonderlands. The wonderlands are particularly striking, usually being composed of enormous versions of various seasonal objects such as reindeer, wrapped presents, menorahs, single candles, groups of carolers, Santas, and (again) Christmas cards and trees.

Because these displays are designed for observation during nighttime driving tours, two features are of critical importance: size and lighting. The objects in the displays must be quite large and all must be brightly lit, either with a profusion of individual lights (as with the cards and trees) or with spotlights (as with objects in a wonderland). Although many of these displays are quite kitschy, this characteristic is part of their holiday charm and actually may contribute to their significance as a necessary part of the Christmas experience.

Besides the monumental displays, countless smaller sites may also be visited in the course of driving tours, including highly decorated commercial buildings in downtown urban centers, but more typically, houses in residential areas. The most popular of these locations are the well-known "Christmas houses" of individual communities. Like the Griswold's house in *National Lampoon's Christmas Vacation,* for these houses the owners have gone quite a bit "over the top" in their observance of the season, sparing no expense in transforming their residences into public spectacles. There are so many lights on these houses that adjacent residential streets look dim by comparison; their lawns are covered with a cornucopia of seasonal blow-mold objects; every available bit of residential foliage is festooned with even more lights; Christmas music may be blasting out of loudspeakers; reindeer-pulled sleighs can be spotted on their roofs; and as often as not, actual Santas are seen waving to gasping motorists stopping to gawk. Invariably, Christmas houses receive significant media coverage, thus heightening their appeal to those taking driving tours; but even without media coverage, their prominence attracts a steady stream of cars — much to the delight of their creators and doubtless to the chagrin of many neighbors, whose own houses are often devoid of all holiday displays.

Almost forgotten beside the more ostentatious sites are the nativity displays that appear during the Christmas festival. As witnesses to the endurance of the Christian context of the holiday, nativity scenes may cause controversy if placed on government property. As a result, they are most commonly found on the lawns of houses (often as blow-mold figures) or in front of churches. Some churches may even have "living" nativity scenes, in which farm animals and members of local congregations assume the roles of characters described in the Christian myth. As Christmas approaches, various parts of the myth may be acted out in these tableaux vivants. Melding together the nativity stories found in the gospels of Matthew and Luke, these performances may include such episodes as the annunciation, Mary and Joseph traveling to Bethlehem, and Joseph's dream. Almost certainly, they will include the angel's message to the shepherds, their arrival along with the magi, and the presentation of the gifts. The actual birth will not be dramatized nor Herod's massacre of the infants. For many Christians, these nativity scenes and dramatic reenactments of the "first Christmas" are important holiday destinations and play an analogous role to Christmas houses and wonderlands for others.

Church services

Of course, for devout Christians, what goes on inside the church reveals the true significance of the season. Not surprisingly, church attendance surges as Christmas nears, making December attendance annually higher than all other months, with attendance on December Sundays and Christmas Eve eclipsed only by Easter Sunday, when an estimated 100 million people attend church.[9] For Protestants, Christmas community events may include church parties and gift exchanges, Sunday school Christmas pageants, visits to shut-ins, Christmas concerts and sing-alongs, collections for the poor (especially toys for disadvantaged children), readings of the nativity myth from the Gospels, and sermons on the Christian meaning of the holiday.

Catholics may engage in all of these activities as well, but for them, one grand tradition stands as the high point of the season: the midnight mass celebrated as Christmas Eve gives way to Christmas Day. Many Protestant communities also have Christmas Eve services that attract large numbers of members and visitors, but in terms of attendance and ceremonial intensity, they do not compare with the Catholic midnight mass. The mass is often a family event and may be prefaced by gatherings with relatives and friends,

---

9. Easter attendance figures from George Gallup Jr., "Easter Draws Americans Back to Church," The Gallup Organization (April 2, 1999), accessed online at *www.gallup.com/poll/ releases/pr990402b.asp* (4/20/01). December as peak level of church attendance from Leo Rosten, *Religions of America* (New York: Simon and Schuster, 1975), 433.

communal meals, driving tours, and the exchange of gifts. As a special treat, Catholics (and certainly interested members of other traditions) may enjoy a tape-delayed broadcast from the Vatican of the pope's Christmas Eve mass. Of course, in some instances, watching this TV show means missing the actual midnight mass at the local parish.

Exchanging gifts

Of all the various seasonal customs, by far the most widely observed is the practice of exchanging gifts, with a recent Gallup poll reporting that 98 percent of the American population planned to give Christmas gifts of some kind in the year 2000.[10] The first of these gifts begin to appear at the same time as the initial ritual acquisitions on Pilgrimage Friday. Among the earliest presentations are to business colleagues, coworkers, and subordinates. As with Christmas cards, we often feel obliged to reply in kind, sharing a gift of our own with the person who has given one to us. As the season rolls along, the giving proliferates; we receive gifts in the mail from out-of-town relatives and friends; neighbors stop by with gifts; and clients drop them off for us at our place of business. Civic groups, elementary school classes, and religious communities may have Christmas parties with "blind" giving, where everyone brings a gift (in some established price range), which is then numbered and given to the person who draws the number. These same groups may acquire gifts for the less fortunate (typically children), sometimes en masse and other times on the basis of individual needs and expectations. They appear under Christmas trees, gradually accumulating through the season. In some instances, they are hidden in secret locations in domiciles, or kept at places of business until the time is right to bring them forth. Such a time may be when extended families gather for communal gift exchanges during the season or on Christmas Eve in domestic settings. From Pilgrimage Friday onward, the giving is incessant, until the grand climax of Christmas morning, when the best, brightest, and most desired gifts are exchanged.

Like tree decorating and card sending, the roots of Christmas gift giving can be traced to the mid-nineteenth century. Prior to then, New Year's had been the customary time to exchange gifts. In fact, in the early nineteenth century, New Year's gift giving was so popular that the holiday occasioned major advertising campaigns by merchants in America's emerging urban

---

10. Based on 2 percent reporting that they would not give any gifts at all in 2000. See Lydia Saad, "More Than Half of Americans Delayed Gift Shopping until Final Pre-Christmas Days," The Gallup Organization (November 23, 1999), accessed online at *www.gallup.com/poll/releases/pr991223.asp* (accessed 4/20/01).

centers. As with the Christmas card and Christmas tree, Americans were emulating their European cousins in their New Year's giving practices. In the 1820s and 1830s things began to change, however, as Christmas and New Year's began to be commingled in advertisements and the popular imagination.[11]

Soon enough, and certainly by mid-century, Christmas had eclipsed its erstwhile gift-giving holiday rival. Leigh Eric Schmidt links the rise of Christmas as the primary gift-giving holiday with the emergence of Santa Claus as a cultural icon. In this regard, he cites Clement Moore's famous 1823 poem, "A Visit from St. Nicholas" (better known as "The Night before Christmas") as a "fateful" event in the development of the American Christmas celebration. As Schmidt observes: "[Moore's] poem suggested the ultimate course of holiday exchanges in the United States as Christmas gradually emerged as the preeminent focus for both gift giving and merchandising" (123) — with Santa Claus serving as the "patron saint" of "the modern Christmas bazaar" (130). In today's postmodern America, under the watchful gaze of the sacred Santa, the average American spends nearly eight hundred dollars a year on Christmas gifts.[12] The question remains, however, is Santa a saint or is he a god? The following chapter takes up this question.

---

11. See Schmidt, *Consumer Rites,* 123.

12. Specifically $797 in 2000. See Mark Gillespie, "Average American Will Spend $797 on Gifts This Holiday Season," The Gallup Organization (November 27, 2000), accessed online at *www.gallup.com/poll/releases/pr001127c.asp* (accessed 4/20/01). Gillespie reports that this was a slight decline from 1999, when the average expenditures summed to $857.

— TWELVE —

The Sacred Santa

In the context of the foregoing discussion, the religious function of Santa Claus can now be explored in greater detail. As noted previously, the High Holy Days over which he presides are foreshadowed by a profusion of myths that appear during Harbinger Weekend. Not incidentally, his arrival at most shrine centers also occurs on this weekend before Thanksgiving. The festival season begins formally on the Day After Thanksgiving, an event here referred to as Pilgrimage Friday. On that day, religious sites of all varieties are crowded with pilgrims beginning their odyssey into sacred time and space. Although a frenzy of acquisition occurs on Pilgrimage Friday and the weekend following, many pilgrims are only surveying the sacred terrain at this time. The vast majority will return and many will return numerous times in the weeks ahead. Others who may have missed the Friday celebration will join them as the season progresses.

After the initial celebratory eruption on Pilgrimage Friday, the ritual process slows somewhat, only to gradually pick up momentum with each succeeding week of December, again becoming frenzied during the week before Christmas Day.[1] Even after the holy day itself passes, the celebration continues until Gift Return Day, which is often observed on the day after Christmas and usually no later than the day before New Year's Eve. The symbolic conclusion of the festival is marked by the disappearance of Santa, which occurs late on Christmas Eve.

Throughout the entire month-long celebration seasonal narratives and holiday traditions support and enhance the distinctly religious activities. Although not explicitly part of the mythico-ritual cycle, these auxiliary stories and customs allow participants to enter even more fully into the spirit of the festival. We closely follow news reports about desired objects of holiday acquisition, watch old Christmas movies on TV and new ones at theaters, put up Christmas decorations, and listen to tales of others who have visited shrines and temples. Above all else, we dedicate ourselves

---

1. As noted previously. See chapter 10, n. 8.

anew to our dharmic obligations, seeking ritual rediscovery of the ultimate truth disclosed in the grand high myth that overarches and defines our culture.

As discussed in part 1, this meta-myth is the sacred narrative of success and affluence, gained through a proper relationship with the economy, and revealed in the ever-expanding material prosperity of society and through the ever-increasing acquisition and consumption of products by individuals. Cosmological in essence and postmodern in form, the reality of this meta-myth is religiously embodied most fully in those mythico-ritual eruptions that occur in conjunction with the holy days and religious festivals of the postmodern liturgical year. The greatest of these events, of course, is Christmas, the prototype for all postmodern holy days and religious festivals. If Christmas is the representative religious event of postmodern cosmological culture, as argued here, then Santa Claus is the apotheosis of the sacred. In short, and in answer to the question posed at the close of the last chapter, Santa is a god. How he came to this high status and what he means to Christmas and culture as a whole can now be addressed.

The genealogy of a postmodern god

Santa did not become a god overnight. Like other cosmological deities, he has a long and rather intricate cultural genealogy. Detailed studies of his lineage can be found in a number of texts,[2] and although the entire genealogy is quite fascinating, my focus here is only on those features that seem most clearly related to his advent as a sacred being.

Although two recent texts make an interesting case for tracing Santa's lineage back to primal shamans and "Wild Men,"[3] more traditional

---

2. For example, see William S. Walsh, *The Story of Santa Klaus* (New York: Moffat, Yard and Co., 1909; reprint, Detroit: Gale, 1970); Penne L. Restad, "Home for Christmas: Family, Religion, and Santa Claus" (chapter 4) and "The American Santa Claus" (chapter 10), in *Christmas in America* (Oxford: Oxford University Press, 1995), 42–56 and 143–54; William B. Waits, *The Modern Christmas in America* (New York: New York University Press, 1993), 120–33; Leigh Eric Schmidt, *Consumer Rites: The Buying and Selling of American Holidays* (Princeton, N.J.: Princeton University Press, 1995), 122–48; Karal Ann Marling, "Santa Claus Is Comin' to Town" (chapter 6), in *Merry Christmas! Celebrating America's Greatest Holiday* (Cambridge, Mass.: Harvard University Press, 2000), 197–242; Stephen Nissenbaum, "Revisiting 'A Visit from St. Nicholas' " (chapter 2), in *The Battle for Christmas* (New York: Alfred A. Knopf, 1996), 49–89; and Russell Belk, "Materialism and the American Christmas," in *Unwrapping Christmas*, ed. Daniel Miller (Oxford: Clarendon Press, 1993), 75–104. For proposals of a pre-Christian ancestry for Santa, see Tony van Renterghem's *When Santa Was a Shaman* (St. Paul, Minn.: Llewellyn Publications, 1995), and Phyllis Siefker, *Santa Claus, Last of the Wild Men* (Jefferson, N.C.: McFarland and Co., 1997).

3. See van Renterghem, *When Santa Was a Shaman,* for Shamans, and Siefker, *Santa Claus, Last of the Wild Men,* for Wild Men. Siefker capitalizes Wild Men.

genealogies trace his origins to a fourth-century Catholic saint, Nicholas (280–342), the bishop of Myra (an ancient city in Asia Minor). St. Nicholas is, in fact, one of the few remaining alternate names for the contemporary god; and with good reason, at least etymologically, since Santa Claus is an Americanized version of *Sinterklass,* an alteration of the saint's name in Dutch — *Sint Nikolaas.*

The contemporary Santa Claus is in many ways quite different from his ancient forebear, but certain mythic affinities nonetheless exist. Among these are stories about Nicholas' generosity, his beneficence to children and families, and his supernatural abilities — all characteristics of Santa as well. Perhaps the most direct mythic congruence between Nicholas of Myra and Santa Claus is the account of the saint supplying the dowries for three daughters of a poor man who could not afford them himself. In some versions of the legend, Nicholas dropped purses filled with gold in the open window of the family's house, where they fell into socks the daughters were airing out under the window. Today, elaborate ceremonial stockings are hung in houses in advance of Santa's visit. The traditional location is above fireplaces, perhaps since this is where northern Europeans hung their socks to dry during the winter. Perhaps, too, this is why the northern European descendants of St. Nicholas, like Sinterklass, entered homes through the chimney.

Iconography of the two religious figures reveals several other notable similarities: Both are in the upper reaches of middle age, have ample white beards and flowing white hair, wear red ceremonial vestments and a distinctive chapeaux (Nicholas a bishop's miter and Santa a nineteenth-century sleeping cap, fringed with white fur). Their most notable distinctions are body shapes and mythic accessories. While both figures are depicted as imposing figures, Nicholas is the taller of the two and often appears gaunt, perhaps due to his reputation for asceticism. Santa is overweight, even bloated. Like Nicholas, his appearance is in perfect keeping with his reputation; in his case, a reputation for indulgence — e.g., the milk-and-cookie myth. Where Nicholas has accouterments appropriate to his office (miter, cope, and staff), Santa, likewise, has accessories suited to his role (a sleigh, flying reindeer, and large bag bulging with an assortment of goods).

To this day, the original St. Nicholas is venerated as the patron of young unmarried women, seafarers, pawnbrokers, and children, to name a few; and the date of his death (December 6) is recognized as a feast day in the Catholic Church. He is also the patron saint of Greece, Sicily, Lorraine, and (together with Andrew the Apostle) Russia. His contemporary American descendant, as noted by Schmidt, is the patron saint of the modern Christmas bazaar, and, as argued here, the incarnate god of the postmodern Christmas religious festival. Before the deification of Santa, however, St. Nicholas had to come to America. To get here, he first had to travel north and west from Asia Minor and take up residence in Germany and Holland. He also had to change.

In the guise of Sinterklass, St. Nicholas apparently made his way to North America, perhaps arriving in New Amsterdam with the first Dutch settlers, although the first published reports of his presence in New York do not appear until the late eighteenth century.[4] By this time, Nicholas, as Sinterklass, had become a gift bearer for Dutch children, usually visiting homes on December 5, the eve of his feast day. He also had acquired a diminutive black servant or slave, *Zwarte Piet,* Americanized to Black Peter or Black Pete. Zwarte Piet's lineage is not as clear as Sinterklass's, although Tony van Renterghem's assertion that he was intended to look like a Spanish Moor seems plausible, as does his and Phyllis Siefker's linkage of him with various nature deities and primal Wild Men of northern Europe.[5] He may also have been related to St. Peter, another northern European holiday visitor. Finally, as discussed below, he appears to have a particularly close kinship with a number of German Christmas figures — especially Knecht Ruprecht.

Whatever his origins may have been, Zwarte Piet's role in the Dutch Christmas celebration is well established. He was to assist Sinterklass in the distribution of presents and treats but also to reprimand children who were not well behaved. In fact, to this day, Black Peter still accompanies Sinterklass on his holiday rounds in The Netherlands, although in recent years Peter's race seems to have become a source of controversy.[6] As the prototype for Santa's legions of contemporary helpers, in traditional enactments of the holiday visit, Zwarte Piet carried Sinterklass's bag of gifts while brandishing a fagot of sticks. The symbolism was obvious, good children got the gifts, bad children got a lashing from Peter. In earlier times, good children were identified by their familiarity with religious teachings and biblical stories. In some versions of the narrative, bad children were put in Zwarte Piet's bag and taken back to Spain, where the saint and his

---

4. Restad, *Christmas in America,* 45.

5. See van Renterghem, *When Santa Was a Shaman,* 91; and Siefker, *Santa Claus, Last of the Wild Men,* 10, 11, and esp. 76. van Renterghem also links Black Pete with ancient cosmological deities, such as Herne, Pan, and Eckhart (Wodan's slave) (e.g., 91, 112).

6. See *Washington Post,* "The Dutch Reconsider 'Black Peter'," as carried in *St. Petersburg Times,* 25A, December 3, 1999.

servant lived. Thankfully, Sinterklass, the ever benevolent saint, made sure that even children who had misbehaved were not punished (at least not too severely). Nonetheless, Black Peter remained a fearsome figure whose very being gave the holiday an eerie edge.

Soon after Sinterklass and Zwarte Piet arrived in North America, other northern European descendants of St. Nicholas immigrated as well. From England came Father Christmas, from France Père Noël, and from Germany Christkindlein, as well as perhaps the most terrifying figure associated with Christmas, Belsnickle. Belsnickle appears to be a German variation of Black Pete, only wilder and much more menacing. The name is derived from *Pelz-nickle* (the German for "Nicholas in Fur"). Like Black Pete, and quite unlike St. Nicholas, Belsnickle often is depicted as dark skinned, fierce in appearance, and threatening in manner. He was likely descended from, or closely related to, an equally ominous figure who might once have been Nicholas's German slave, Knecht Ruprecht ("Rupert the Servant").[7] In fact, Belsnickle and Ruprecht appear virtually indistinguishable, with Ruprecht most likely being the prototype for Belsnickle as well as other German Christmas visitors.

Unlike Pete, however, Belsnickle and Ruprecht were autonomous figures. There was no generous and tolerant St. Nicholas to temper the punishments they might administer. There also were no bags of gifts. Instead they might have pastries or fruit to give to good children, but they always had a stick or whip to punish those who misbehaved. Moreover, unlike the diminutive Black Pete, the Germans were normal-sized adult males, often larger than others in group depictions, thus suggesting that not only would their punishments be severe, they would also probably be inescapable.

Dressed in outlandish vestments, Belsnickle or Ruprecht appeared on the night before Christmas or New Year's Eve. For many of the German homes they visited, there would be no subsequent visit by St. Nicholas or any of his northern European progeny. I suspect that this was largely due to the influence of Martin Luther, who opposed the tradition of giving gifts in celebration of the feast of St. Nicholas.

By doing away with the generous saint in the sixteenth century, Luther appears to have given freedom to his punitive helpers. Prior to this time, we might presume, these erstwhile servants had been kept in check by Nicholas, in much the same way he had restrained the violent inclinations

---

7. For Belsnickle as "most certainly based on" Ruprecht, see Nissenbaum, *The Battle for Christmas*, 99. For Pelz-nickle as related to Ruprecht, as his Bavarian counterpart, see van Renterghem, *When Santa Was a Shaman*, 103.

of Black Pete. With Nicholas gone, however, the servants had no master to control them. This is most obviously the case with Knecht Ruprecht, whose name identifies him as a servant, but curiously, he is never depicted with his master and seems to serve no one at all. To the degree that Belsnickle is patterned on Ruprecht, as images and legends about him indicate, he too functions as a fully autonomous punitive figure. Released from control by their kindly old master, Ruprecht and Belsnickle (as well as other German Christmas figures) were free to do as they wished, and this was a scary proposition for children in the German communities where they wandered. In early America, the largest concentration of these communities was in eastern Pennsylvania.

Stephen Nissenbaum tells us that in later years, Pennsylvanian Belsnickles became a concern to adults, as bands of rowdy youth dressed in the character's garb began making rounds of houses and businesses demanding holiday food.[8] As Phyllis Siefker observes, this tradition coalesced with the English Christmas customs of wassailing and mumming, resulting in Philadelphia's Mummers Parade.[9]

While Luther may have been indirectly responsible for the emergence of the Belsnickle/Ruprecht tradition, he was definitely the source of yet another German precursor of the postmodern Santa. This was *Christkindel,* who in later years would be Americanized and greatly domesticated as Kris Kringle. Although Luther did not approve of saints, and especially gift-bearing saints, he did condone and, in fact, promoted giving gifts in commemoration of Jesus' birth. To Luther we trace the origins of Christkindel — literally, the Christ Child.

Interestingly, by the time this figure immigrated, he had become virtually indistinguishable from Belsnickle and Ruprecht. As described in a letter of 1821, excerpted by Penne Restad, Christkindel arrived on Christmas Eve: "Dressed 'in ludicrous masquerade,' and carrying 'a rod [in] one hand & nuts & cakes in his pockets,' this 'Christkinkle,' awarded the rod to the 'idle & ignorant' and gave favors to the deserving only after they had repeated 'a tremendous round of [D]utch prayers.'"[10] This Christkindel was a far cry from the baby Jesus suggested by the figure's name, yet it was in perfect keeping with the German tradition of the punitive Christmas visitor. So powerful was the spell of this tradition that it seems to have transformed all mythic German holiday visitors into the same character — Knecht Ruprecht, Rupert the (erstwhile) Servant.

---

8. Nissenbaum, *The Battle for Christmas,* 101–2.
9. Siefker, *Santa Claus, Last of the Wild Men,* 22–23.
10. Restad, *Christmas in America,* 50.

The extent to which this tradition has controlled the depiction of figures in the German holiday mythology is revealed in a story shared with me by an individual who grew up in a German-American home in the 1950s. In this person's household, the Christmas visitor was not one of the more well-known German figures discussed here, but rather, none other than *Schwarze Peter,* the German incarnation of the Dutch *Zwarte Piet* — Black Pete, St. Nicholas's helper. Yet this *Schwarze Peter* was no Black Pete, he was just another Ruprecht: scary, large, black, punishing, and *sans* Santa. He was the stuff of sleepless nights, and the original nightmare before Christmas that played in the theater of the mind, long before Tim Burton's postmodern film by this title made it to movie screens in 1993.

The most immediate cultural descendant of this wide assortment of nightmarish German Christmas figures was Kris Kringle, who came on the scene in Philadelphia in 1842. His relationship to his namesake, Christkindel, however, extended no further than his name. Instead of the Ruprecht-like being described in the 1821 letter excerpted earlier, Kris Kringle had no menacing features whatsoever. In fact, he closely resembled the American Santa Claus, who had appeared two decades before.

The 1821 date of the letter describing Christkindel is significant, for in that year the world of Belsnickles and Christkindels, Sinterklasses and Black Petes would begin to contract. The event that signaled the beginning of the end of the European descendants and associates of St. Nicholas was the publication of a Christmas poem in *The Children's Friend.* What made the poem so important was its articulation of a distinctly American version of the December gift-bearer. Three elements were especially critical: the identification of the gift-bringer as "Santeclaus," his arrival on Christmas Eve, and his use of a reindeer-pulled flying sleigh as a means of transportation.[11]

Notably, in this first truly American Santa Claus myth, the hero is not St. Nicholas, Christkindel, Father Christmas, or any of the other options then available; he does not bring his gifts on the eve of St. Nicholas' Day or New Year's, but rather Christmas Eve; and finally, his flying sleigh was an entirely new innovation. With *The Children's Friend* the American Santa Claus was born, and two years later (in 1823) he would burst upon the cultural scene with the publication of another children's poem, Clement Moore's famous "A Visit from St. Nicholas" (better known as "The Night before Christmas").

---

11. For text of the poem, see Nissenbaum, *The Battle for Christmas,* 73. For further analysis, see Nissenbaum, *The Battle for Christmas,* 72–76; Schmidt, *Consumer Rites,* 123; and Restad, *Christmas in America,* 54 and 144.

Although Moore's poem anachronistically refers to "St. Nicholas" as the Christmas gift-bearer, his depiction was to become synonymous with Santa Claus and the basis of all other narratives about the postmodern god. In Moore's account we find nearly all the primary features of the Santa Claus story as it is known today. Building on *The Children's Friend*, Moore's Santa arrives on Christmas Eve in a reindeer-pulled flying sleigh. In addition, it is the night of a full moon and a fresh snowfall — perhaps the first White Christmas. There are eight reindeer, and each is named — Dasher, Dancer, Blizten, etc. Rudolph came to the team later, initially as a Montgomery Ward holiday promotion in 1939.[12] The magical flying properties of the reindeer and the sleigh are dramatically stressed as is Santa's supernatural ability to enter houses with a bundle of toys through a chimney.

Moore's description of Santa's appearance also supplied most of his now classic physical features. His eyes "twinkle," his nose and cheeks are flushed, his beard is white, his face is broad, he has a "round belly" in addition to being "chubby and plump," he is jovial, and, of course, he leaves gifts in stockings. Only two features in Moore's poem are not included in our contemporary conceptions of Santa. One is the pipe, which apparently has been discarded because of health risks associated with smoking; the other much more significant feature is Santa's size. Where Moore depicted him as diminutive (his sleigh is "miniature," his reindeer are "tiny," his round belly is "little," as is his mouth; he is, in fact, an "elf"), the postmodern Santa is a large man, imposing in breadth if not in height, and corpulent if not clinically obese.

The increase in Santa's size and girth is attributable to the work of Thomas Nast. Just as Moore's poem became the basis for the foundational mythic narrative of Santa Claus, Nast's vivid artistic renderings became the template for all subsequent iconography. In the words of Restad, as a result of Nast's work, we "have something of an official portrait of Santa."[13] In this regard, the well-known work of Haddon Sundblom serves as both a fine example of the orthodox tradition in Santa iconography and also its capacity to adapt to contemporary culture. Where Nast's Santa smokes a pipe, Sundblom's Santa drinks a Coca-Cola; Nast's Santa is loaded down with toys to give to good children, while Sundblom's Santa is benevolently watching as good children place newly acquired beverages in a refrigerator.

Nast's most famous depiction of Santa first appeared in *Harper's*

---

12. Schmidt, *Consumer Rites*, 147.
13. Restad, *Christmas in America*, 146.

Weekly on January 1, 1881. Long before this time, however, the artist had devoted himself to depicting the mythology of Santa Claus. In 1863 he prepared the illustrations for an edition of Moore's poem, and shortly after the Civil War he published a series of Santa scenes in a book titled *Santa Claus and His Works* (1866). Here we find Santa "at home, in his ice palace, in his workshop, and looking through his telescope for 'Good Children' " (146).

Already the Santa in these images has begun to take on the appearance of the classic 1881 icon. He is the size of a normal adult, corpulent, dressed in red, jolly, longhaired, full bearded, and apparently in the upper reaches of middle age (perhaps in his early sixties). For thirty years, Nast devoted himself to the creation of "an entire world for Santa" (146). By the time he was finished, not only had he stabilized the iconography of Santa Claus, he had also further embellished the myth itself. Adding to Moore's original account, Nast (and others) gave Santa "ledgers to record children's conduct," "a home at the North Pole," elves to assist him, a wife, and "by some accounts, children" (147). With these final touches, the distinctly American Santa Claus came into full view. Together, Moore and Nast, along with many others who followed their lead, had fashioned an entirely new holiday visitor. More supernatural than his predecessors, the American Santa Claus was also kinder, gentler, more prosperous, and capable of generating far more material goods than any of his European rivals. He was, thus, the perfect embodiment for the emerging American Christmas festival.

Apotheosis

Leigh Eric Schmidt tells us that the first physical appearance of Santa Claus most likely occurred in 1845.[14] This apparently isolated incarnation, at the Ladies' Favorite Store in Philadelphia, was a portent of the future. By the 1880s and 1890s, he was regularly incarnating at such well-known sacred temples as Macy's and Wanamaker's (140). Looking like Nast's images and conforming to the established mythology, in his first incarnations Santa was confined behind display windows where he presided over Christmas scenes. In spite of the fact that he was physically separated from would-be worshipers by plate glass windows, with these annual manifestations at sacred temples, the apotheosis of Santa had begun.

---

14. Schmidt, *Consumer Rites,* 135. He is the source for the location of the first appearance, given in the next sentence.

In the same decades, Santa began to make regular physical contact with worshipers — mostly children, it appears. Schmidt reports a specially arranged location for such contacts at a sacred temple — J. Lichtenstein and Sons, a store in New York City (140). The store's announcement of the 1888 incarnation "cordially invited children 'to come and see a real live Santa Claus,' who was in residence at the store day and evening in his very own grotto" (140). And come they did, so much so that by the turn of the century "these sorts of grottoes, thrones, cottages, and workshops for Santa Claus amounted to a store tradition, a Christmas rite all their own" (140). In fact, not long after the first physical contact, "providing children with this encounter with Santa Claus was something the stores [temples] took with an almost religious seriousness" (141). I would modify Schmidt's description only slightly, suggesting a deletion of "an almost."

By the turn of the century, avatars of the American Santa were a routine occurrence at most temples in major urban centers. He was also firmly established in the consciousness of the nation. In myth or in actual theophany, Santa was the personification of Christmas for an American culture just coming of age. A mature yet quite robust figure, he typified the expansive energies of the nation's emerging middle class. He embodied affluence and abundance, assurance and achievement. He was a factory owner, the employer of industrious elves, whose mass production of goods surpassed all the assembly lines in America's rapidly industrializing society. He smoked, he enjoyed the good life, and he may have imbibed, judging from his ruddy, often flushed complexion.

Obviously this American Santa worked hard, but he never seemed to be working. He also never was tired. Perhaps he was an idealized version of the capitalist master of industry. If so, he also was a kind and generous sort of master; generous beyond belief, *miraculously* generous — more generous, in fact, than the incredibly generous economy that was making millionaires of many and consumers of everybody. And like the economy, we came to believe in him, and we encouraged our children to do so as well. To the degree that he was still thought of as St. Nicholas, he was our kind of saint; but St. Nicholas was fading fast in the land of mass production and mass consumption. For many and soon enough most, Santa would be our kind of god.

By the early twentieth century, Santa, the god, had come into his own. With the same vigor exhibited by Zeus and the Olympians in dispatching Cronus and the Titans, Santa and his family dispatched all would-be rivals to his cultural throne. By mid-century his cultural dominance was complete. Most of the older Christmas entities had disappeared, and those who remained were weak and ineffectual shadows of their former selves.

As America entered the postmodern era, one had to look long and hard to find a Sinterklass or Père Noël. St. Nicholas still remained, but essentially as another name for Santa Claus. All the various alterations of Nicholas had certainly vanished by this time: St. Aclaus, St. Iclaus, Sancte Klass, and several others.[15] Long gone by this time was Black Pete, along with his nefarious German cousin Belsnickle. And Knecht Ruprecht, if he had ever even arrived, had long since been sent back to Bavaria. Pete became a Caucasian and he multiplied, becoming Santa's legion of elves, none of whom would ever lift a switch to reprimand a child. He swallowed Father Christmas whole and changed Kris Kringle into a surrogate of himself. He took a wife, unlike his less virile predecessors. Whether or not he had children is a matter of debate. But, then, he had no real need for children of his own; he had all the children of the industrial world. He even had the Christ child, or so it seemed to many.

Santa today

As Santa became increasingly sacred, he also became the target of attacks by Christians who complained that Christmas had lost its meaning. This lament began as early as the late nineteenth century and has continued on ever since. Seen as the embodiment of "commercialism" and the secularization of the holidays, Santa seems to make an easy target. Yet, aside from a small number of true believers (certainly some subgroup of the 2 percent of the population that does not give Christmas gifts), the criticism has failed to have any adverse effect on the High Holy Days or on Santa Claus.

The polemics miss the mark because they misunderstand the target. Santa is not the embodiment of secular "commercialism." He is the embodiment of our culture's greatest religious myth: the myth of success and affluence, right engagement with the economy, and the acquisition and consumption of images and objects. Santa is the incarnation of this myth. For this very reason he functions as a profoundly religious figure in our postmodern cosmological culture. This reason may also account for his seeming immunity to criticism from a religion still following the cultural logic of a previous time. In short, Santa is not secular. He is sacred. To attack him as secular is to attack his shadow.

---

15. Restad gives these and other names. See Restad, *Christmas in America*, 51.

Just as he is not secular, so too he is not pagan, at least insofar as paganism is linked to natural powers and energies. Santa is quite divorced from nature and the earth. The city is his home and the grand high temples of the city are his shrines. He is the product of the industrial age, but he has become the god of a postindustrial culture. He was born when industrialization was in full and furious emergence, but he really began his reign when the spirit of consumption desacralized the engines of production in the West. All vestiges of a meaningful paganism were gone by then.

Santa's sacred character is revealed in many ways, perhaps most clearly in his profound unreality. As the perfect deity for our culture, he is certainly godlike in his powers. More importantly, he is a god who allows himself to be demythologized. Curiously, of all the Santa myths, the most pervasive is the one that explains why he is not real. This is a coming-of-age narrative in our culture. Nearly all of us at one time believed in the actual, physical reality of Santa; yet most of us were also disabused of this belief at a relatively early age.

As a personal aside to this discussion, in the course of researching and writing this book, I have been quite surprised by the number of persons who have expressed some concern or genuine disbelief that I should be proposing that Santa is an actual deity. It appears that it is of some importance to many that his "unreality" be maintained. In this regard, the question of whether or not Santa is an actual deity is left to the judgment of readers. Suffice it to say, he seems to satisfy most of the criteria for cosmological deities; he especially meets the criteria of a deity in a postmodern/late capitalist cosmological culture, the most important of which is the willingness to be dismissed, radically denied, and demythologized, and yet remain totally unaffected by any of this. Although often accepted without reservation by children, once a child reaches a certain age Santa ceases to be real; curiously, though, he never fails to return. Santa always comes back, every Christmas season, every year, right on time.

For many, his presence is first noticed on Pilgrimage Friday, but he has usually arrived a little before then, typically on Harbinger Weekend — the weekend before the Christmas festival begins. He needs to prepare. Over the course of the festival, these High Holy Days of postmodern culture, he will be extremely busy. During this time he is always close at hand, and throughout the season we usually find him nearby — if not as a living avatar, then on greeting cards, in the tertiary myths of newspapers and TV, in sitcoms and sitdramas, in old movies, as blow-mold figures on the lawns of neighbors, and as peel-off appliqués on our children's homework assignments or on their faces. He is everywhere. Inevitably, he appears as jolly as ever, white-bearded but vigorous, bespectacled yet all-seeing, as distant as our youth and as close as our desires. As the personification of the sacred spirit of acquisition and the reigning deity of the Christmas festival, he is at once the literal embodiment of the meta-myth of our culture and the symbolic representation of the sacred ideal of success and affluence.

Once upon a time, when the world was young to us, we told him our desires. Perhaps we visited him in a shrine center, maybe not as elaborate or luxurious as the shimmering temples of today, but a sacred place nonetheless. Sitting on his lap, we whispered to him of things that we wished for and of products filling our dreams. He always listened attentively. If we did not or could not find the great man himself, we wrote letters to him, listing our longings and indexing our wants. Today we encourage our own children to do so as well. Then as now, these longings and wants center on material products, items to be acquired through ritual performances at sacred sites. And, lo and behold, we meet with him at just such a site. This is his home, after all, and for a short time every Christmas it is our home as well. As it was in our own beginning as sacred consumers, so it is now and ever will be at Christmas time — for children of all ages, as the adage goes.

Santa reminds us of this — that we are all consumers after all. If he does not do so consciously, then he does so subconsciously; if not seriously, then playfully; if not literally, then symbolically and metaphorically. In point of fact, we do not have to take him seriously at all. Then again, we cannot ignore him, even if we would like to. Trying to have our children ignore him is even more difficult, more difficult perhaps to shield them from Santa than to shield them from Christ — should we desire to shield them from either or both.

Far more profoundly than Jesus, the annual rebirth of Santa is seen, felt, and celebrated in the season of their overlapping advents. Santa, not Jesus, signals the beginning of the Christmas holy-day cycle, arriving with the season and announcing the formal commencement of its mythico-ritual cycle. After Harbinger Weekend his presence becomes increasingly prominent. By Pilgrimage Friday, he is ubiquitous. He shows up on television specials and in holiday films, at football games and holiday basketball tournaments. He is seen with the president. We find him wherever we turn: in songs on the radio and songs our children sing, on greeting cards, at churches and hospitals, riding in parades, ringing bells for the poor and ringing up sales for Wal-Mart and Sears. Above all, we find him sitting in palatial splendor at the sacred center of every shopping mall in the postmodern world. Like the great seasonal gods of antiquity, he has made his annual return; with this theophany, the High Holy Days begin. Every year, we are there to greet him, even as he is there to greet us.

Santa and the religious nature of culture

As stated in the introduction, *The Sacred Santa* offers a reinterpretation of the long-standing secularization thesis that interprets postmodern culture as a battleground between secular and religious values. I have argued that the struggle is actually between two distinct and distinctly different religious systems and have further contended that some rather clear indications are that the traditional religion of America and the West, Christianity, has been eclipsed by a contemporary version of cosmological religiosity.

The validity of this thesis awaits further study and evaluation, and in a very real sense, the passage of time. Short of any conclusive confirmation, however, the value of this thesis, as I see it, is in the twofold question that it poses: first, about the extent to which Christianity still functions as a viable religion in postmodern culture, and second, about the extent to which our seemingly secular culture may actually be profoundly religious in character.

In light of this two-part question, I am certain that the thesis of this book will be found to be quite challenging to persons with a strong commitment to Christianity. Some will simply reject it out of hand. Others may offer reasoned rebuttals, contesting my premises, questioning the structure of the argument, citing omissions, disputing the conclusion. Still others may find *The Sacred Santa* of religious value as a resource for cultural critiques, a call to intensified evangelism, a reason for greater piety at Christmas time.

Such responses are legitimate and entirely to be expected. Christianity is, after all, the affirmed religion of the majority of Americans, and Christmas is the second most important holy day in Christianity. Because *The Sacred Santa* raises questions about the integrity of Christian belief and the religious significance of Christmas, it would be surprising if the book did not engender these types of reactions from the faithful.

Aside from the out-of-hand rejections, I believe the various reactions that Christians may have to this book are a sign of Christianity's vitality, and to the degree that the book prompts responses among the faithful, I will count it a success. This comment should not be interpreted, however, to be an endorsement of any particular response or of Christianity per se. My aim is not to move Christians to action or even to suggest that the eclipse of Christianity by postmodern cosmological religion is undesirable.

I leave the judgment of the matter up to people of faith, and not just Christians, but persons of all religious traditions. The call, after all, is theirs to make. In the end, I am fairly confident that this will happen, for religious persons, and especially Christians, are very good at making calls in matters such as these. For believers, then, the question is not perhaps so much one of *making* a call as *heeding* one already made to them.

•

Santa is a profound and compelling figure, whether or not we believe he is real. His ontic status actually raises some important and quite helpful epistemological questions for students of postmodern popular culture and for students of religion as well. Among these is the question of just what it takes for a deity to exist — in the postmodern world or any other. As noted previously, the answer is left up to readers. But in closing, let me offer the following reflection on just how and why it might be that the Sacred Santa does exist.

Like all powerful (and some not so powerful) cosmological deities, Santa commands our attention. He is a shape-changing god, one who can be in numerous places at the same time. He is also omniscient. As we all know, he sees you when you're sleeping and knows when you're awake. He brings both rewards and sometimes punishments (although rarely the latter today) in a way that seems much like playful interactions with humankind. In this regard, he is like Zeus or Vishnu. He can multiply material objects, fold space in his travels, and inspire the assistance of animals and humans. His flying reindeer are like the vehicles of any major South Asian god, perhaps most of all like the mouse ridden by the great Hindu god of prosperity and success, Ganesh. Santa, in fact, resembles Ganesh in many ways. But, then, Santa resembles many gods.

Yes, he has a high degree of actuality for children, but in spite of the seeming denial of his reality by adults, he nonetheless continues to function as the representative figure of the central religious event of our culture. It is striking to observe how willingly parents allow their children to believe in Santa, then how suddenly they disabuse them of the belief after they reach a certain age. Yet all of us remain comfortable with the myriad symbols of Santa as well as the legion of shamanlike humans who represent him during the sacred season.

We take our children to his throne in the sacred precincts of our culture, encourage them to tell his shamanistic agent (or what we presume is his shamanistic agent — how do we know after all?) what they desire. We dutifully encourage them to sit on the lap of the great being, something we would never allow them to do with an unknown male of Santa's seeming age. Trust underlies all of this. We take pictures of the event to share with our own parents or simply to treasure. Professional photographs cost extra, but we can pay by credit card. The visit is a meaningful event.

Back at home, we tell our children to be on their best behavior because Santa is omniscient, which they already know from the songs about him on the radio. Like contemporary Black Peters, we may threaten them with warnings that they had best be good because Santa is either watching them or somehow keeping an inventory of their deeds. On the eve of the fateful visitation we tell them that offerings of food and beverage should be left for him. Later we tell them that it is he (not we) who has satisfied their desires (although later, if the ruse is discovered, we tell them that we are in fact his agents).

Finally, when they are older, we tell them that it is all just a fiction, or at best, that Santa is something like "the spirit of giving," the "spirit of the season" — or best of all, "the spirit of Christmas." Usually this clarification and correction occurs around the same time that children begin asking serious questions about ultimate reality and things like death, the afterlife, and various transcendental narratives of divinity. Yes, Virginia, there is a Santa, we just do not know what to make of him.

Indeed we do not. In point of fact, we are not making him; he is making us, and what he is making us is participants in a month-long adventure in the throes of sacred space and time. He is ubiquitous in this season, yet he remains entirely unknown in our purposeful denial of his existence. From youth to old age he inspires us to join in the spirit of the season and participate in the process of acquisition-consumption-disposal, yet he cannot be actual, for no beings of this type exist in either our seemingly secularized world or our increasingly anachronistic transcendental universe. He is a god in a culture that denies gods; and so he is entirely appropriate, domesticated enough to dwell in our midst yet strange enough to threaten if need be. Adults, I have noticed, tend to keep at a distance from Santa. Yet what would Christmas be like if he failed to appear?

He embodies the democratic ideal in its late capitalist guise; he knows no distinctions, save economic ones. Rich and poor all enjoy his largesse, but to the rich he brings high-end items, and to the less well-off he brings goods from the lower end of the production cycle. He routinely appears in the December issues of *Playboy* and *Penthouse,* which annually outsell all other issues of the magazines.[16] He visits the White House. He receives tons of mail.

His image appears on greeting cards and soda displays, in the windows of stores and on public grounds where other religious images are not allowed. Fully secularized (if that word has any meaning in all of this), the Sacred Santa is profoundly religious as well. He lives in both worlds and shows us how they are really one. Ever jolly and generous, he inspires Christians to write critiques and deliver polemical sermons, thus letting them engage in their own religion, while nevertheless overshadowing their celebration of the birth of their God. He may or may not be real, but he certainly is coming to town.

---

16. Belk, "Materialism and the American Christmas," 83.

— A P P E N D I X   A —

Citation and Description of Sources Used to Analyze Consumer Spending

Two source documents were used in the book for the analysis of consumer spending:

1. The Bank of Tokyo-Mitsubishi (New York) and UBS Warburg Weekly Chain Store Index[1]

2. The United States Census Bureau Monthly Retail Trade Survey

For the period of my study (1990–99), the weekly index was produced by the Bank of Tokyo-Mitsubishi (New York) in affiliation with Schroder Wertheim. In the text, this source is cited as "The Bank of Tokyo-Mitsubishi (New York) and Schroder Wertheim Weekly Chain Store Sales Index" and abbreviated "BTM/SW." Data contained in the BTM/SW index is now included in the Bank of Tokyo-Mitsubishi (New York) and UBS Warburg Weekly Chain Store Index, which has superseded BTM/SW.

The weekly index was begun in 1989 and based on "comparable store sales," meaning stores that have been open for at least one year.[2] The "week" in the index is Sunday through Saturday. Near the midpoint of my survey period (August 1996), the BTM/SW index was based on the sales patterns at "about 12,645 stores" of major retail chains, such as Wal-Mart, Kmart, Target, JC Penney, Sears, and others.[3]

In the words of Michael Niemira, vice president and senior economist, the Bank of Tokyo-Mitsubishi (New York), "point changes in the sales index are like point changes in a stock price index," so that "it is correct

---

1. UBS is a corporate name. It is derived from the abbreviation for Union Bank of Switzerland. As communicated by Michael P. Niemira, vice president and senior economist, the Bank of Tokyo-Mitsubishi (New York). E-mail 3/1/02. I am most appreciative for Mr. Niemira's willingness to share the Bank's data and to assist my research assistant in interpreting the data.

2. E-mail, 3/8/02, from Mr. Niemira. For "comparable store" definition, see "Chain Store Sales Snapshot" (New York: Bank of Tokyo-Mitsubishi, Ltd., 1996), 3.

3. "Chain Store Sales Snapshot," 1. Specification of chains supplied by Niemira, E-mail, 3/1/02.

to say that a 1 percent rise in the index represents a 1 percent rise in dollar sales — 'comp-store' — for the industry."[4] In other words, fluctuations in sales at these stores are indicated by changes in the index's numerical value from week to week. Thus, weeks in which there are increases in the numerical value of the index indicate a net increase in sales for the week at the stores in the index, declines in the index indicate a decline in sales.

As noted in the text and explained more fully in Appendix B, I used fluctuations in retail spending reported in the BTM/SW index as measures of ritual activity. Because the index offers weekly reports, it allowed for the correlation of fluctuations in sales relative to specific holiday periods; and because it is based on a representative sample of major chain stores it was suggestive of the sort of "large-scale" ritual activity that I specify as a criteria for designating postmodern holy days. Further, although there is not an exact correlation between the BTM/SW index and the U.S. government's comprehensive survey of overall monthly consumer spending, the relationship between the BTM/SW's weekly report and the government's GAF category is significant enough to allow the index to serve as a fairly accurate guide to total spending in this critical area of consumer commerce.[5] Appendix C contains a summary of the percentage of change in the BTM/SW index in connection with specific holidays over the ten years of my survey. It also contains a bar chart representing the average change during these holidays as compared with the average overall weekly change for the period. For more information on this index, go to the Bank of Tokyo-Mitsubishi homepage (*www.btmny.com/*).

The second source document that I used was the United States Census Bureau's "Monthly Retail Trade Survey" (MRTS). The MRTS reports total retail sales in a vast array of consumer spending categories — from building materials to alcoholic beverages. As of January 2000, the survey was based on data received from "about 13,300 retail business."[6] On the basis of this data, the Census Bureau extrapolates the total national sales figures in the various categories of consumer spending monitored in the MRTS. The MRTS is used by government agencies such as the Bureau of Labor Statistics to "develop consumer price indexes and productivity

---

4. Niemira, E-mail, 3/8/02.
5. The Bank of Tokyo-Mitsubishi reports that although the index is "first and foremost a monitor of the retail chain store industry . . . as a bonus [it] also mirrors the trends of GAF store sales and non-auto sales." See "Chain Store Sales Snapshot," 3. "GAF stores" are stores that sell general merchandise, apparel, furnishings, and "miscellaneous shopping" items. See n. 8, below.
6. U.S. Census Bureau, "Monthly Retail Trade Survey: Overview," 1 (accessed online, 1/4/00, at *www.census.gov/mrts/www/overview.html*).

measurements," the Bureau of Economic Analysis to "calculate Gross Domestic Product," and the Bureau of Economic Advisers to "analyze current economic activity."[7]

Of particular interest to my study was the GAF (general merchandise, apparel, and furnishings)[8] category of the MRTS since this category correlates closely with the BTM/SW index, and GAF comprises "those retail formats where the bulk of consumer goods shopping occurs."[9] From time to time, I used other categories (such as vehicular and grocery store sales). A chart of MRTS reports on GAF sales for the period of my study (1990–99) is found in Appendix C. For more information on this index, go to U.S. Census Bureau "Monthly Retail Trade Survey: Overview" (*www.census.gov/mrts/www/overview.html*). For a sample annual report, go to "Monthly Retail Trade Survey: 1999 Retail Sales" (*www.census.gov/mrts/www/data/html/sal99.html*). For other years, simply substitute the last two numbers in the year between "sal" and ".html" in the Web site address.

---

7. Ibid., 2.

8. Also included in the survey are "Miscellaneous Shopping Goods Stores." U.S. Census Bureau, "Monthly Retail Trade Survey: Explanatory Materials," 9 (accessed online, 1/4/00, at *www.census.gov/mrts/www/explanat.html*).

9. See report of National Retail Federation, "Holiday Data" (accessed online, 12/13/99, at *www.nrf.com/hot/holiday/dec99/default.htm*).

Methodology for Discerning the Holiness of Holidays

The primary document used for my analysis of ritual consumption during the holidays was the BTM/SW index.[1] For purposes of my analysis, the week-to-week data supplied by the index was of primary importance because it (1) indicated specific weeks in which sales increases occurred relative to a previous week and (2) allowed for tracking of sales during specific weeks across a number of years. These two features served as the foundation for my analysis of ritual activity and the basis for the methodology I used to designate other holy days besides Christmas.

The development and application of this methodology can now be outlined. My interest was not in long-term economic analysis or really any traditional type of formal economic analysis at all. I was not concerned with annual trends, long- or short-term; whether spending was higher in one year than in another; or if the overall index was lower or higher in the same week of one year than it was in the same week of some other year. I was interested only in weekly fluctuations and annually repeating patterns of weekly increases in retail (ritual) spending.

Using reports for a ten-year period (1990 through 1999), two considerations guided my use of weekly fluctuations in retail spending to designate holy days. First, and most obviously, I used it to isolate weeks in which there were increases in retail spending compared to the previous week. Such weeks would meet the minimum criteria of a holy day as a time of increased ritual activity. As indicated by Appendix C, weeks when there was neither increase nor decrease were counted as increase weeks for purposes of analysis and classification. This was done in order to account for the fact that the BTM/SW index uses only "comparable-store" sales and thus does not include increases from new store sales.[2] Second, in order to

---

1. See Appendix A for description of this index.

2. As reported by BTM, the index includes only "same store" (stores opened for more than one year) sales, whose sales "generally grow more slowly than new stores." For example, in the

specify certain days or periods as distinctive holy days, I used the index to isolate those weeks that revealed sales increases on a consistent annual basis — i.e., in at least 70 percent (seven or more) of the years in the sample period.

On the basis of these two criteria, a select number of weeks and sequences of weeks emerged as especially apt candidates for designation as holy days. To fine-tune my study and test the hypothesis that these "provisional" holy days were related to the holidays of American culture, I compared the weeks and sequences of weeks that had annual increases in the BTM/SW index to (1) the calendrical date of a holiday and (2) the beginning of advertising related to the holiday in a given year.[3]

The day of the week on which a holiday occurs largely determined how they were evaluated relative to advertising and BTM/SW weekly (Sunday-Saturday) sales data. On this basis, I classified the holidays in three categories: Those that occur on Sundays, those that occur on Mondays, and those tied to specific dates that can occur on various days of the week. Thanksgiving does not fit any of the categories because it always occurs on a Thursday; and due to patterns in Christmas advertising and spending, I included it in the Christmas cycle. As discussed in the text, a number of the holidays included in my analysis do not satisfy all holy-day criteria.[4] They are, however, notable for various reasons. These include increased advertising but no significant increase in sales, increased sales but no significant increase in advertising, high sales in areas outside the GAF category, and notable increases or declines during a specific period in the ten-year study. I used the term "feast day" (and "memorial day" for the King Day holiday) to classify these non-holy-day holidays.

Because the BTM/SW recording week ends on Saturdays, in order to measure the impact of holidays on consumer spending I compared the BTM/SW index from two or three Saturdays prior to a given holiday with the Saturday just before or just after the holiday. This allowed me to cap-

---

five-year period between 1990 and 1995, new store sales accounted for increases of between 6 percent and 7.5 percent annually. See "Chain Store Sales Snapshot" (New York: Bank of Tokyo-Mitsubishi, Ltd., 1996). There is thus an overall increase in sales that is not reported in the index. On the basis of this unreported general increase, for purposes of this study, I classified weeks with 0 percent increase as increase weeks.

3. My analysis of advertising was based on a two-year study of TV commercials and advertisement supplements in Sunday papers. The years of my study were 1998 and 1999. Three Florida newspapers were used in my research: the *St. Petersburg Times,* the *Tampa Tribune,* and the *Orlando Sentinel.* From time to time, I also consulted newspapers from other regions of the country, including Denver, Chicago, and San Francisco.

4. See also Appendix C for data on spending increases and declines during all holidays analyzed in the text.

ture the increase (or decrease) in sales in the week(s) leading up or through the holiday — i.e., the period when holiday advertising and holiday spending are at their peak. As described below, the choice of Saturdays for comparison was contingent on specific characteristics of each holiday.

The two major exceptions to this general method were Back-to-School and Christmas. I extended the duration of these two holidays largely because of two considerations: (1) the extended length and expanded volume of advertising associated with the holidays and (2) the significant increase in shopping activity I observed at stores during these periods. Back-to-School was measured using GAF data from MRTS and comparing GAF figures for August with those of July — the one exception to my use of BTM/SW. For the sake of continuity, a Back-to-School column is included in Summary A, with sales fluctuations during the period based on a comparison of BTM/SW figures for the first Saturday in August with the second Saturday in September. The affect of Christmas was measured by comparing the Saturday before Thanksgiving to the Saturday after Christmas.

All Sunday holidays, with the exception of Easter, were measured by comparing index figures from two Saturdays prior with the Saturday just before the holiday. This method captured sales increases (or decreases) for the week before the holiday. Because of the high level of holiday-specific and spring-related advertising well in advance of Easter, I extended the Easter holiday period to two weeks, comparing index figures from three Saturdays before the holiday with those of the Saturday immediately prior. Monday holidays were measured by comparing figures from two Saturdays prior to the holiday with those from the Saturday after. This method captured the change in the index over a two-week period and allowed for inclusion of sales on all days critical to shopping in connection with Monday holidays (Fridays, Saturdays, and Sundays before the holiday and, of course, the Monday holiday itself). It also included sales during the week after the holiday, and in this regard it must be noted that nearly all Monday holiday advertisements specify a sales period that includes the week after the holiday.

For date-based holidays I used a modification of the method used for holidays that fall on Sundays or Mondays. If the date-based holiday occurred on Sunday or Monday, I used the measurement model described above for Sunday or Monday holidays, respectively. If the holiday fell on a Saturday, I compared the index from the Saturday prior with the Saturday on which the holiday occurred. If the holiday fell on any of the other four days of the week, I compared the index from the Saturday prior to the holiday with the Saturday after. I used this method as the result of an analysis of advertising in advance of the holidays and observations I made of the volume of shopping activity at stores and malls in the week prior to the holiday. On the basis of these two considerations, I concluded that when these holidays occurred from Tuesday through Saturday, the bulk of holiday shopping occurred after the previous Saturday, and is thus best quantified by comparing the previous Saturday with the Saturday of or after the holiday. The one exception that I made was for Halloween. Because of the high level of holiday-specific advertising and my observations of holiday shopping activity well in advance of Halloween, I extended the study period an extra week.

Applying this method of analysis resulted in several significant findings. First, some holidays fail to generate regular annual increases in consumer spending, thus failing to satisfy a key criteria for holy days. Second, and more importantly, certain holidays not only yield consistent annual spending increases indicative of holy days, these are the only times when spending routinely increases in any given year. Third, and even more significant, the spending increases coinciding with these specific holidays *alone* accounted for the overall net increase in spending during the ten-year period and in all but one of the individual years in the period surveyed. In other words, without the spending increases directly traceable to these holidays, there would have been an actual decline in spending during the ten-year period and in nine out of the ten years.[5] In short, only during certain distinct and clearly identifiable holiday periods does retail spending accelerate on a routine and consistent annual basis. These holidays are the ones I have designated holy days in *The Sacred Santa*. Appendix C contains a summary of spending increases during holidays and a chart comparing average fluctuations in holiday spending to the overall average change during the ten-year period.

As noted above, besides the BTM/SW index, I used the U.S. Census Bureau's comprehensive "Monthly Retail Trade Survey" (MRTS), and especially the GAF category. In addition to using the MRTS to analyze GAF

---

5. From the first week of 1990 to the last week of 1999 (the period of my study) the BTM/SW sales index went from 247 to 369.9, an increase of 122.9 points, or 49.75 percent. This translates into an average weekly increase of approximately .095 percent. During this period, the three major holy days designated in the book alone accounted for a 148.6 point (or 60 percent) increase in the index. Factoring in the other holy days brings the total increase because of the holy days to 199.5 points (or 81 percent). Thus if the holy-day increases were removed from the total increase for the period (i.e., 122.9–199.5) there would have been a net decline in the index. This same phenomena is reflected in nine out of the ten years in the study. See Appendix C for charts of fluctuations in holiday spending.

sales, I used its data for two other purposes. First, because the MRTS reports consumer spending on a monthly basis, I used the survey to measure fluctuations in spending from month to month and season to season. Second, because it supplied information on spending in a wide array of SIC (Standard Industrial Classification) areas, I used MRTS to research relevant areas of consumer spending not covered by the BTM/SW index. In the first instance, the MRTS allowed analysis of the liturgical year as a whole and in the second it served as a source for data in spending categories relevant to certain holidays — e.g., grocery-store sales during Memorial Day and jewelry-store sales during Mother's Day. In a general sense, then, MRTS data was used to support and enhance BTM/SW data and also as a source for the study of retail commerce by month, season, and spending category. A summary and chart of MRTS reports on GAF sales for the period of my study (1990–99) is found in Appendix C.

— APPENDIX C —

Supporting Summaries and Charts

The summaries and charts that follow offer supporting documentation for the analysis of holidays presented in the text. They are listed here in order of their appearance in this appendix.

"Summary A" presents percentage changes in the BTM/SW "Weekly Chain Store Sales Index" during holidays in the years 1990–99. Percent changes were determined following the methodology described in Appendix B and applying the standard formula for measuring percentage changes in index figures — for example, the formula used to determine percentage changes in the U.S. government's "Consumer Price Index."[1] The computation process (using arbitrary index numbers) is as follows:

Index number for holiday Saturday	295.2
Less index number for a prior Saturday	293.7
Equals index point change	1.5
Divided by index figure for prior Saturday	293.7
Equals	.0051
Result multiplied by 100	.0051 x 100
Equals percentage change	.51

Figures in the yearly columns (1990–99) represent the percentage of change in the index during the holiday cycle for the given year. Ten-year averages for each holiday are given in the last two columns. Figures in the first of these columns indicate the average *total* percentage change for the holiday cycle during the ten-year period. Figures in the second (final) column represent the average *weekly* percent change during the cycle, which is computed by taking the average total percentage change and dividing by the number of weeks in the cycle. Figures for holidays

---

1. See Bureau of Labor Statistics, U.S. Department of Labor, "Consumer Price Indexes: How to Use the Consumer Price Index for Escalation" (last modified 10/16/01; accessed online, 2/6/02, at *www.bls.gov/cpi/cpifact3.htm*). The computation process given in Appendix C is based on the model given in this report.

with a one-week cycle are the same in the total and weekly columns. For holidays with a two-week cycle, the weekly column is one-half the total column. For Back-to-School and Christmas, weekly column figures were derived by dividing the total figure by six (the maximum number of weeks in each festival cycle).

As noted in "Summary A," the overall average weekly percentage change during the period was +.095.[2] The summary also indicates that the average weekly change during most holy-day cycles exceeded this change, often to a very considerable extent — e.g., Valentine's Day averaged a change of +.79 percent, Presidents' Day a change of +.40 (for two weeks), Easter +.73 (for two weeks), and Christmas +.44 (for five to six weeks, depending on the year). On the other hand, New Year's revealed a decline, with a ten-year weekly average of -.32.

"Chart 1" presents the ten-year average of total percentage changes for each holiday in the form of a bar chart. "Chart 2" presents the average weekly percentage change. For purposes of comparison, the holidays are indicated by vertical bars and the average weekly change (+.095 percent) by a horizontal line.

"Summary B" presents the monthly sales figures for the GAF category of the U.S. government's MRTS during the years 1990–99. The numbers in the summary represent sales in millions of dollars. Sales figures for each month are given by year, and the average for each month over the ten-year period is given at the end of the month's column. "Chart 3" presents the ten-year average of the months in "Summary B" in the form of a bar chart.

---

2. For more details, see Appendix B, n. 5.

Summary A

Total and Weekly Percent Change during Holidays Based on BTM/SW Weekly Chain Store Sales Index (1990–99)

Overall Average Weekly Percent Change for Period = +.095%

	1990	1991	1992	1993	1994	1995	1996	1997	1998	1999	total%	wkly%
New Year's		-1.61%	-1.36%	-1.88%	0.62%	0.90%	0.52%	-1.02%	0.69%	0.23%	-0.32%	-.32%
Martin Luther King Jr. Day	0.24%	-0.08%	-0.22%	0.72%	-0.92%	-0.07%	-1.75%	0.34%	0.84%	1.54%	0.06%	.03%
Super Bowl Sunday	0.40%	0.31%	0.11%	-0.21%	0.28%	-0.72%	0.00%	0.19%	0.96%	1.04%	0.24%	.24%
Valentine's Day	0.16%	0.12%	0.45%	0.04%	0.65%	1.45%	2.69%	1.67%	0.56%	0.14%	0.79%	.79%
Presidents' Day	0.00%	0.31%	0.19%	-0.43%	1.21%	-0.40%	1.61%	1.39%	1.86%	2.35%	0.81%	.40%
St. Patrick's Day	0.20%	-0.50%	-0.40%	1.20%	-0.07%	0.56%	1.19%	-0.06%	0.69%	0.51%	0.33%	.33%
Easter	0.20%	1.56%	0.92%	2.00%	3.71%	0.30%	1.64%	0.57%	1.15%	2.62%	1.47%	.73%
Mother's Day	0.24%	0.23%	-0.15%	0.57%	-1.47%	0.37%	1.95%	-0.03%	-0.59%	0.26%	0.14%	.14%
Memorial Day	-0.08%	0.00%	0.63%	0.86%	0.61%	0.30%	0.00%	-1.95%	-0.81%	0.40%	0.00%	.00%
Father's Day	0.00%	-0.12%	3.17%	0.57%	0.00%	-0.69%	0.00%	0.03%	0.17%	-0.16%	0.30%	.30%
Fourth of July	0.00%	0.42%	-0.22%	0.07%	-0.34%	-0.10%	0.22%	0.09%	0.31%	0.11%	0.06%	.06%
Back-to-School	0.24%	0.31%	1.21%	0.42%	0.30%	0.03%	0.09%	0.21%	0.09%	-0.66%	0.22%	.04%
Labor Day	-0.12%	0.42%	1.10%	0.24%	-0.87%	0.66%	-0.41%	0.24%	0.78%	0.16%	0.22%	.11%
Columbus Day	-0.04%	0.46%	0.25%	-0.03%	0.20%	0.79%	1.09%	-0.12%	-0.54%	-0.83%	0.12%	.06%
Halloween	0.51%	0.38%	0.15%	0.21%	0.10%	-0.16%	-0.19%	-0.46%	-2.06%	-0.79%	-0.23%	-.12%
Thanksgiving	0.20%	1.37%	-0.22%	-0.10%	0.70%	-0.46%	-0.22%	0.46%	0.15%	0.74%	0.26%	.26%
Christmas	2.31%	3.62%	3.42%	1.20%	0.40%	7.13%	3.77%	1.04%	1.33%	2.23%	2.65%	.44%

Summary B

GAF Category of U.S. Census Bureau's Monthly Retail Trade Survey (1990–99)
In millions of dollars

	1990	1991	1992	1993	1994	1995	1996	1997	1998	1999	10-Yr Avg
Jan	$30,329	$30,111	$32,849	$35,350	$36,499	$39,919	$41,205	$44,520	$47,647	$50,819	$38,925
Feb	$30,128	$30,484	$34,260	$34,596	$37,419	$39,408	$43,785	$44,748	$48,216	$51,924	$39,497
Mar	$36,745	$37,747	$37,646	$39,802	$45,140	$46,724	$49,343	$52,441	$53,942	$59,867	$45,940
Apr	$35,929	$36,567	$39,393	$42,185	$44,361	$46,893	$49,313	$50,074	$55,921	$59,102	$45,974
May	$38,232	$40,074	$41,142	$43,974	$45,976	$49,513	$53,240	$55,309	$58,858	$62,664	$48,898
Jun	$37,785	$38,144	$39,871	$42,951	$46,686	$49,958	$51,404	$53,164	$56,880	$61,346	$47,819
Jul	$35,364	$37,323	$39,774	$43,455	$45,593	$48,096	$50,125	$53,080	$56,872	$61,124	$47,081
Aug	$39,645	$41,877	$43,395	$45,813	$49,933	$52,481	$56,191	$58,284	$60,814	$64,487	$51,292
Sep	$36,329	$37,104	$40,238	$43,567	$46,852	$49,722	$50,524	$52,398	$55,631	$60,810	$47,318
Oct	$38,049	$39,616	$43,558	$45,992	$49,542	$50,254	$53,943	$56,508	$59,939	$63,572	$50,097
Nov	$45,458	$47,086	$49,984	$53,724	$58,180	$61,456	$63,257	$65,939	$69,426	$73,940	$58,845
Dec	$67,604	$69,306	$77,120	$81,637	$88,066	$90,325	$92,669	$96,780	$103,014	$112,063	$87,858
	$471,597	$485,439	$519,230	$553,046	$594,247	$624,749	$654,999	$683,245	$727,160	$781,718	$609,543

Chart 1
Average Total Percent Change during Holidays
in BTM/SW Weekly Chain Store Sales Index (1990–99)
Overall Average Weekly Percent Change for Period = +.095%
(indicated by dotted line)

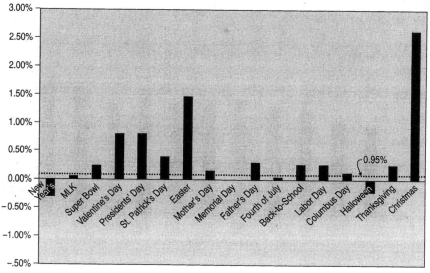

Chart 2
Average Weekly Percent Change during Holidays
in BTM/SW Weekly Chain Store Sales Index (1990–99)
Overall Average Weekly Percent Change for Period = +.095%
(indicated by dotted line)

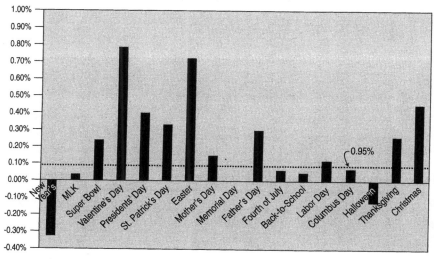

Chart 3
U.S. Census Bureau Retail Trade Survey:
GAF Monthly Average 1990–99
(in millions of dollars)

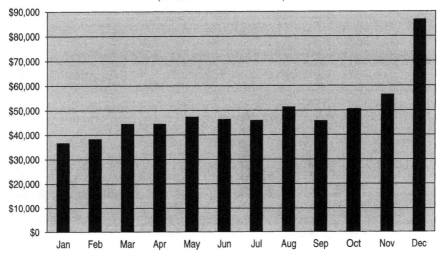

Index

215